Wood Block
Clare Romano
"New Jersey Landscape"

The Complete
PRINTMAKER

John Ross

Clare Romano

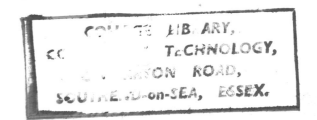
The Complete PRINTMAKER

THE ART AND TECHNIQUE OF THE RELIEF PRINT, THE INTAGLIO PRINT, THE COLLAGRAPH, THE LITHOGRAPH, THE SCREEN PRINT, THE DIMENSIONAL PRINT, PHOTOGRAPHIC PRINTS, CHILDREN'S PRINTS, COLLECTING PRINTS, PRINT WORKSHOP

THE FREE PRESS, NEW YORK
Collier-Macmillan Limited, London

To Christopher and Timothy

THE FREE PRESS
A Division of the Macmillan Company
866 Third Avenue, New York, New York 10022

Collier-Macmillan Canada, Ltd., Toronto, Ontario

Library of Congress Catalog Card Number 72-77151

First Printing August 1972

ACKNOWLEDGMENTS

We are indebted to a number of people whose energies and interest served to help our own. Many artists gave their time and knowledge in their special areas. They include Peter Milton, Fritz Eichenberg, Andrew Stasik, Ansei Uchima, Lynd Ward, Antonio Fraconi, Toshi Yoshida, Carol Summers, Jack Sonenberg, Norio Azuma, Al Blaustein, Fred and Hilda Castellon, Rudy Pozzatti, Warrington Colescott, Jacob Landau, Richard Anuszkiewcz, Herman Zaage, Paul Bruner, James Lanier, Michael Ponce de Leon, Herbert Youner, and David Finkbeiner.

The basic manuscript was copy edited by Linda Mattison, whose suggestions were thoughtful, constructive and gratefully received. Marie Nolan patiently typed the major portion of the text with assistance from Mary Thompson. We wish to thank Sarah Sprague for compiling the index and checking the photos and captions. Douglas Howell demonstrated the process of making rag paper, Edmund Desjobert permitted us free rein in his lithographic workshop in Paris, as did Jeff Stone at the Bank Street Atelier in New York City. Donna Moran of Pratt Institute, Irvil Sloan of Multiples, Donna Stein of the Museum of the Modern Art, and Elizabeth Roth of the New York Public Library were all willing with their time and expert help. Valri Pozzatti translated a little known letter from Felicien Rops, Sylvan Cole and Aldis Browne of Associated American Artists were generous in their assistance; Andrew Fitch and Walter Bareiss, both kind hosts as well as dedicated collectors, were pleasant and informed and shared their enthusiasm with us. Theodore Gusten of I.G.A.S. was cooperative and patient, as were Donald Karshan, Edna Blank of Andrews/Nelson/Whitehead, and Elke Solomon of the Whitney Museum. Timothy and Christopher Ross were willing models, printers, photo technicians and general assistants. Most of the photographs and all of the drawings are by John Ross, except where noted in the captions. Modernage Photographic Services processed the bulk of the photographs, both in black and white as well as in color. Our special thanks to Lewis Falce, President of Algen Press, for his interest and care in printing the color sections.

PRODUCTION CREDITS

The Complete Printmaker was designed by Sidney Solomon,
who also planned and supervised the production through all its stages.
Picture layouts: Bob Vari
Typesetting: V & M Typographical, Inc.
Black-and-white presswork: Murray Printing Co.
Color printing, jackets and endpapers: Algen Press Corp.
Paper: Starflex Enamel Dull by Oxford Paper Co.
Binding: The Book Press

PREFACE

The Complete Printmaker developed out of our work with collagraphs in the mid nineteen-sixties. After several assignments as artists-in-residence with the U.S.I.A. exhibition "Graphic Arts U.S.A." in Yugoslavia and Romania, we realized how much interest there was in new methods and approaches in printmaking. There seemed to be little published material on the newer techniques and our students constantly requested information about them. Fellow artists and art historians from various parts of the country wrote to us for details concerning the collagraph, helping to convince us to write down our methods and experiences. Sidney Solomon, whom we first met when he was Director of Design for the Macmillan Company, was involved with the Free Press at that time. He saw our new work and was excited with the new direction and experiments. He prodded us to put some material together for a book on our use of this new technique. He became our editor, designer, and production director, and it was only through his constant interest and encouragement that this book has become a reality.

As an explanation of the collagraph and other new methods evolved, we soon realized that we had to cover both intaglio and relief processes in depth to present properly the potential of the mediums. An understanding of new processes depends, in part, on a knowledge of traditional techniques; these had to be presented too. Over two decades of work as printmakers and painters and fifteen years of teaching have enabled us to explore every major printmaking medium. At this point we decided to compile a book that would be as complete as possible in the format of a single volume.

The emphasis in this presentation is on the workshop approach to printmaking. This postulates that one learns best by doing, and that a flexible approach is more productive than a highly structured, dogmatic sequence of problems designed to impart information in an academic way. The student develops his own ideas at the pace that suits him. An individual artist selects the method that best suits his esthetic intention. It will be helpful to him if he understands the possibilities of other techniques, so that his range of expression can be expanded when necessary. The diversity of work that takes place in a workshop atmosphere is stimulating to many artists, and can create an exciting environment for new and experimental projects. The possibility of combining techniques in a mixed-media statement is enhanced when working in a shop where many methods are being exploited simultaneously. Though small groups are better than very large groups, too few people are also a disadvantage. There should be enough activity in the shop to stimulate ideas and provoke reaction to new directions. In this kind of situation the organization and planning of the workspace is of prime concern; thus we include diagrams and photos.

The present intensity of interest in the fine print is directly related to the advancement of technology in this century. A whole battery of new materials and procedures is open to the adventurous artist who wants to expand his imagery into the world of prints. Photographic processes and three-dimensional prints are recent developments which indicate that even more possibilities will be uncovered before long. The print is changing in its technology and, therefore, in its expressive power. The magic of the print becomes that much more intensified with the expansion of means. The artist who is interested in these possibilities must learn to exploit the new procedures and techniques to his advantage.

JOHN ROSS
CLARE ROMANO
Englewood, New Jersey
June, 1972

CONTENTS

BLACK & WHITE REPRODUCTIONS

COLOR REPRODUCTIONS

THE RELIEF PRINT

The Woodcut

INTRODUCTION AND HISTORY

Of all the forms of expression in printmaking, the woodcut is the most ancient. Its early beginnings in Egypt and China came from the use of wooden stamps designed to make symbolic or decorative impressions in clay and wax. With the development of paper on the Chinese mainland in the second century A.D., the stamping devices gradually evolved into wood blocks.

As plank wood was utilized by the artist and the craftsman, he was able to cut and print more sophisticated and complex designs. Many of the earliest images were for popular Buddhist religious use.

The woodcut came to Japan from China, in the wake of Buddhism, in the sixth century A.D. The early Japanese woodcuts were also religious in subject matter. It was not until the 17th century that a more highly developed art began to come forth. The Japanese printmaker's concept of the symbolism of subject matter, asymmetric composition, the use of flat color, pattern, and line were a great influence upon the work of Gauguin, Van Gogh, Lautrec, Whistler, and others.

The woodcut in western art evolved as a later expansion of the utilitarian printing of textiles from wood blocks used extensively in the early 14th century. Though paper from the east was known in Spain in the 11th century, it was not until paper was produced in large quantities in France, Italy, and Germany in the 14th century that the art of the woodcut began to unfold. In southern Germany, woodcuts began as primitive religious figures. Their directness, simplicity of line, and economy of means made them very powerful. They were handbills for veneration, sold for pennies to pilgrims visiting holy places and to the populace on religious feast days. Woodcuts of Christ or the Virgin Mary were often pasted inside traveling chests or onto small altar pieces and frequently sewn into clothing to give protection from evil forces.

As the invention of printing from movable type became a reality in the mid-15th century, the woodcut began to appear in more highly developed forms as illustrations for religious

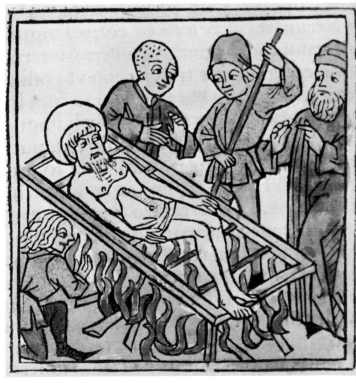

Jacobus de Voragine
Martyrdom of St. Lawrence, ca. 1474
From Legenda Sanctorum (Golden Legend)
Brooklyn Museum

1

books. By the late 15th century the great artists of the time, Durer and Hans Holbein in Germany, Lucas von Leyden in the Netherlands, and Titian in Italy were using this new medium with great eloquence.

After the mid-16th century, the woodcut began to decline in importance as a vehicle for esthetic expression. The richness and flexibility of line engraving and etching attracted most of the major artists dealing with the print. The woodcut and, later, the wood engraving became a means for reproducing popular painters and was used extensively for book, magazine, and newspaper illustrations. It was not until the revival of the woodcut as a sensitive, personal art form in the late 19th century, that it regained its place as a major expressive form. The prints of Gauguin, strongly influenced by the Japanese prints being exhibited in Paris, the prints of the German Expressionists who were returning to the simplicity of the early German Medieval woodcuts, and the prints of the Norwegian expressionist Edvard Munch greatly helped to renew interest in the woodcut as a serious contemporary art form. With this revival of the woodcut as a fine print medium came a new spontaneity and creative use of the material.

Until the late 19th century the woodcut was in a sense reproductive. The woodcuts of the German Renaissance, including those by Durer and Holbein, had often been cut by

Emil Nolde
"The Doctors" 1922
Woodcut 19⅞" x 27¾"
Dain Gallery, New York

highly skilled craftsmen from drawings made by the artists directly on the blocks. The prints became very fine facsimiles of exquisite pen drawings, having little relation to the quality of the wood. Line became the important element, mass or wood grain was rarely used. However, the artist-craftsman system, with the artist doing the creative work and the craftsman the cutting, enabled Durer and his contemporaries to produce a tremendous number of prints. Japanese printmakers also developed the same system. The artists designed the images, and the skilled craftsmen cut and printed the blocks. In succeeding years, with the artist so removed from the wood and the creating in less gifted hands, it was inevitable that the print became a reproductive image until the new approaches of the late 19th-century artists.

Because the contemporary artist uses the wood more freely with a real sense of the material and usually cuts and prints his own blocks, a more complete knowledge and respect for the material's potential comes forth. The aesthetic freedom of the 20th-century artist has enabled him to make new discoveries through experimentation and given him a richer utilization of the medium.

WOOD FOR RELIEF PRINTS

Pine

The most commonly available wood suitable for the technique of the woodcut is pine. It is soft, easily bruised, and requires very sharp tools if it is to be cut cross grain. Clear pine costs about twice as much as common pine but offers no knots. It is possible to buy pine boards up to 18" in width and occasionally up to 24", but larger sizes must be joined by edge gluing, which requires special clamps. Because of pine's softness, lines that are too thin are rounded or bruised in printing; in general, it is not a suitable wood for fine black line work. Sometimes it is advisable to coat the wood with a thin layer of shellac and sand it when it is dry. Thin the shellac with 50% alcohol to help it penetrate. It will harden the surface and make cutting easier. The wood is sometimes oiled to help prevent warping. Linseed oil may be used, but it should be applied some time in advance of cutting to allow the wood to dry.

Poplar

A medium soft wood with good cutting characteristics and even grain and not brittle is available in many lumber yards as whitewood (poplar); it is used extensively in inexpensive furniture. Poplar is slightly harder than pine and therefore it is possible to cut a little more detail on it. It is also used as backing wood for blocking copper or zinc line cuts and photoengravings. In the larger cities it should be possible to buy poplar blocks from the same manufacturer who supplies these backing blocks. It can be obtained type high (.918" thick) if enough is ordered to warrant a change in the planing machine. These type-high blocks may be printed on a Vandercook or other printing press (as discussed in section on press printing). Because poplar blocks are normally made from two or three inch strips, edge glued, they will not warp and they tend to retain a level surface.

Cherry and Pear Wood

These fruit woods are hard and dense and are suitable for very fine lines and long printing. Cherry blocks were, and still are, used by the traditional Japanese cutters in the Ukiyo-e tradition because of their resistance to splitting, their even grain, and their ability to withstand printing pressure and abrasion. Cherry is used for backing photoengravings even more often than poplar, and it is more easily available than poplar from blocking manufacturers. Pear wood is readily available in Europe but is a hardwood specialty item in the United States. It is quite similar to cherry in its characteristics.

Other Woods

Maple is so hard and dense that it is difficult to cut, but it yields extremely fine detail when properly worked. Oak is hard, stubborn, and full of a characteristic open pore texture that is disturbing. Mahogany is soft, very brittle, and has an open, pecky pore surface that is monotonous. Spruce and hemlock are soft, brittle, and mushy but can be used for color areas and knotty textures. Fir and redwood are brittle and flake off and chip when cut.

Plywood

When large areas are to be cut, plywood is the only answer. Fir plywood has a characteristic wild grain that is very dominating and hard to manage. However, pine plywood and gum plywood when available are quite usable for large woodcuts. Bass wood is also good. Cedar is too brittle to cut well. Birch is hard and has good even grain. A good birch plywood prepared for woodcutting is available from a Chicago supplier listed among the sources in the back of the book. Walnut is very hard, expensive, and has enough density to take fine even lines.

As many kinds of wood may be used in making woodcuts, the artist will choose that available wood which best suits the image he is cutting. Even old, worn, discarded boards are usable. Some artists save boxes full of old box wood, charred or burned pieces, knotty or rough sawn logs, and other wood which may yield interesting textures and shapes. With the correct procedure any piece of wood can be made to yield a good print.

WOODCUT TOOLS

A sharp nail will scratch the surface of a wood block, and the scratch will print as a white line on a black ground. Almost any object that is harder than wood will bruise or indent it, causing the indentations to print as white marks. Hard pencils will score most woods; paper clips will impress the surface; keys, tin cans, screwdrivers, needles, screws, dental tools, forks, pizza cutters, and plastic swizzle sticks will leave their impressions on the receptive surface of a piece of wood. All these implements can be used by the artist to create textures and designs that will print by the relief process. However, when good control of a shape or an area is needed, the knives and gouges come into their own and demonstrate why they have been used for so many years.

Objects that may be hammered or impressed into soft wood: A. Small brads. B. A leather punch with cross design. C. A hexagonal nut. D. A washer. E. Circular chuck. F. Staples.

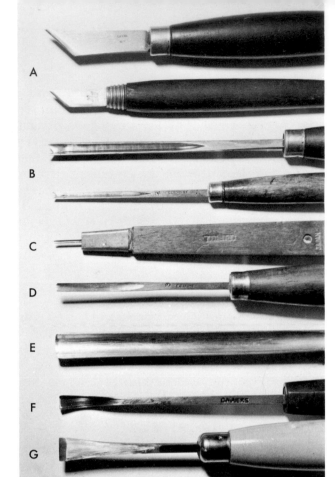

A

B

C

D

E

F

G

Some of the basic tools in woodcutting are shown top to bottom: A. Woodcut knives in two sizes. B. Raked V gouges, large and small. C. Small Japanese C gouge with movable steel gouge. D. Small shallow scoop or gouge. E. ⅜″ C gouge. F. Unusual rectangular gouge. G. Fish-tailed straight chisel.

The Knife

The knife has long been considered one of the prime tools of the woodcut artist, and justifiably so; it can perform cuts that no other tool can make and is one of the most useful instruments in the woodcutter's kit. It should be made of the best quality carbon steel, raked back from the point at about a 45° angle, and kept very sharp on the arkansas stone. The edge should be sharpened so that it is straight, not rounded; the point must be precise and keen if any small cutting is to be accomplished. There are many different sizes and styles of handles; choose one that is comfortable and workable and grips the knife blade very tightly so that it does not twist or wobble.

A few simple techniques will help you properly to cut with the knife. For broad cutting of large masses and long shapes hold the knife to cut at an angle of 45° to 60°. It takes four cuts with the knife to make one black line; in order to minimize the constant turning of the block that would be necessary if you held the knife at a constant angle you should learn to make the second cut by swinging the knife to the other side in order to release the cut splinter. Do not cut too deeply or you will tire quickly, and the fluency and responsiveness of your line will be impaired.

The knife is unexcelled for the clean cutting of inside small shapes where great control and accurate joining of lines is required. The tip of the knife does the most careful work. For this kind of cutting the tool should be held somewhat as a pencil between the thumb and the forefinger and be twisted and turned in the direction of the cut. As you can see the forefinger of your other hand can be used to push the knife into the wood and can be a great help, when your hand and arm are not strong enough to maintain the right pressure.

Hold the knife as shown above. Make the first cut at about a 45° angle.

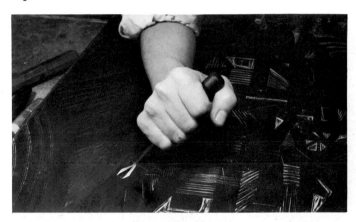

Turn your knife to the opposite side. Make the second cut, again at a 45° angle. The sliver of wood should curl up out of the cut. This method is for broad, fast cutting of large forms.

To cut smaller shapes and details, hold the knife somewhat like a pencil. Push it with the thumb of your other hand.

Turn the knife to the opposite angle. When you make the second cut the small sliver of wood should be loosened. Inside corners are easy to cut with a sharp knife.

The depth of cut does not have to exceed ⅛" except in large areas. This block has been cut by Antonio Frasconi.

Antonio Frasconi uses a small scoop to clear out an area on a block. Most of these tools are of Japanese manufacture.

Frasconi pushes the gouge with both hands for maximum control.

In addition to the traditional cutting, the knife can be used to achieve linear and textural qualities. It may be used to score the wood to create very fine lines either across the grain or with the grain. The knife can be used to bring up the grain if you hold the blade perpendicular to the block and scrape against the grain. It can be used as a chisel to shave away the wood. Its point can develop dot tones. Some very proficient artists use the knife as their only tool for all kinds of cutting, including cleaning out large areas of wood. However, other tools such as gouges and chisels are more efficient for this purpose.

Gouges and Chisels

You should have several kinds of gouges and chisels in your tool box. The most useful gouge is called the raked V gouge; when it is properly sharpened it will cut cross grain without tearing and is a joy to use. You can buy raked V gouges in various sizes from E. C. Lyons in New York City. It is handy to have two or more raked V gouges, the smaller one for detailed lines and the larger one for gouging areas and coarser textures.

A C gouge is indispensible for general cutting, and many sizes and shapes are available. When the curve of the gouge is very deep it becomes a U gouge and must be sharpened to a razor edge to cut effectively. There is an artist in Romania who has made over 1000 woodcuts in the past 30 years using almost exclusively a small C gouge for the entire image on each block. When any tool is used to this degree it makes the textures monotonous, and the forms themselves become constricted by the limits of the tool. Certain shapes and areas demand different tools, and for sensitive work it is necessary to have at least 3 or 4 varieties of gouges at hand.

A small flat chisel is a very helpful tool for getting soft grey edges when you do not want the typically hard-cut edge that is so characteristic of the woodcut knife or gouge. Study Antonio Frasconi's subtle and effective use of the flat chisel, and see the prints of Gauguin for soft edge effects.

Inexpensive Japanese Tools

The cheap sets of Japanese woodcut tools widely sold in the United States are useful for certain kinds of work. Although the steel is very soft and will not hold an edge for any length of time, the small knives are good for detail work, and the gouges will cut well for a while. Munakata uses them until they are dull and then throws them away. However, the greatest value of these tools lies in their ability to demonstrate the cuts that a certain type of tool will make before you spend a lot of money on a good quality tool. By testing the cuts of certain shapes of gouges and chisels you can determine which tools are best suited to your work and then buy a good high-carbon steel tool of that shape. As the cost of a complete set of twelve Japanese tools is less than $2, you can save the entire price with the discreet purchase of two good tools.

In any case, your tools should be kept in a tool kit or in a canvas tool roll in order to protect them and to keep them available.

Large wood cutting gouges and chisels can be stored in a canvas kit.

Rolled canvas tool kit. This type of storage is better for the cutting edges than throwing all the tools into a metal box where they slide around.

Sharpening

It is easy to resharpen your old straight V gouges to the correct angle of rake as shown on the diagram. Grind the tool to the desired angle on a coarse carborundum stone or on a small grinding wheel. If you use a wheel, do not over-heat the tool or you may lose the temper in the steel. Once the correct angle is obtained, sharpen each side of the V gouge as you do a knife, making sure that the two edges meet at exactly the right angle. This point does the cutting, and it must be precise and true for the most delicate work.

The curved gouges are very difficult to sharpen, and it will take a great deal of practice and patience to master the technique. Hold the tool as shown and slowly turn the tool between your thumb and forefinger while keeping the same angle of tool to stone. It will take a number of turns before the edge can be ground evenly. The edge of the gouge should be rotated in small circles on the stone. When the tool is held in front of a light the edge should not be visible. If it reflects light on any one spot that area will need more stoning. There are a number of stones, both india and carborundum, with concave indentations of various curvatures for different-sized gouges. These are helpful to the beginner but scorned by old timers, who still insist that the flat stone is sufficient and the human hand is the best instrument for controlling the tool. Use enough fine oil to lubricate the stone and float off the tiny particles of steel that eventually will clog the stone. Pike oil, Three-In-One, or any light machine oil will work. Do not use linseed oil.

CUTTING IN RELATION TO IMAGE

If the beginning woodcutter experiments freely with a variety of tools, he will begin to develop a preference and feeling for certain tools. Through selectiveness and growing experience in cutting, a personal manner in handling the tools will show itself, much as style develops in handwriting and drawing.

A good way to start to familiarize yourself with the tools is to prepare a series of small blocks without planned image. These blocks should exploit many cutting and texture possibilities inherent in the tools. By freeing yourself of imagery and finding out what the tools can do in the hand, you will

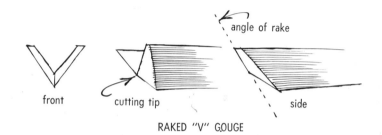

RAKED "V" GOUGE

To sharpen a curved gouge keep the angle of bevel steady. Move the gouge in small circles, rotating the shaft of the tool between the fingers.

develop a basic cutting vocabulary and also understand the vast potential for tonality through textures. These experimental blocks can then be rolled up and printed to create a guide to future cutting.

Cutting methods, of course, vary in relation to the idea expressed. A good guide is to cut in the direction of the flow of the form. However, with images as varied and personal as they are in contemporary expression, any fixed rules would be impotent. One sure caution, however, is to avoid overcutting and to undercut wherever possible. It's easy to become carried away with the physical movements of cutting and to forget that each cut will appear as a white area. This is why undercutting and proofing are so important. Developing the block through the proofing is as important as the cutting on the block. If frequent proofs are pulled in developing stages and the proof is worked on with white paint to see how new areas will evolve, or with black paint to remove cutting, a freer concept can develop. Do not hesitate to sacrifice the drawn image on the block to constant proofing. The image can be easily re-indicated, and it is far more time-consuming to have to correct the overcut block.

Another caution is to try to keep a certain consistency in the scale of cutting. Again, this would apply to certain imagery and not to others. For instance, in an abstract concept, the scale of cutting would not need to be consistent. However, if certain special qualities were to be introduced in relation to landscape or figurative images, the scale, the weight of cutting, and therefore the sizes of the gouges or cuts would be very important.

Developing tonality or greys through the black-and-white print can be achieved in a variety of ways. The early woodcuts of Durer never relied on texture or wood grain. Form and tonality was developed in his woodcuts as it had been

Edvard Munch
"The Kiss" (1902)
Color woodcut, block 18⅜" x 18⁵⁄₁₆"
Collection, The Museum of Modern Art, New York
Gift of Mrs. John D. Rockefeller, Jr.

Opposite:
John Ross
"Commercial Street" 1963
Color woodcut 23⅛" x 16½"

Brass brush, flat knife, and sandpaper emphasize granular structure to extent shown.

A brass suede brush, made for cleaning shoes and leather clothing, can subtly accent grain. Run in the direction of the grain.

A steel wire brush gives a rapid, coarse texture.

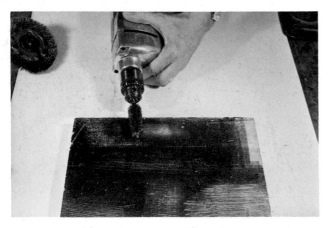

The electric drill with a wire brush of brass will scour the surface of a block, accenting the grain.

conceived in his pen drawings. Today's expression in the wood is comparatively free. Line can of course express tone and form, but so can the great variety of textural cutting possible with the numerous cutting and textural tools used. Wood grain can play an extremely important role in the development of the image. Sometimes it has been used as almost the total image, as in Munch's *The Kiss*. Often it is the rich combination of grain, line, black mass, and texture that fulfills the wide potential of the wood.

Developing Grain

Many methods can be used to bring out the grain. When the image is expressed almost totally through the grain, a careful control must be exercised. One method is to hold the blade of a woodcut knife perpendicular to the block and lightly scrape the straight edge against the grain. Sometimes a thin scoring with your knife around the area where the grain is to be brought up will help you to keep within the form where strong grain quality is desired.

Where less control is necessary, a wire brush like an ordinary suede brush or a copper gun-bore cleaner is useful. In this method, the brush is rubbed with the grain.

Sandpaper in varying degrees of roughness may also be used, again rubbing with the grain. Pumice may be used in the same way.

A power-driven metal brush can be used if a rough texture is desired.

In all instances, the scraping, rubbing, or sanding wears away the soft particles of wood between the harder areas of grain, forcing the grain to become more prominent.

ROLLERS OR BRAYERS

Rollers present one of the greatest problems to an artist attempting the relief print. You will soon find that one roller will ink a certain block properly but will not work as well on another block. You will eventually need many different rollers, differing in size and in hardness of materials. There are a number of materials used in the making of rollers, ranging from gelatine, soft and hard rubber, composition, plastic, leather, and linoleum to lucite or plexiglas. It is necessary to understand what are the advantages and disadvantages of each type.

Hard Rubber Rollers

The small hard rubber rollers that are usually sold for use in printing linoleum cuts are of very little value to the serious printmaker. They are rarely of even diameter and ink an irregular, blotchy pattern at best. The most useful hard rubber rollers are made of cylinder rubber stock, which usually comes in outside diameters of 1½", 2", and 3", and

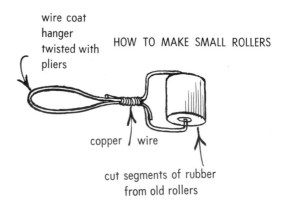

wire coat hanger twisted with pliers

HOW TO MAKE SMALL ROLLERS

copper wire

cut segments of rubber from old rollers

with an inside diameter of ½", in lengths of 24". This material can be cut with a hand hacksaw or on a power saw with a hollow-ground blade, using a slow feed. The inside ½" diameter should be filled with a ½" maple dowel cut about ¼" longer than the length of the roller. This wooden core can then be drilled and mounted in a handle made from flat iron stock of approximately ⅛"-thick bar stock about 1" wide. If the iron bar stock is first scored with a hacksaw it will bend precisely at the proper place to fit the roller.

A hard roller of even diameter will ink the surface of a relief block without inking the shallow gouged or lowered areas. If you want a "clean" print without a lot of gouged texture, then a hard rubber roller is the proper choice.

Smaller rollers may be made with handles of stiff wire, such as the wire from coat hangers, bent into the proper shape with two pairs of pliers. As the most difficult part of the roller to make is the handle, it is desirable to save any suitable handle and simply replace the roller section. It is worthwhile to buy wallpaper rollers with a wooden or plastic roller and throw away the roller section. Then you may cut a section of cylinder rubber with a dowel insert to fit the handle section. The metal brackets may be bent inward to fit smaller rollers.

Soft Rubber Rollers

Soft rubber rollers are now obtainable from the Hunt Mfg. Co., Philadelphia, Pennsylvania, and are called speedball soft rubber rollers. They come in a variety of lengths from 1½" to 6". The smaller sizes are particularly handy for color areas. As the rubber composition is quite soft, they are useful for collage prints and for inking uneven blocks. They deposit ink on gouged areas in a very great amount and should be used with discretion. The rollers are too soft for blocks that are not very deeply gouged unless you want lots of gouging texture to print. They are also too soft for finely cut blocks, as thin lines fill in. The small diameter of these rollers is a handicap when you are inking a large area.

Gelatine Rollers

A very sensitive and useful brayer is made from gelatine. It gives a smooth, even distribution of ink. The disadvantages of gelatine are so numerous that it is rapidly being replaced by more durable materials. Gelatine pits very easily, melts in contact with water, will sag out of shape in very warm weather, will indent if left standing on a slab overnight, and is, in general, such a delicate and destructible material that it becomes very expensive to have your rollers recast every year, as is the custom in commercial printing shops.

Plastic Rollers

Soft plastic rollers are now being manufactured that combine the even inking qualities of gelatine with the more durable characteristics of hard rubber. They can be cast in an enormous variety of sizes and are the most useful rollers in the studio. As would be expected, these rollers are quite expensive. A 6" brayer with handle costs around $12. They are made of polyurethane or polyvinyl chloride and are very durable. They will withstand an amazing amount of abuse, and we recommend them highly. Large sizes are very expensive but are worth it.

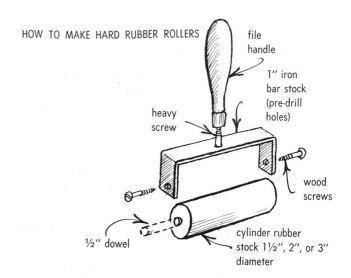

HOW TO MAKE HARD RUBBER ROLLERS

file handle — 1" iron bar stock (pre-drill holes) — heavy screw — wood screws — ½" dowel — cylinder rubber stock 1½", 2", or 3" diameter

Small rollers, many homemade, in varying sizes.

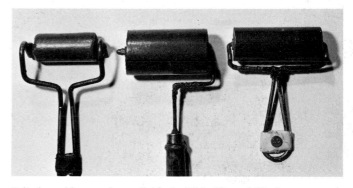

Cylinder rubber stock, available in 1½", 2", and 3" diameter stock, is very useful in the making of hard rollers. Handles can be made from coat hangers, wallpaper seam rollers, dowels, and the like.

An overhead roller rack is a great convenience when located over the work table. Rollers are always available and are out of the way when not in use.

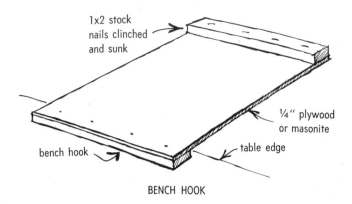

1x2 stock
nails clinched
and sunk

¼" plywood
or masonite

bench hook

table edge

BENCH HOOK

Bench Hook

A bench hook will hold the block from moving while the gouge is being forced through the wood. You can make a bench hook, using a piece of ¼" plywood, ¼" Masonite, or similar thickness composition board as a base. Glue or screw two pieces of 1"-thick wood on each end but on opposite sides of the base. Countersink the heads of the screws very deeply in order to avoid damage to the cutting edge of your gouge. One edge of the bench hook fits on the front of your table and the other side holds the block in position. It is a good idea to have several in various sizes because a small block simply won't work in a large bench hook.

C Clamps

You may clamp a large block to your table by using a carpenter's C clamp. The pressure of the threaded clamp will indent the block unless several layers of cardboard are used to protect the soft surface of the wood. Clamps are not as flexible as bench hooks because they must be loosened every time you want to move the block.

Gouging Jigs

Another useful tool is the gouging jig. If you are cutting a number of blocks it may be worthwhile to drill a number of ¾" holes in your table, spaced to receive ¾" dowels that have been glued to a strip of wood shaped as shown.

The right-angled corner is essential to keep the wood from slipping off the strip. The advantage of this method is that the holes may be drilled at the angle you prefer and the jig may be shifted easily to accommodate small blocks as well as large blocks.

The table on which you work must be either heavy enough not to slide all over the floor or prevented from moving by being placed against a wall or another piece of furniture. When a large amount of deep gouging is necessary, it may be helpful to use a small wooden mallet to help drive the gouge or chisel through the wood, particularly if you are working in a hardwood like cherry or pear.

Texturing Tools

The soft surface of the wood may be indented or scratched by an enormous variety of things, from nails and screws to washers, bottle caps, punches, dog combs, drills, rasps, wire screening, and sandpaper. These can be hammered or tapped into the surface of the wood, and the indentations will print as white against the black surface of the block.

Multiple gravers made with a certain number of lines to the inch, ranging from 40 to 120 or more, are available from E. C. Lyons and E. C. Muller in New York City. These tools are made for photoengravers but are useful in the coarser sizes, i.e., 45-55-65, in obtaining closely textured grey tones. They work best with the grain.

Sculptors' tools, the small metal rakes with small teeth, also produce interesting textures.

Often a tool or implement designed for other purposes can work marvellously well. A dressmaker's sharp-pointed wheel for marking patterns, a little texture wheel for pastry mak-

A bench hook holds the block in position and keeps it from sliding around when you gouge.

Push the gouge with your right hand. The other hand acts as a guide and as a restraint against the tool and helps to keep it from slipping out of control.

The C clamp method of holding a block in position does not allow as much freedom of cutting as does the bench hook. Be sure to place a few pieces of cardboard between the block and the jaws of the clamp to prevent bruising the wood.

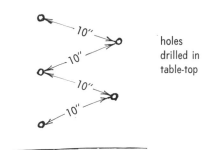

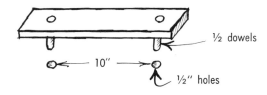

holes
drilled in
table-top

½ dowels

10"

½" holes

BLOCK SUPPORT IN TABLE
BY DRILLING HOLDS

Another method of keeping the block in position is to drill holes in your table top. Make a corner angle from an old canvas stretcher, insert two dowels through the stretcher, and fit the dowels into the holes in the table. If you make several holes you can adjust the angle to suit your block.

This shows the corner angle in use. The wood is held in place by the dowels, and the block cannot slip.

Ernst Kirchner
"Alpine Shepherd" 1917
Woodcut
Brooklyn Museum

ing, a sharp-edged pizza cutting wheel have all been useful tools in our studio. Look around you, in your workshop, basement, attic, kitchen, hardware or ten-cent store and discover texture-making tools that relate to your own images and you will introduce some freshness into your work.

Power Tools

Several types of power tools are very useful to the artist. The most easily obtained is the electric drill, which can be used with steel drill bits, wire brushes, and other tools. The block must be securely fastened to the table, or the force of the drill will move it around.

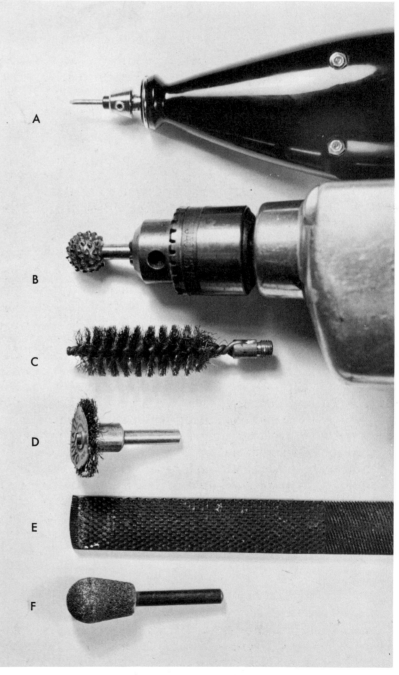

Auxiliary tools in woodcutting, top to bottom:
A. Multiple scratchboard tools, 40 lines to the inch. B. A screw-thread cutting tip that can make multiple grooves. C. An Exacto knife. D. A pie trimmer, which makes a zig-zag line. E. A glass cutter. F. A pattern wheel makes a dotted line. G. A leather punch for sewing seams. H. A sculptor's rasp makes multiple grooves. I. A dog comb, useful for coarse multiple strokes. J. A brass brush that can accentuate grain or texture the wood surface.

Other tools for texturing wood:
A. A motorized Vibro-tool which can be used on metal, wood, or plastic. B. An electric drill with circular bit. C. A brass gun cleaning brush. D. A wire brush for the electric drill. E. Wood rasp. F. A circular drum of carborundum.

A vibrating-point tool has been developed recently which has great potential if used with skill and care. There are several brands such as Vibro-Tool and Vibro-Graver. They can be used with a variety of points, from carbide or diamond tips to files and brushes. This tool is also useful for working in the intaglio methods on zinc, copper, or lucite plates. The stroke of the vibrating point is adjustable, and it can be used for many types of lines and textures.

A flexible shaft hooked up to a small electric motor is a very handy addition to an artist's workshop. There are a number of bits, grinding wheels, rasps, wire brushes, and other points that can be used.

All these tools are simply devices for easing the demands on the artist's strength and time. They are as much a part of a printmaker's equipment as the pencil or the knife.

Rubbing Tools

The choice of rubbing tool is often as personal as the choice of cutting tool. We have known artists to select from a wide range of objects hardly designed for printing use. These have ranged from an ordinary kitchen wooden spoon to the electric light bulb that a Romanian woodcut artist staunchly upheld as the best.

The traditional rubbing tool of the Japanese is the baren. It is a flat, circular disk backing a spiral of cord about 5½" in diameter covered with a sheath of bamboo. It is very sensitive for printing water-based inks. See the section on the Japanese method.

We have found a most useful rubbing tool to be two ordinary square wooden drawer pulls glued together. These may be purchased in many well-equipped hardware or 10¢ stores. One serves as a handle and the other as the rubbing tool. The handle can be selected for the size of the hand. The rubbing portion is usually most useful in the 4" dimension. Because the wood is quite raw, it is best to rub a little linseed oil into it in the beginning so that it glides easily over the back of the print and will not tear the paper. After a few printing sessions you will find a lovely patina developing. The flat of the knob is especially easy to use for large areas. The handle is excellent for small areas. Some of our students have fashioned their own tools by using a jigsaw and whittling a piece of wood to the desired shape.

Another excellent tool is a Japanese rice spoon made of bamboo. This can be purchased in a Japanese novelty shop for as little as 25¢. The flat end may be used for larger areas, the handle for smaller ones. Its great advantage is that it fits very comfortably in large and small hands. See the section on hand printing woodcuts.

The circular rasp produces a rough, uneven texture.

INKS FOR RELIEF PRINTING

The oil-based printer's inks normally used for the relief print are available from a large number of ink manufacturers. It is much easier to keep this ink in tubes than in cans. The small extra charge for the tubes is well worth it. However, as many colors are not available in tubes and can be obtained only in cans, it is good practice to replace the circular waxed-paper liner carefully, pressing it down and

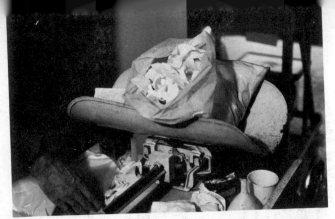

Douglas Howell weighs cotton rags on a scale to prepare the raw materials for paper manufacture.

leaving no air bubbles, before sealing the can with the lid. Wipe the rim clean, too.

The water-based inks are much harder to use because they dry so quickly. Oil inks are much more flexible and are preferable to water-based inks. However, water-based inks are discussed in a later section on the Japanese method. See section on color inks for relief printing.

PAPERS FOR RELIEF PRINTS

The wide variety of papers available to the printmaker working in the United States offers great flexibility and choice in every medium. The papers most suitable for printing relief blocks are handmade in Japan from the inner bark of the mulberry tree and other plants and bushes, such as the hibiscus and the hydrangea. Almost all the papers are used unsized and not dampened. Some of the characteristics of the most useful Japanese papers are listed in the chart on papers.

For very fine lines, such as in delicately cut wood engravings and relief etchings, it may be better to use machine-made papers. The handmade papers vary in thickness and have much more surface texture than most machine-made papers of rag content, and the fine detail is somewhat harder to print on rough stock. Many domestic papers are suitable,

The rags are reduced to a pulp, called stuff, in the beater. Howell controls the length of the fibers by the duration of the beating.

The wire mesh screen or mold used to make each single sheet of paper. The water mark of copper wire is in the upper corner.

Below: The screen is immersed in the stuff to a certain depth, then it is removed as shown. It is shaken in two or more directions in order to interlock the fibers by Howell, acting as vatman.

The deckle is removed from the screen while excess water drains off.

Below: The pulp or stuff has been formed to the shape of the screen, making a sheet of paper.

including Mohawk text, Strathmore all rag Book in wove surfaces, and Strathmore bond wove. Some of the European papers are very good for fine detail in press printing. These include Basingwerk light, Arches text wove, Maidstone, Rives light wove, and Opaline, a parchment paper. Most of the imported papers can be obtained through Andrews-Nelson-Whitehead in New York or Aiko Company in Chicago, if ordered in quantity.

See the paper chart in the back of the book for further information.

PUTTING THE IMAGE ON WOOD

Painting on the Block

Wood lends itself exceptionally well to mass, both solid and tonal, and to the use of strong line. The density of the wood and the direction of the grain are factors to be considered in the planning of the image. If you keep this in mind, the preparation can be approached in a variety of ways depending on your esthetic direction and your needs as an artist. The inspiration for a particular image may vary considerably for each artist. Working directly on the block can be especially interesting. Take special care to select wood that has an interesting grain, knot, or rough-sawn texture that can help evolve the image.

One way to proceed is to paint directly on the wood surface with India ink, working with verve and speed. When the ink drawing is dry, tint over the block with a diluted oil-based ink, rubbed in with a rag. As an alternate method you can take the block (prepared with a thin coat of grey poster color, rubbed on with a rag, so that the wood will not become too wet nor the pigment too thick) with you as you would a sketch pad or drawing paper. You can paint directly on the block with a Japanese brush, a pointed sable, or a

The newly formed sheet has been couched on a stack of felts, called a post. The mold is removed with a rolling motion.

Below: The felts absorb moisture from the sheets and impart a texture to them. Douglas Howell makes only fine rag paper.

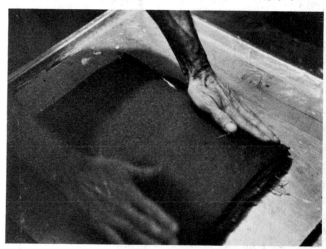

Painting directly on the block with india ink and brush is a good way to keep the image fresh and strong.

When the ink drawing is dry, tint the entire block with a dilute mixture of printers ink. Red, grey, blue, or some color of intermediate tonal value is rubbed over the drawing. Pour some varnoline or benzine on a rag, and thin the ink enough to tint the surface.

magic marker. Keep some of the grey poster color handy for making changes. You may use two instruments, a brush or pen with black to indicate positive forms and a brush with grey to make corrections. This method is extremely free and spontaneous. You may analyze the drawing back in the studio and develop it further just as you would a drawing on paper. Felt pens in a variety of sizes or speedball pens in an assortment are also very useful for attaining fluidity of line and quick development of mass.

Material for Painting on Block

India ink
Poster color—black and white
Brushes, flat and pointed and Japanese
Felt pens, assorted thin and thick sizes
Speedball pen nibs, #6 and #8
Sharpened stick, pen holder, or brush handle for stick drawing
Two mixing tins
Oil-based ink (red, blue, or grey)
Rags
Water
Wood, large 15″ or 18″ width of clear or common pine or poplar, ½″ or 1″ thick

Cutting Without Sketch

Another approach, related to the method just discussed, is cutting directly into the block without a previously prepared sketch. This is a very personal manner and seems to be most successful when the artist has a clear mental concept of his image. The block should be blackened with a rag dampened with India ink, diluted with a little water, so that the cut marks can be easily seen. The very act of cutting becomes an important part of the evolvement of the block. The physical motions themselves help to achieve a certain freedom. A student at Pratt Graphic Center worked on huge pieced planks or large drawing boards in this manner. He blackened his block with India ink and, with perhaps only a rudimentary positioning of forms with white chalk, would proceed to cut large expressionistic, figurative images with gouges and knives. However, the beginning artist of the woodcut must not confuse the size of the block or the gouge or the expressionism of the image with a result that will necessarily be free or spontaneous. Unless great control of design and composition and tool is part of the artist's experience, this method, if attempted without taking time to get the feel of the materials, can often result in large, impetuously cut blocks without enough organization. It is often better to start with medium-sized blocks and some planning.

Materials for Cutting Directly into Block

India ink, rag, mixing tin, water, white chalk
Wood, large 15″ or 18″ width of clear or common pine or poplar, ½″ or 1″ thick
Variety of cutting tools

Charcoal Offset Drawing

In this method, the drawing can be prepared in line on tracing paper with a compressed charcoal pencil, (a soft 6B

A very quick transferring procedure uses a drawing made with soft pencil or charcoal pencil. Do not fix the drawing. Turn it over, face down, on the block and tape it in position. Rub the back of the tracing with a spoon or a wooden drawer pull.

Below: If more pressure is needed rub the back of the tracing with your finger nail.

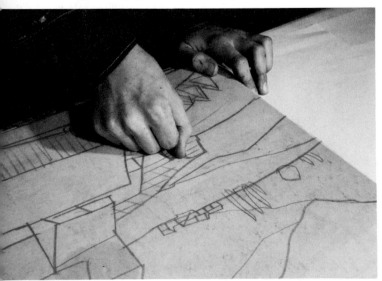

General's or Wolf's are very good), keeping in mind the need for simplicity and directness. The charcoal pencil should be used full strength without reliance on smudging effects. After the drawing is completed, it can be placed face down and taped to the block. The block should be tinted beforehand with sepia or grey poster color or printing ink diluted in varnolene, so that the cut marks will be seen easily. The back of the tracing is carefully rubbed with a rice spoon or drawer knob with strong pressure. The dense black compressed-charcoal pencil transfers itself quickly to the block with excellent readability. A good spray of fixative will keep the drawing from smudging, and cutting may begin. Any good brand of spray fixative such as Krylon or Blair may be used. Because the drawing is reversed when it is placed on the block, the finished print will read as the drawing was made on the tracing paper. There will not be a mirror image such as occurs when the drawing is painted directly on the block.

Tracing-Paper Transfer Method

In this method the drawing can be prepared on paper or illustration board in a manner that would relate well to the simplicity of line and mass of the woodcut. Use some instruments that have a relationship to the medium, such as brush or speedball pen and ink or felt pens. After the drawing is developed to your satisfaction, a tracing in mass can be made with a 6B General's or Wolf's compressed charcoal pencil, drawing every line and mass with the sharpened charcoal pencil. After the drawing is completed, it can be placed face down and taped to the block and rubbed with a rice spoon, a drawer knob, or your finger nail.

A variation on this method is to make a linear tracing of the prepared drawing with a medium soft pencil. The tracing is then placed face down with a piece of carbon paper between block and tracing. The block may also be prepared with a light tint, as described in the first discussion of the indirect method of preparing the image. The drawing may then be traced with a medium pencil so that the carbon paper deposits the image with sufficient strength onto the block. Be careful not to trace with too much pressure because the wood indents easily. This method is the least satisfactory because of the additional step required in the use of carbon paper and because tracing the linear image of a drawing is alien to the concept of the woodcut and becomes too reproductive.

Materials for Charcoal Offset and
Tracing-Paper Transfer Method

    6B General's or Wolf's compressed-charcoal pencil
    Tracing paper of very transparent quality
    Medium H pencil
    Carbon paper
    Masking tape
    Small spray can of fixative
    Japanese rice spoon or wooden drawer knob for rubbing
    Wood cut to size

Japanese Transfer Method

Still another transfer method is used by the Japanese traditionalists. It requires a carefully done tracing of your

The pencil drawing has been placed on the block. When the block is cut and printed it will be "flopped" back into its original position as on the drawing, a great advantage of this method. Lettering is easy to do by this method.

Another method for transferring a drawing is the carbon-paper technique. Tape a tracing of your shapes to the block. Slip a carbon-paper (typewriter carbon is O.K.) under the tracing and trace through the drawing so that it is transferred to the block. *Below:* Check the block. Use a soft pencil. A pencil that is too hard will indent the wood and those indentations will print as thin white lines.

design. The process is described in the section on the Japanese method under "pasting the drawing on the block."

Proofing the Woodcut

Pulling an impression of the cutting, no matter how rudimentary it may be, is an important aspect in developing the woodcut. Proofs may be made without using ink at all. One useful method is to rub the raised cut surface thoroughly with a large stick of graphite. Place a piece of Troya proofing paper over the area and rub with a suitable rubbing tool. A clean, sharp, readable impression of the developing block should be visible. Observations and changes can be easily made right on the proof with white and black poster color if the graphite impression is sprayed first with some fixative. The graphite method is useful for small areas when the block is in very early stages. When cutting is more advanced, ink is more advisable. The graphite may be readily removed from the block by rubbing with a rag sprinkled with a small amount of varnolene. Another process is to place paper over the block and then to rub it with a stick of graphite to produce the image.

Another method of proofing is to roll up the block with a light even coat of black ink and again to pull a print on Troya paper. A useful method is to pull two proofs if there is to be some extensive correcting with black and white poster color on the proof. One proof with painted changes and one proof to show what exists on the block can be very helpful in finding the areas to be corrected.

Developing and changing the block through proofing eliminates a great deal of the hazard of overcutting and enables the artist to realize the potential of the wood in a clearer, faster way. The greatest surprise always seems to come after the beginner has lovingly cut the block, which becomes a thing of beauty in itself, a bas relief, where every cut seems to have meaning because of the texture of the wood and the play of light on the relief surface. Then with the first proof, the unhappy revelation comes: None of these nuances are evident! It becomes a flat relation of white line and mass against black. The whites are invariably cut too heavily, too deeply, and too much.

Cleaning the block without dirtying the recessions on the block can be achieved if only a dry rag is used to clean away the ink. If this is insufficient for proper cleaning, then a rag with just a few drops of varnolene should do the trick.

CORRECTING ERRORS IN RELIEF BLOCKS

Wood Blocks

It is rather difficult to correct mistakes in wood, and great care should be taken not to overcut your blocks or to damage areas that should print. However, certain things can be done to repair small damages and bruises. These methods have distinct practical value and will save many a damaged block.

Plastic Wood

The easiest and fastest method to repair broken lines, overcut textures, and general overcutting is to fill the area

It is possible to take a quick "proof" of a cut block by rubbing a piece of paper with litho crayon or pastel when it is positioned on top of the cut area.

with fresh plastic wood, applied in as many coats as necessary to fill the holes. Allow each coat to dry. Don't allow each layer to exceed a thickness of about ⅛". Apply plastic wood to rough, new wood that has not been soaked with oil or ink. A clean base is essential for the plastic wood to stick properly. If this is not possible, since most errors or the need to make changes are not discovered until after a proof is pulled, clean the block well with solvent, especially in the recessions, and dry it well with a clean rag. It often helps to roughen the surface to be repaired with scraping movements of a knife. This will help the plastic wood to bind to the block. The final coat should be slightly higher than the level of the block but not excessively high or it will be too time-consuming to lower the plastic wood back to level. Sand the high spots with fine sandpaper, wrapped around a rectangular block. Sand with the grain only, keeping the pressure even and working carefully in order not to damage the surrounding areas.

Plastic wood will not withstand rough treatment, and occasionally the material falls out, particularly if the inking brayers are gelatine. Press printing also tends to pick out loose areas of plastic wood. For long editions and permanent work it may be better to plug the block or to cut a new block. With plastic wood, it is relatively easy to fix spots that have not been too thoroughly gouged out. If a section has been completely ruined by excessive cutting and it extends over a large area, it may be preferable to try the next method.

Planing Areas to Correct Mistakes

When the offending section extends to the edge of the block, it may be better to plane the whole section down to fresh wood. This is radical surgery, indeed, and will work in only a few cases. Plane with the grain and go deep enough to expose enough good wood to allow for proper recutting. When you have finished planing, sand the entire area with fine sandpaper to even out the plane marks. A block treated in this way can be printed only by hand rubbing and will never print properly on a press.

Plugging

When a line or two has broken and the block must be printed for a long edition, the best repair method is to cut a plug of a wedge-shaped piece of wood several inches long. Cut a deep tapered groove through the line that is broken, removing all the wood to be replaced. Hammer the wedge into the tapered cut until it is forced in very tightly. Cut off the excess with a hacksaw blade, sandpaper down to the level of the block, and recut the line. The wedge will fit so tightly that it need not be glued. If you need a larger area than the wedge will cover, you can cut a block shaped to fit a deep incision in your block. The depth of the incision should be over ¼", and the sides should be cut vertically. This piece will have to be glued in position with Elmer's or carpenter's glue, sanded level, and then recut to gain the desired effect. The bottom of the incision should be level enough to have the glue hold the repair block in place.

It is possible to drill circular holes with a bit and then glue in pieces of wooden dowel to fit the drilled holes. This method does not make a good joint and can only be used for small, isolated repairs.

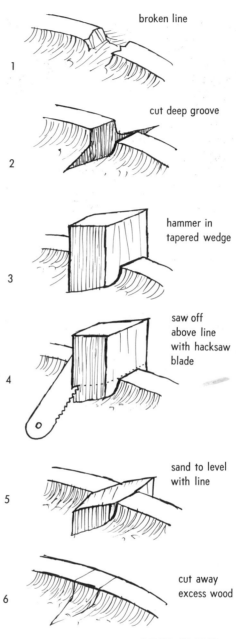

1 broken line

2 cut deep groove

3 hammer in tapered wedge

4 saw off above line with hacksaw blade

5 sand to level with line

6 cut away excess wood

REPAIR OF BROKEN LINES IN WOODCUT

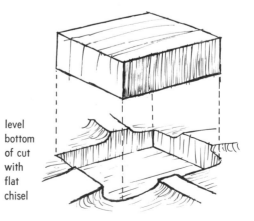

cut a new plug precisely to fit. Drive in with mallet. Recut lines

chisel out the offending portion. Cut straight down

level bottom of cut with flat chisel

PLUGGING A WOOD CUT

The brayer (or roller) should spread the ink evenly over the surface. Good distribution of ink is vital to a clean impression.

Ink the block thoroughly. Move the roller in many directions, building up the ink gradually. Too much ink will fill the fine textures and delicate cutting.

Below: Here a Japanese rice spoon, made of bamboo, is used as the rubbing tool. The flat side covers large areas quickly.

Repairing Other Relief Blocks

The repair of a relief etching is a rather tricky process. When a zinc plate is etched, it is often necessary to change poorly drawn or incorrect passages.

If this happens, scrape the entire area evenly to eliminate all ridges and bumps, turn the plate face down on a polished metal plate, such as an inking platen or ¼" steel plate, protecting the face of the relief etching with newspaper, and hammer the back of the plate over the offending area until the zinc has been forced into the proper level again. You must hammer fairly vigorously, using a rounded hammer. With careful work you can force up a considerable amount of zinc and make repairs by re-etching the scraped out areas. Use wooden calipers to locate the proper spot to hammer on the back of the plate. This process is called repoussage.

A linoleum cut may be repaired easily. Simply cut the bad area out and reglue another piece of linoleum on the backing board. Cardboard collage and other collage relief plates are so easy to repair that this quality is a very positive factor in their wide acceptance and popularity. You can glue new pieces in position very quickly with any one of a number of good adhesives, such as polymer gesso, Elmer's glue, thickened lacquer, model cement, and the like.

HAND PRINTING

The printing of the woodblock is almost as important as the cutting. Without a doubt, sensitive printing through careful inking and rubbing can reveal all the nuances of line and tonality that may be inherent in a block. Heavy inking and a heavy hand at rubbing with an improper tool can make a sensitively cut block look inept.

A few careful steps that should be followed can help to produce prints with excellent printing quality. First, it is important to set up for printing. The cutting table should be thoroughly cleaned with a dust brush of all wood chips. The block should be brushed off with a soft wire brush to eliminate any possibility of tiny chips of wood clinging to the block and being picked up by the roller and redeposited onto the block. If these little chips become lodged between paper and block, rubbing the paper during printing soon produces tears in the paper and ruins a good print. All tools used in the cutting process should be put aside. Only the block, a tube of black printing ink, a palette knife, a slab for rolling, a good roller, one or two rubbing tools, and enough precut paper should appear on the work table.

A word might be said here about choice of roller and ink. The quality of softness or hardness of the roller is important in relation to the quality of the cutting. If the block is finely cut with considerable detail and tonality, then a hard roller and stiff ink is very important. If the cutting is in free large forms, a softer roller and less stiff ink may be used.

Squeeze a moderate amount of ink onto the slab. Pick up some ink on the roller and roll it out on the slab in horizontal and vertical movements. Be sure the ink is distributed evenly on the roller and the slab. When there is a thin even layer on the roller, begin to deposit it on the block in a variety of horizontal, vertical, and diagonal movements in order to distribute the ink evenly. This process can be repeated three or four times from slab to block until there is an even, tacky, moderate deposit of ink on the block. Avoid too much ink. Overinking will fill in thin lines and produce a too-thick uneven deposit on the paper.

When the block is properly rolled up, place the paper carefully on the block, leaving even, two-inch margins, and rub moderately with the palm of the hand to smooth out the paper and adhere it to the block. Rub with moderate to heavy pressure from the back, with the Japanese rice spoon or the wooden door knobs or whichever rubbing tool feels comfortable for you. Rub in small even strokes from the center of the block outwards, with consistent pressure rather than long, broad strokes that are more difficult to control. Hold the paper down with your free hand. Pick up a corner of the print, being careful not to disturb the registry, and check the quality of printing every now and then. If the paper is of a medium to thin variety, some of the imagery will show through on the back, which will often indicate that there is proper pressure and proper amount of ink. If the block has been too lightly inked it sometimes can be carefully reinked if the paper is picked up in small areas at a time, holding the adhered area down with the other hand, and the rerolling done without disturbing the registry.

Two hands give more pressure to the bamboo rice spoon, helping to give emphasis to certain areas of the block.

Place the paper in position, using a register frame if you want consistent margins. The register frame is optional for one color prints but essential for color register work.

Below: Rub the back of the print with good pressure. The rubbing instrument is two drawer pulls, glued together.

Use the edge of the spoon for greatest pressure and, therefore, the strongest impression.

Below: Check the printing by lifting the corners after you have rubbed the major part of the block. You can replace the paper and reprint the light areas.

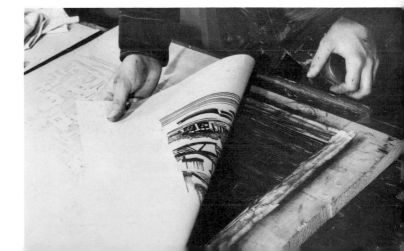

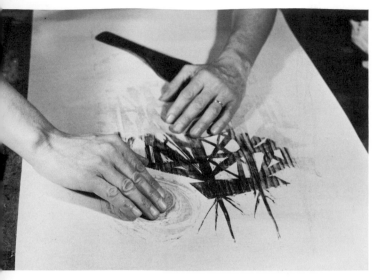

If you want very light tonality, use only the pressure of your fingers.

The finger-rubbed area is much lighter than the spoon-rubbed shapes.

An etching press may be used to print woodcuts if the roller can be raised high enough to accomodate the block. In this case the Brand press is equipped with springs for this purpose. Ink is applied with a brayer.

Tonal qualities can be achieved through printing, and tones can vary in the same print, again through printing. If one area in a print is supposed to be black and another grey, rub the black area heavily with the rubbing tool, and in the grey area, rub lightly with just the fingers. Even more controlled greys can be achieved by inking lightly in some areas and more heavily in others and again using a combination of fingers and rubbing tool for printing.

PRESS PRINTING

The sensitive control that is possible when you are printing by hand-rubbing or spooning the back of the paper is a tiring, time-consuming operation. Some prints can be achieved only through this method. However, if you need a large edition or want to print the block together with type, it may be possible to plan the block for printing in a press. There are four or five types of presses that might be used.

Relief Printing on an Etching Press

The most commonly available press is the typical etching press, with a bed passing between two steel rollers. If the upper roller can be adjusted upward to one inch or more above the bed, you may easily print a woodcut on this type of press. The inking may be done with hand brayers or rollers. More than one color can be rolled onto the block if the areas to be inked are separated enough to avoid overlapping.

The block need not be perfectly level for printing on the etching press. Slight cupping or curling is no great disadvantage because the contact area between the steel printing roller and the inked block is a thin line, about ¼" wide. This contact enables the block, even though warped, to print evenly if the block is placed on the press so that the grain runs parallel to the length of the press roller. Use a newsprint or other packing paper, such as a blotter to keep the blanket clean. Normally one blanket is plenty, and the pressure may be much lighter than that used for intaglio print-

Below: Light packing is used for level blocks. Newsprint and a blotter are put under a thin blanket. The pressure is controlled by micrometer gauges.

ing. Now we are merely printing from the surface of the block.

Smoother papers tend to print more accurate detail and texture than rough papers. If you use thin Japanese papers such as Mulberry, Sekishu, or Moriki, the ink may be forced through these porous papers, soiling the blankets. Heavier stocks need less packing and are easier to handle.

Avoid handling the inked block while it is in position on the press bed. You may tape paper to the bed and mark, with a pencil, the corners where the block fits. It is easy to make little cardboard stops and tape them to the bed to indicate the precise position of the block. The paper may also be controlled in this way, making possible an even margin throughout the edition. When you are involved with color work, it is possible to have a color register system with taped cardboard stops.

Press printing yields longer editions than hand printing because the pressure is evenly distributed over the entire length of the block instead of being localized in small areas by the hand rubbing method.

Relief Printing on the Vandercook Press

Editions of several hundred or more in several colors are feasible if you can obtain the use of a Vandercook press for printing. There are many models, depending on size and inking facility. The older models are relatively cheap, because every printer had a press of this kind for proving his typographic matter. Many models have no inking rollers and the inking must be done with brayers, and only the impression is performed on these presses.

Some older Vandercooks have no grippers, and these presses are much more difficult to use for larger editions than models with grippers. It is possible to do color register work with gripperless presses by linking enough rubber bands to form two strings. These bands are wrapped around the cylinder and fastened with string or paper clips. The paper to be printed may be slipped under these rubber bands, taking care to see that the printing surface does not come in contact with the rubber bands, or it will be damaged. Mark the packing sheet with pencil as a guide for the paper, so that successive sheets may be placed in a similar position. The register obtained by this method is not as precise as that obtained by more recent presses.

These newer presses have inking rollers attached to the printing cylinder, and these rollers ink the block in the instant after the printing drum has passed over the block. Some presses have motor-driven inking rollers that automatically distribute ink over the surface of the rollers. These presses are ideal for longer editions.

Lock-Up on the Vandercook

The block must be fixed in position within the bed of the press, in order to prevent slipping and insure even margins. The easiest way to fix the block is to use an automatic lock-up bar, supplied by Vandercook in different lengths for the varying beds that are manufactured. They are expensive, however, and a 19-inch lock-up bar costs over $75.

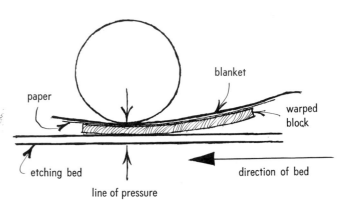

HOW TO PRINT A WARPED BLOCK ON ETCHING PRESS

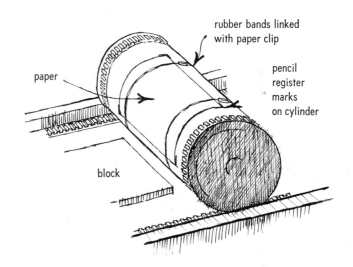

REGISTER CONTROL ON SIMPLE PROOF PRESS

To print an edition on the Vandercook 25 press, the block is locked in position using plywood furniture and conventional quoins. The block must be level.

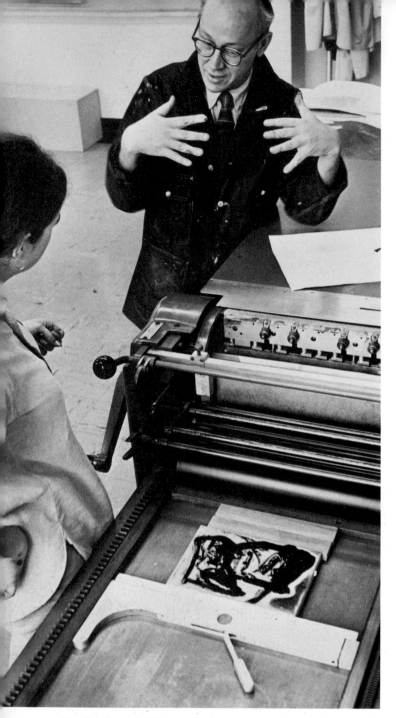

The Vandercook 219 press has a motorized inking roller assembly which speeds the distribution of ink. An automatic lock-up bar holds a zinc relief etching in place for Kathy Herbeck of Manhattanville College.

The cylinder and attached inking rollers pass over the block, inking it twice between impressions.

The cheapest lock-up is made with pieces of square wood, called furniture, held in place with keys and quoins. Wooden furniture is cheap, available everywhere, even secondhand, and most job printers get rid of their old furniture from time to time. Metal furniture is better than wood, and plastic furniture is better than metal but is very expensive and not yet commonly available. A great convenience if you do much press printing is to have some magnetic metal furniture handy. You may use this material to lock the block in position temporarily, for a few proofs. It is not suitable for a lock-up that is going to be printed for a large number of impressions.

Make-Ready on the Vandercook

If you use type-high (.918″) wood that is quite level, you will find good impressions are easy to obtain. Slight variations in printing surface may be remedied by gluing thin pieces of strong tissue paper (called make-ready) on the packing sheet over the printing cylinder. Use Sphinx paste, and if the edges of the paper cause a sharp line to print, sand the edges with fine sandpaper in order to smooth the edges. Better still, tear the paper instead of cutting it with scissors. This will usually solve the problem. It may be necessary to glue more than one level of make-ready paper to the packing sheet in order to bring the printing surface to proper height. Discard the packing sheet when the edition is finished. Don't attempt to reclaim it for your next print because it will be ruined by the glue.

If you use wood that is less than type high, slip a few sheets of thin cardboard or oak-tag under the block in order to build up the height of the block. Cut these sheets slightly smaller than the block so that they do not stick out and ruin your lock-up.

Wood that is warped or curled may present too much difficulty to print, and make-ready will not suffice to correct this handicap. Therefore, your blocks should be level from the start when printing on a proof press, because it is fixed in position and cannot adjust to the rollers as on an etching press. The best source of level blocks is from a manufacturer of backing wood for photoengravings. These blocks are usually of cherry or poplar, both very good for woodcuts.

It is possible to print from relief etchings made from zinc or copper plates or from collage plates made from cardboard, paper, cloth, and other materials. If these plates are to be press printed, care must be taken to get the surface of the plate as level as possible, otherwise the make-ready will be an enormous task. The collage plates should be well sealed and thoroughly glued in order to withstand the suction of the inking rollers and the pressure of the impression cylinder.

Printing on the Vandercook

The quality of impression possible from the Vandercook is excellent, depending upon the proper preparation of the make-ready and the right distribution of the ink. Too much ink will fill the fine texture of the block and clog the fine lines. It is better to start with a thin film of ink and build it up rather than to put too much ink on the rollers and then have to remove it, necessitating a wash-up of the block, too.

To print a large sheet of paper without slurring or blurring of the edges of the printed matter, it may be necessary to hold the trailing edge of the paper tight against the cylinder as it prints.

Printing from the Columbian or Albion Press

The use of the Albion press has dwindled to a very low point in fine printmaking. It is suitable for small blocks, however, and some wood engravers still find them helpful. The block must be inked with a brayer. Because the edges of the blocks usually print darker, make-ready should be done with care for each block, building up the packing with thin sheets of paper pasted to the packing sheet with Sphinx paste. The make-ready paper should be torn or the edges sanded in order to have a gradual transition in thickness. The block must be placed in the center of the bed of the press; and while the bed is being rolled in and out for alternate inking and printing, care must be taken not to cause bumping or jogging that may loosen the block and cause slurring or blurred prints.

The pressure exerted by one of these old platens is considerable and may easily damage a block if it is excessive. Therefore the pressure should be built up gradually by increasing the number of pieces of paper or cardboard under the block to raise it to proper printing level. Pressure may also be increased by adding to the packing sheets placed between the tympan sheets. These packing sheets cushion the pressure and distribute it somewhat over the surface of the block. A tiny speck of lint or sand can cause pitting or denting of the block in any press, including cylinder and platen presses, and great care must be taken to keep the inking slab and roller clean.

A bookbinding press may be used to print small woodcuts if the edition is limited. The pressure is usually good, but the amount of manipulation is quite time-consuming. Hand rubbing is faster.

Printing from a Low Relief Surface

It is possible to print from a surface where the depth of relief is too low for normal methods, such as with an underbitten relief etching. Instead of inking the plate directly with the roller, which would almost certainly contact the lower areas where they are not deep enough, ink a piece of heavy oak-tag paper evenly and completely. Then place the inked surface on and facing the plate, place a piece of mat board or smooth cardboard on top of that, and, and run it through the etching press with reduced pressure. You will find that only the raised areas will receive the ink. It is possible to use this process without the press by burnishing or spooning the back of the oak tag carefully and with heavy pressure. This will ink the plate, which must now be printed onto your paper either by spooning or by using the etching press. You may use heavy acetate or vinyl instead of tag paper, as it cleans easily and may be reused. The William Blake relief etchings were very shallow and were printed by a similar method.

When the cylinder is run to the foot of the press the paper is placed in position, resting on the slanted paper support. The grippers will pull the paper through the printing cycle.

When the cylinder has returned to the head of the press the grippers release and the printed impression may be checked for flaws.

The Color Relief Print

Color in the woodcut was first used in the West to hand tint the early black and white woodcuts of saints and the designs of woodcut printed playing cards. It was a cheap means to supply colored pictures to the widely illiterate public of the late Middle Ages. The use of color from several wood blocks was introduced in western Europe in the second half of the 15th century for heraldic cuts, initials, and printer's marks. The method of printing pictorial color woodcuts from separate blocks, known as "Chiaroscuro," appeared in 1508 in Germany in the earliest dated print. However, according to Hind, the first of the Italian Chiaroscuro woodcutters, Ugo Da Carpi, about 1455–1523, was no doubt making prints much earlier. These prints, though printed from separate blocks, were tonal and interpreted the line and wash drawings of the period. Da Carpi and other fine woodcutters worked from designs by Parmigiano and Raphael and were essentially reproductive. The emphasis was on various tones of one color but sometimes included browns, yellows, and greens on the same print.

Some woodcuts with color as a unifying structural element were made by the Chinese as early as the 17th century. However, it is the multicolor prints of 18th and 19th century Japan that have given us such an eloquent concept of color in the woodcut. The ukiyo-e prints (the pictures of the Floating World, the World of Everyday Life) were made by major artists with great refinement and taste for the generally poorer classes and the uneducated. They were bought for a few yen, with little value attached to them, much as the medieval woodcuts were purchased in Northern Europe in the 16th century. They were souvenirs, pasted in homes, bought by travelers. The subject matter covered a wide range: girls, actors, genre scenes, popular landscapes. Utamaro, Sharaku, Harunobu, Hokusai, and Hiroshige were among the great names.

There are many tales of the Ukiyo-e prints first arriving in Paris as packing material for art objects. However, as early as 1775 a Swedish naturalist, Carl Peter Thunberg, spent considerable time in Nagasaki and made a collection of Ukiyo-e. Dutch sea captains in the early 1800s formed extensive collections that were known in Paris. In 1860, the British magazine *Once a Week* contained articles of a voyage in Japan illustrated with some of Hiroshige's landscapes. By 1862 a Japanese curio shop opened in Paris and sold many of the Ukiyo-e prints. In 1867 the Paris Exposition Universelle exhibited a large quantity of Ukiyo-e, and the Paris art world became profoundly aware of the new art forms.

Opposite: Kitagawa Utamaro
"The Awabi Fishers" (from a triptych)
Color woodcut 15½" x 10¾"
Collection of the authors

It was from this exhibition that many western artists incorporated the concepts of the Ukiyo-e into their work. Though the art was declining in intensity and quality in Japan, it was a great influence on the creativity of the avant-garde in Paris. Gaugin, Van Gogh, Mary Cassatt, Toulouse-Lautrec, Whistler, Degas, Manet, and Pissarro came under the influence of the asymetric compositions, strong design, and stylized form. The flat color, pattern, and line as intrinsic compositional elements were deeply inspiring to those artists.

Though the early influence of the Japanese print was felt more directly in Western painting, it also rapidly affected the approach to color in printmaking.

Gauguin's use of the woodcut had a strong Japanese influence. His blocks were conceived in black and white, but the use of color in the print interested him. He experimented with printing a block in black, then reinking it in another color, usually brown, and printing it slightly off register. In some prints he added brilliant color through stencils or hand colored the prints. Gauguin's innovative approach with the woodcut influenced the woodcuts of Munch. Gauguin's probes into the use of color in the print no doubt helped Munch to explore the color print even further than Gauguin had taken it. In some instances Munch used separate blocks for each color, in others he used one block cut into separate color areas, inked separately, and reassembled for printing with one rubbing. These are powerful prints, where color and form are synonymous.

Another major innovation occurred with Picasso's lino-cuts of the 1950s. His use of one block for a multicolor print was probably the first time anyone had devised a reduction method for cutting and printing each color out of one block.

Since the late forties and fifties, color in the relief print has become increasingly adventurous and freewheeling. Michael Rothenstein in England and Carol Summers and Seong Moy in the United States were early experimenters.

The flexibility of the cardboard relief print and the collage print along with inventive ways of inking with small rollers has expanded the use of color. Op and Pop images have also loosened conceptual ideas about color and have helped to break down old taboos about color in the print.

USE OF COLOR

The use of color in the development of the relief-print image should help to clarify the visual idea and express form. Employing color as mere decoration or as a "tint" to a black-and-white print will not normally produce an exciting or satisfying work. If the artist understands and exploits the great potential of color in a relief print a work of high expressive power can be resolved. The woodcut block itself has a quality that makes the colors take on vibrancy and intensity. It is easy to cut separate blocks for each color and to print them in correct register to achieve the final impression of many colors in one image. It is also possible to use a single block to print all the colors in a design. This method, known as the *reduction* or *subtractive* method, was the one used so eloquently by Picasso in his linoleum color prints. This process will be discussed in the section on reduction prints. The procedures an artist uses in the color relief print are extremely personal and are dictated by his own esthetic direction. We will discuss various methods that have been found logical and useful at various times for our own work and for the work of other artists.

Key Block Method

Some artists will cut a block that contains most or all of the dominant design elements. This block is called a *key block,* and it can be proved in a strong color after it is cut. These proofs may serve as trials for color samples that may be painted directly on the proof, using poster color, water color, or ink to develop the color relationships. From these sketches the other blocks may be cut. The drawback of the key-block method occurs when too much emphasis is placed on the first block and the succeeding colors become only incidental to the design rather than essential to it. The Japanese Ukiyo-e prints used a key block with the major elements in black line and the areas of mass and pattern in successive color blocks.

Color on Block Method

Another approach is to develop a color sketch directly on a block, painting the image with poster or tempera paint, using thin pigment so that the grain is not filled with color. After the design is completed, make a careful tracing of it as a record, then cut the most important color on the block. This first block serves as a master that may be proved in register onto the successive blocks. The tracing you have made will enable you to cut the shapes of the next colors. The drawback of this method is that you destroy your color sketch when you cut the first block. However, it eliminates one transfer and keeps the first block very vigorous and fresh, which is a very positive factor.

The Separate Color Sketch

The most complete control is obtained when a carefully worked out color drawing is completed on a separate sheet. This is an excellent means for those who must have a completely realized solution before they start. The sketch should be made in a medium that can reflect the transparencies possible in color overprinting. Watercolor is good, colored inks are better, and poster color or tempera are suitable if used properly. As poster colors are opaque, the basic colors of each block may be mixed in small dishes and used to mix smaller batches of the secondary colors that will be fairly close to the finished print from the blocks.

Pastels may be used for the same result, as may pencil crayons. These are excellent for small-scale work if used on tracing paper. The color range is quite good in the larger artist's sets. Colors may be applied over each other to approximate the quality of overprinted inks. Felt pens, using dyes, are excellent, although they tend to fade after a few months. Colored paper can be used in making a collage sketch to serve as a guide for a color relief print. With any of these methods, a tracing will have to be made of the completed sketch to serve as the master guide for all the blocks to be cut. The results from this method are not likely

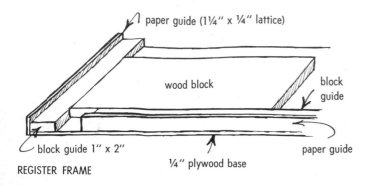

paper guide (1¼" x ¼" lattice)

wood block

block guide

block guide 1" x 2"

¼" plywood base

paper guide

REGISTER FRAME

to be as fresh and spontaneous as with other, more direct approaches. However, the increase in control of color relationships has certain advantages for those artists who desire complex color statements. The choice of method is really directed by the personal direction of each artist, and the success of each procedure depends upon his enthusiasm and drive.

COLOR REGISTRY METHODS

Register Frame

After your preliminary color sketch is completed and your first block is cut, it is necessary to place this first image on each successive block, in proper register or juxtaposition, in order to have each color area in proper relation to the other. A register frame is easily constructed; on a base of ¼" plywood or pressed wood or composition board, nail or glue two pieces of 1" by 2" wood, as shown. These pieces are at right angles to each other and hold the block in place. If you habitually use cardboard or linoleum or other thin blocks you can make the frames from thin stripping. In any case they should approximate the thickness of the blocks that you are printing. Along the edges of this wooden angle nail or glue two strips of thin ⅛" by 1" wooden stripping to serve as a paper guide. Take care to leave an open corner when you fasten the stripping so that the thumb can comfortably adjust the paper. Two wooden 12" rulers make excellent paper guides.

The first block, after it is cut, is inked fairly heavily and placed in the frame. Slide the block against the long edge of the frame until it touches the other, perpendicular side. Make sure that the long edge is firmly fitted in the frame. This position must be duplicated every time the block is printed. If the block is square both edges may fit securely, but it is more likely that the block is slightly out of square and one side fits solidly while the other edge touches at one point only. When the block is in position, tape a piece of tracing paper to the edge of the frame.

When printing color blocks, always place the block into the register frame in the same way for each printing to achieve a consistent register, using the block guides.

To transfer a design cut into a block to another block in order to achieve color register, ink the block, then place it in the register frame. Put a piece of nonabsorbent paper (tracing paper or bond paper) in position with masking tape. Rub the paper with the spoon to print the inked design.

Below: Now turn the block over or place a new, uncut block in the register frame, leaving the taped tracing paper in position.

Offsetting onto Additional Blocks

Tracing paper is used in preference to all other papers because it is not absorbent and will hold a great deal of ink on its surface in order to offset the cut image onto the other uncut blocks. Let the tracing paper drop down over the well-inked first block. Rub your hand over the back of the paper to hold it firmly. Now rub the back of the tracing paper with a rubbing tool to obtain a strong image on the tracing paper.

Lift up the tracing paper with the imprint of the block on it, being careful not to remove the paper from the frame. Slip out the block that has just been printed. Turn the block over to the uncut side and slip the block back into the register frame carefully in the same position.

Drop the tracing paper onto the block. Rub it with the hand to adhere it and then with a rubbing tool to achieve a strong image on the uncut block. Lift up the tracing paper again, remove the block, and slip in the next uncut block

until the first cut image has been successfully transferred, in position, onto each uncut block.

Let the offset images of the first block dry on the uncut color blocks. Wash off the ink from the first cut block with varnolene so that the pores of the wood will not be clogged. After the offset images are dry, the second color can be indicated with chalk or traced on the block from a drawing, in direct relationship to the first color. Care must be taken to make the image of the second color a little larger to allow for an overlap of colors so that no gaps of white paper will appear between forms. This technique is called *trapping* and requires an overlap of $\frac{1}{16}''$ or so. After the second color is cut, the transfer is repeated, placing the image onto tracing paper and then onto the third or fourth blocks that are to be cut. This time, instead of using a dark ink, use a light red or green ink to roll up the second block so that it can be seen clearly in relation to the first color offset.

An aid in using this method is to avoid cutting any of the blocks completely; thus the composition can develop organically, and changes can be easily made after first proofing. When printing an edition from the register frame, the paper should be trimmed in advance to have two straight sides, at right angles to each other. These sides fit into the paper guides on the frame and must always be placed in the same manner, from block to block, in order to maintain the same relationships. The best way to hold the paper is by diagonally opposite corners, which gives you the most control. Slide the paper along the long edge of the paper guide until it hits the side guide. Then lower the paper on to the inked block and print it by rubbing. Once the ink has adhered the paper to the block, it may be moved out of the guides for the printing process. The inking should also be done with the block away from the frame edges in order to keep them clean and to help keep margins clean.

Japanese Method

The Japanese register method requires blocks somewhat larger than the printed area because the register guides are cut into each block. The white margin around your print is established by the register guides. Small right-angled key stops are cut into one corner and one side of the block. They do not have to be cut very deeply, as they must hold only the edge of the paper. About three times the thickness of the paper you are using is enough. See drawing for details. The

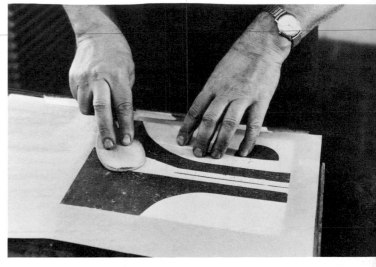

Transfer the wet ink from the tracing paper to the uncut block by rubbing with the spoon. The tape will keep the paper in the correct position.

The design has been transferred, in register, to the new block. This will enable you to see exactly where the first block will fall in relation to the new block.

The paper is placed in position over the inked block, using the paper guides. Use the same placement throughout the edition for consistent register.

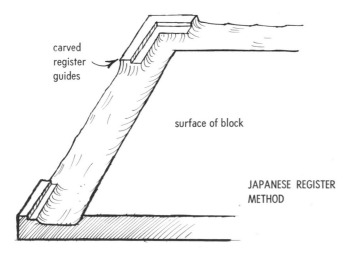

carved
register
guides

surface of block

JAPANESE REGISTER
METHOD

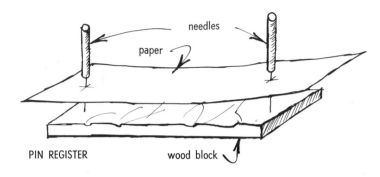

PIN REGISTER   wood block

Antonio Frasconi places small blocks on a marked cardboard sheet in order to control their register for a color print. It is not necessary to cut the same size blocks for each color of a color print.

REGISTER FOR THICK RELIEF PRINT OBJECTS

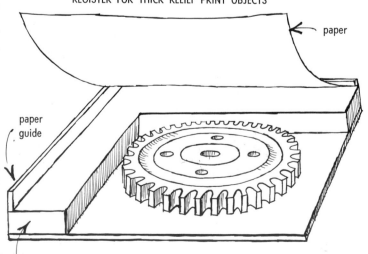

paper is fitted into these stops each time an impression is to be pulled. These registers are cut into each block in succession, as the blocks are cut. The previously cut block is transferred to the uncut blocks either by the Japanese method of gluing the key proof to each block or by the western method of transferring a proof inked on tracing paper or nonabsorbent bond paper by rubbing the back of the proof, while the ink is still wet, on to the next blocks. See the section on the Japanese method. This method restricts the size of the prints, and most western printmakers do not use this technique.

Pin Register

An adequate method for registering small prints uses two long needles. Common pins are usually too small for any but tiny prints. After the first block has been cut, take a heavily inked proof on a strong, tough paper. While the paper is still on the block, punch two needles through the paper into the block. The holes must be close to the edge and far enough apart to insure adequate control. Remove the needles, then the inked proof. Place the proof, image down, on the next block, transfer the image by rubbing the back, punch holes into the new block through the same holes in the paper that you first made. Now cut the second block, and continue this process until all the blocks are cut. When you print using the needle method, you may need help to keep the paper taut and away from the inked surface until the needles have found the holes in the wood. The disadvantages of this method are so great that only small editions may be printed before the process becomes too tedious. Large prints are very difficult to handle, too. The pinholes in the paper are usually easy to burnish closed when the print is dry.

Small Blocks or Pieces

You may need to register a small block or found object into a certain position on a color print. If the block is of thin material, such as cardboard, engraving metal, cloth, or the like, it may simply be glued to a base block of plywood or masonite or chip board. However, if the block is of thicker material, such as ⅞" wood or ¾" plywood, or cannot easily be glued in place, you can make a base board out of heavy paper or cardboard. Cut this material to the size of the key block or the size of the print. Mark the position of the small block on the base board so that you can return the block to the correct position each time it is inked.

When you are printing from very thick material such as rough-sawn planks or log sections, machine parts, and the like, you may have to make a special jig or frame to hold these pieces in place.

Jigsaw Method

An interesting method of making a color print from one block should be mentioned here because it eliminates registry yet enables the artist to use a multiplicity of color. This approach was used by Edvard Munch, the gifted Norwegian expressionist painter and printmaker who lived from 1863 to 1944. His work with color in the print was unique for his

Antonio Frasconi
"Portrait of Sioux Chief Sitting Bull"
Color Woodcut 36" x 24"
Terry Dintenfass Gallery

Carol Summers
"Rainbow Glacier" 1970
Color Woodcut 36½" x 37"
Associated American Artists Gallery

Pablo Picasso
"Woman with Hat" 1962
Linocut 13¾" x 10¾" (reduction print)
Barney Weinger Gallery

time. He used it boldly and symbolically in his images. Although he used four or five colors in one print, they were often printed from one block sawed into separate pieces very much like a jigsaw puzzle. After inking each separate piece, he would fit the elements back together again and print the complete image quite easily with one rubbing. *Two Beings* was printed from one block carefully sawn into two separate pieces. The two simple elements, the couple and the ground, and the sky were each cut along the edges of their forms. A thin dividing line appears in the print where a slight space occurs between the forms. This line becomes an integral part of the design and seems to preview the appearance of white separating lines that appear so frequently in contemporary intaglio plates that are cut into separate pieces and inked and reassembled in printing. To produce this effect, mat board or cardboard may be cut into segments, inked separately, and then reassmbled into correct position for printing. Of course, the surface of the mat board should be sealed with lacquer, shellac, or polymer gesso before inking.

Reduction Print

The reduction method is best described by its name. One block is reduced in numerous stages to a multicolored print. It is an interesting and creative procedure for the experienced artist. However, it would be best for the uninitiated to prepare a careful color sketch that will help to clarify the sequential cutting of areas.

The first color is sometimes printed from the whole block. Sometimes a minimal amount of wood is removed to designate the first color. The number of the edition must be determined with the printing of the first color, as there is no possibility of reprinting. After printing the first color, remove all the ink from the block, indicate the second color on the block, and cut away all the excess wood. Ink the block with the second color and print it over the first color. Repeat the cutting and inking until a satisfactory image develops. With this method the area of the block is reduced with each cutting so that the larger areas of color must be cut first. The final block will, of necessity, contain only a small percentage of the area of the block.

Picasso completed a fine series of vibrant color linocuts between 1961 and 1963 that are reduction prints and interesting to study in preparation for using this method.

COLOR INKS FOR RELIEF PRINTING

The chemistry involved in the production of today's printing ink is so complex that a new profession has evolved, that of ink chemist or engineer. Some manufacturers go to great lengths to keep their formulas secret, and the technology of ink manufacture has become so sophisticated that the artist and printmaker should not attempt to make his own color, except in rare cases. It is suggested that you buy ink from a well-establshed commercial firm and conduct a few simple tests of the permanence of some key colors. You will probably find that the great majority of color is relatively permanent and a small number of colors fade quite rapidly and are unsuitable for use.

In general, the earth colors such as the ochres, umbers, and siennas are usually permanent. The cadmiums, yellow, orange, and red, are also permanent in most cases. When you add black, white, transparent extender, and the phthalo blues and greens, you will have a pretty fair palette.

The colors that tend to fade are the reds, magentas, purples, and certain blues. The pigment used in the manufacture of the ink is responsible for the fading in almost every instance. It is usually not specified which pigment has been used in the composition of the ink and it is difficult to predict which exact color is not permanent. When in doubt, roll out a thin film of ink onto a few white matboard cards. Place one in the sun, one in a shady spot, and file another away in an enclosed book or file. After a month or two you will see the amount of fading in each case. Very few colors will pass the sun test without some fading, but all should pass the shade test. Use the best pigments you can get.

As the artist printmaker has a prime interest in the permanence of his colors, he will have to take proper care to guarantee that all his inks are stable. Many artists mix their own colors. They add a good quality oil paint (one without excessive filler, binder, or extender) to a transparent white ink extender in order to get the proper viscosity. Oil paint directly from the tube, although made of high-quality ground

Clare Romano
"Rocks of Truro" 1962
Color woodcut 17½" x 26"
Collection, Brooklyn Museum

pigments, rarely has enough stickiness to roll out properly when inking a relief print. The amount of transparent extender (basically a varnish) will vary according to the viscosity required. In any case, add only the minimum extender needed to achieve good rolling quality. A small amount of dry magnesium can be added to the color to make it stiffer.

It is not so useful to purchase inks in a transparent state, such as transparent lemon yellow, as to buy ink in the opaque state and purchase a separate amount of transparent white. It is not a white pigment at all but a transparent varnish of tannish color that does not alter the intensity of other colors. The transparent white will enable you to control the amount of transparency and to add transparency to any color that you choose. The primary colors, called the process colors by ink manufacturers, will produce a wide range of hues and used with black and white, can extend your palette to a very wide spectrum. However, such colors as emerald green and intense magentas and purples may have to be purchased specially in order to gain maximum brilliance and intensity.

Unless you use ink rapidly, you should buy it in tube form. Many makers put up a good range of color in large tubes (about 1½" in diameter by 7" long). Tube ink is slightly more expensive per pound than ink in cans but is much more convenient to use. We have some tubes of ink that are ten years old and still in good condition. Replace the caps carefully, after cleaning the cap with a rag or palette knife. If you do use canned ink, and it is cheaper, you should wipe the rims and lids and replace the circular waxed paper by smoothing it over the ink in the can, eliminating the air bubbles. When the ink skins over, the top must be scraped off and discarded. Even a small piece of dried ink skin can be an annoyance when printing. Another aid in storing partially used ink cans is to fill the remainder of the can with water to retard the drying-out process. Spray cans of sealers for cans of ink can also be purchased from ink companies and are useful in keeping ink from drying out. A thin film is sprayed over the ink surface.

COLOR PRINTING

Sensitive printing of the color blocks is a vital step in the completion of the final image. A thorough knowledge of the use of overprinting and color sequence can exploit the use of color with variation and inventiveness.

Transparency and Sequence

The use of transparencies in overprinting is an important aspect of the color woodcut. It enables the artist to achieve a wide color range with just a few colors and to use the full potential of the blocks.

Clare Romano
"Summer Garden" 1958
Cardboard relief 18¾" x 24"

A varnish-like material called transparent white is manufactured by many ink makers. When it is added to the color inks it will make them transparent. It is often tannish in color but it does not appreciably alter the color quality of the inks when mixed with them. From 40% to 60% transparency may be added to an ink to achieve the desired quality. The transparency should be added to the ink on the mixing slab and mixed well with a palette knife. The amount of transparency is determined by the color. A lemon yellow or bright orange needs little or no transparency because of the natural transparency of the color itself.

You will find that it is much easier to roll up a block with the color inks because they are of a softer consistency. Less ink is required on the block and less rubbing in printing. If delicate cutting is to be printed, you may find it desirable to add some powdered magnesium to the ink in order to stiffen it.

Generally speaking, the dark colors are printed first and the light ones last in order to achieve the most effect from overprinting with transparent inks. However, there are times when a dark or black block is a key block and it is necessary to the design to print it last.

The color quality of a color print can be greatly changed if the sequence in printing is reversed. Experimentation will lead you to the varied possibilities that exist through sequential printing. Colored papers can also be used with a wide range of effects. Light colors can be printed over black and off-black papers. High-key colored papers and subtle colors can all be used with very surprising qualities.

Wet and Dry Printing

Wet and dry printing is very important in proving. Usually when transparency is used the colors are printed wet over dry or semidry inks. Sometimes when two colors are close in value, even with some transparency added to the second color, they must be printed wet on wet for best transparency results. It is difficult to make firm suggestions in this area. Experimentation with the blocks is of prime importance. So much depends on the color value. Best results can be achieved after a few possibilities are tried.

Exploration of Texture

Interesting color variations can be achieved by overprinting a combination of a smooth block and a textured block or two textured blocks. Flecks of pure color will appear in whatever pattern the textures make.

Use of Small Rollers

There are other possibilities in the printing and the planning of color blocks. Two or three colors can be easily printed on one block if the color is in isolated areas. Small rollers can be used very successfully for these places. There are some small Hunt rollers that come in sizes from 1½″ to 6″. There are also smaller Craftool rollers of 1″ in length and ½″ in diameter. All these rollers are quite soft and very good for non-detailed work. If a harder roller is desired, it is best to make one's own. Check sources and methods under section on rollers.

Split Fountain Printing

An interesting way to print more than one color at a time involves a press. A Vandercook, Kelly, or other flat press works very well. The colors are placed on the rollers, not too close together, and the inking rollers are then worked until the ink has been distributed evenly. The colors will merge and blend where they overlap, and this effect can occasionally be used to great advantage. As the ink keeps on blending, there is a limit to the number of prints that can be made before the color is merged or changed. Of course, this effect can be obtained with hand brayers, too, if the length of the roller is long enough to take the blending effect. The method is tricky, however, and can be easily overdone, becoming quite flashy or commercial-looking if not used with discretion.

Carol Summers Method

A unique method of color printing from separate blocks that is worth mentioning has been developed by the New York artist Carol Summers. Summers works with large, simple, stylized or abstracted forms, very often of landscape or architecture. He cuts his blocks fairly deeply, usually of ¼" plywood. After the blocks are cut he places them in a register frame, lays a piece of woodcut paper down on the uninked block, and rolls a thin film of oil-based ink on the paper with small rollers. Separate blocks are inked in this manner. When all the blocks are printed and the ink is still wet, Summers sprays the whole print with a thin film of varnolene with a mouth atomizer or a spray gun, allowing the colors to run together slightly, giving a watercolor effect to the printed image. Sometimes Summers combines the traditional method of rolling ink on the block with rolling ink on the paper. At times he prints on the back of the print so that the image is diffused. The resulting prints are very handsome and quite similar to rubbings.

JAPANESE WOODCUT METHOD

We have touched on some of the history of the Japanese woodcut, the ukiyo-e, in our introduction to the woodcut. It is not our function to involve ourselves in its rich history in this chapter, but to give some of the basic technical methods that the Japanese have used so eloquently in their prints. It would be well to mention the vast difference in the basic approach to printing the color woodcut in the Japanese Ukiyo-e prints as compared with our contemporary woodcuts that use the woodgrain as an important element and relate the printing to overprinting colors. The use of the water-based inks in the Japanese prints and the application and blending of watercolor washes directly on the blocks enabled them to achieve amazing watercolor qualities and impressions that would seem to us to be closer to monotypes. However, the application was so skilled that the printers were actually able to repeat complicated wash effects and still have consistent multiple editions.

The traditional approach of the Japanese artist to the use of his materials is quite ritualistic. The mastery of manual skill that was demanded of the Ukiyo-e artisans is an impossibility in our culture. However, it is very possible for the contemporary artist to adapt some of the methods for his own expression and with this intent in mind we will try to give some rudimentary information on materials and procedure.

Materials

Wood (cherry, poplar)
A good cutting knife
V gouge
2 sizes of C gouges
Small chisels
Large chisels
Whetstones for sharpening tools
Baren for rubbing
Dosa (sizing for paper made of water, animal glue, and alum)
Animal glue in stick form for making dosa
Alum, 3 to 4 oz. for making dosa
Tube of library paste or rice paste
Pigment
Brushes, large and small horsehair, for applying color
Brush for sizing, called a dosabake
Sumi ink
General equipment for stacking
Paper, boards for cutting, bowls, and the like

Wood

Cherry or yamazakura wood (a species of wild cherry) was almost the only kind of wood used by the traditional ukiyo-e artists. Cherry is a very hard wood and difficult to cut but was very necessary for the fine lines and great detail so prevalent in the ukiyo-e prints, as well as the common large editions.

The traditional ukiyo-e blocks were always cut with the grain. The selection of wood was a very important aspect of the preparation of the block. The wood was most often cut from the central portion of the tree between the heart and the bark, and a regular grain was preferred. The blocks were allowed to season for a few years to make them quite dry, as it is important in working with water-based pigments that the blocks absorb some of the color during printing.

The contemporary Japanese artist is very likely to use any wood that relates to what he wishes to say. Bass plywood is one of the woods most commonly used. It is inexpensive and easy to cut and comes in large sizes. Its unobtrusive grain also makes it desirable. American plywoods such as birch and fir are available and can be successfully used. Birch plywood in ¼″ and ½″ thicknesses, imported from Finland by Stewart Industries in Chicago and listed under our source list, is ideally suited for the woodcut in general and for the Japanese method in particular and is quite inexpensive. In addition to plywood, boards of pine, poplar, or fir can be used.

Tools (For Cutting)

The tools used by the Japanese are few and simple. They do not differ much from the ones suggested in our section

Mallet, chisels, and gouges used by Ansei Uchima in cutting his blocks (frequently made of birch plywood).

Uchima sharpens his tools on a smooth Japanese whetstone (*toishi*), using water as a lubricant.

Two barens, the one on the right with a split in its bamboo sheath cover, which will be replaced.

Below: The baren taken apart: on the left the old cover about to be replaced, at the top center the coil bamboo cord. At the bottom center is the backing paper that gives the baren its circular shape. The piece of bamboo sheath on the right will be shaped and trimmed to form a new cover for the baren.

on the western manner of the woodcut, but we do list the traditional ones here and suggest that they be used as described in that section. Their use by the ukiyo-e artisans was ritualistic. Certain tools were used only for certain kinds of cutting. The cutters themselves were divided into very distinct areas of work. There were separate cutters for figure work. The highly skilled workers cut the heads and the fine lines of the features and hair. Other cutters worked on the bodies and the pattern of drapery. Less experienced cutters worked on color blocks or unimportant areas. Their training took as long as ten years, and only a few achieved the skill necessary to work on the delicate faces, hair, and hands.

A good knife is essential for cutting lines. It is one of the most important tools. Tiny areas can be cleared with assorted small knives.

Chisels in small sizes are used for cutting out small areas of wood. The larger broad chisels are used for cleaning out large areas and for making *kento* (registry) cuts on the blocks. Sometimes a wooden mallet is used to hit the back of the chisel in order to clear areas in hardwood blocks.

The V gouge and C gouges were not used by the ukiyo-e artists but can be useful additional tools to define forms and to clear small areas.

Whetstones

Whetstones have traditionally been used by ukiyo-e artisans for sharpening tools. They are available in rough, medium, and smooth surfaces and are used with water for sharpening the tools. The stones used extensively by western printmakers use oil as a lubricant.

The edge of the knife or the gouge or chisel is held parallel to the surface of the whetstone. Water is applied so that the stone's surface is always wet. Use a smooth whetstone to finish off the sharpening. Do not change the angle of the tool during sharpening or the edge will be uneven.

The V gouges or C gouges can be sharpened on whetstones with grooves to hold variously sized tools. They can also be sharpened on a flat whetstone, but care must be taken to keep the edge of the curve flush with the stone's surface and to rotate it evenly to keep the edge and the curve at the same time.

Baren

The baren is the pressing and rubbing tool used for printing. It is an ingenious, simple tool that is beautifully designed for use on the porous Japanese paper. It consists of flat, coiled cord strands, strips of bamboo sheath, and a backing disk. The backing disk, about 5½" in diameter, is made of many layers of Japanese paper, molded on a form, covered with silk tissue, and lacquered. The backing disk holds the coil of cord, and the bamboo sheath used as a covering and as a rubbing surface on one side is twisted into a secure handle on the other side.

Barens come in different weights depending on the thickness of the cord used. The thicker it is, the stronger the pressure it can exert in printing. Only a few traditional printer-artisans can make a proper baren; however, all the Japanese artists cover their own barens. The inside of the baren lasts

for years and can be recoiled. The bamboo sheath covering must be replaced often because of the constant rubbing. For the western artist who is not ready to cover or make his own baren, adequate ones are available in art supply stores. The baren can be used for some printing of oil-based inks when the print does not require too much pressure. It works best when used for water-based pigments.

Pigment

At the core of the difference between the Japanese method and the western method is the use of water-based pigment by the Japanese and oil-based inks by western artists.

A variety of kinds of water-soluble paints must be experimented with before the artist can decide which will best express his image.

In choosing a black, you will find quite a difference in printing quality between sumi black, watercolor black, gouache, or poster black. The sumi ink is more of a dye and really penetrates the paper. Water color is a bit more uneven but does penetrate the paper too. Gouache penetrates less but prints strongly, and its colors are of excellent quality and not fugitive. Poster color can print unevenly with some of the color penetrating and some lying on the surface.

Any good quality tempera or water color such as Windsor Newton or Grumbacher will work well.

The fine brushes on the left are used for applying the water color to the block in the Japanese method. The coarse brush at right serves to mix the rice paste into the water color prior to its application to the block.

Brushes for Applying Pigment

Brushes instead of rollers are used for applying pigment to the block. Two types of brushes are used, one for applying pigment over large areas and one for small areas. These brushes are also used for blending and grading color. The brushes are made of horsehair and wood or bamboo. Most Japanese artists soften the hairs of their brushes by rubbing the hair against a piece of sharkskin with a little water for a half hour or more to soften the ends and split the hair tips. Care must be taken to wash the pigment out of the brushes.

Larger water color brushes (called *enogu-bake*) for putting the color on the block. All the brushes and tools shown are used by Ansei Uchima.

Paper

The choice of paper for the Japanese method is in many ways more important than when oil-based inks are used. The degree of absorbency of the paper is important in relation to the kind of effect desired in the image. The strength of the size used on the paper can be a controlling factor in absorbency. Hosho, Torinoko, and Masa papers are all easily available in this country and produce good results. Hosho has especially fine qualities for water-based printing. It is absorbent, yet strong, and allows the printer to rub it extensively without tearing. Because it is so tough, it also seems immune to shrinkage and expansion, a very useful characteristic in the Japanese method.

These wide flat brushes are *mizubake* and are used for applying water or sizing to the sheet of paper.

Below: The ends of the hairs in the brushes are split and softened by rubbing them against a piece of sharkskin nailed to a board.

Sizing

Presized paper is available with one or two sides sized from Nelson Whitehead, Aiko, or direct from Japan. Kizuki-Bosho, the paper used by Ansei Uchima, is sized on both sides and is made by a Tokyo papermaker whose family has

Cover the stack with a piece of wet cotton fabric and leave overnight.

You will soon know how to judge the proper amount of moisture in the paper after a little experience. Dry weather and humid weather affect the paper and must be taken into consideration. As necessary either add more water or place newsprint paper between every two sheets. If margins become too dry during printing, they must be moistened. If printing must be suspended for any reason, care must be taken to cover the paper with thick wet paper and wet cotton fabric.

Applying Pigment

Pigment is placed on the block with a small bamboo brush. A small quantity of paste is placed on the block, and pigment and paste are mixed and spread over the block with the horsehair applicator brush, adding a few drops of water if necessary. Mix only pigment and paste on the block. Allow the brush to become saturated with pigment and move it in every direction on the block. First use a circular motion to insure mixing the paste and the pigment. Next, use a straight motion across the grain to make the application uniform.

For gradations, rub the block with a wet rag in the area where a fading quality is desired. Dip only one side of the brush in the pigment and rub the brush back and forth over the block a few times to produce a graded tone from the wetness of the block and the pigment.

Use of Baren

Use four fingers to grip the handle of the baren, with the thumb over the handle. Pressure on the baren should be exerted from the palm of the hand so that the force of the rubbing is not just from the wrist but from the whole arm. Stroke the back of the sheet lightly with the baren moving in a circular motion to secure the paper on the block. Next dip a cotton-tipped stick into the camellia oil and dab it over the bottom of the baren. Before each printing rub the baren on a cotton cloth to remove any excess oil

Try to use the weight of the whole body in the rubbing. Start from the righthand corner nearest the printer and continue in a zigzag motion moving forward. When the top of the sheet is reached, start at the bottom again, until the whole sheet is rubbed. Use the baren in short strokes. Proper printing quality is achieved when the pigment penetrates about one half the thickness of the paper. Before removing the paper, rub the edges well and across the grain to be sure the image is uniform.

Remove the print carefully with the left hand from the right corner. Place it carefully on the paper board and examine it for printing quality and color relationships.

Toshi Yoshida, in a demonstration in Provincetown, Mass., applies water color to a cherry wood block with an *enogu-bake* or color brush.

The paper is placed on the freshly inked block and then is rubbed with the baren by Yoshida to make the impression.

Wood Engraving

HISTORY

The history of wood engraving should not be separated from that of the woodcut, as wood engraving was an 18th-century offshoot of woodcutting. However, for our purposes, it is simpler to present the history of wood engraving as an introduction to the section discussing its technique.

Until the 18th century, woodcut images had always been cut into wooden boards, vertical length cut from a variety of medium soft to hard grain trees, from poplar to cherry. Thomas Bewick, the 18th-century English engraver, is often given credit for first using the end grain of the wood. He cut his images in white lines directly into the wood with gravers, instead of knives and gouges and printed from the relief surface of the block. In the woodcut, the image was developed through an intricate pattern of black lines as the positive image, and white negatives areas were removed with gouges as in Durer's woodcuts. There is no doubt that other artist craftsmen experimented with this wood engraving method before Bewick gained fame for his outstanding book illustrations. However, he used the method so extensively and developed it with such skill and sensitivity that there are no contenders for his position as innovator. Its possibilities for detail and tonality soon made it the most popular and practical method to produce illustrations in great numbers for books, magazines and newspapers. The durability of the wood engraving, due to the close grain of the end grain of such hard woods as boxwood and maple, allowed enormous numbers of impressions from one block. A copperplate engraving of the day would begin to break down after fewer prints. One of Bewick's blocks, an illustration for a Newcastle newspaper, produced an edition of 900,000 prints without wearing down. Another great advantage was the ease of locking up the wood engraving and the type in one unit and printing it in one operation.

The application of wood engraving for a growing printing industry hungry for illustrations soon proved to be destructive to original creative expression. Numerous craftsmen of unbelievable skill worked to reproduce drawings and to interpret paintings for mass consumption through wood engravings. Scores of volumes of classics illustrated with Gustav Dore's wood engravings and cut by highly skilled craftsmen had a ready market among a rising middle-class audience. The craft flourished as a purely reproductive process until the late 19th century when photoengraving began to replace the use of the engraved block.

Creative wood engraving was revived in the 20th century through the use of the medium by imaginative book illustrators in England, Germany, and the United States, with notable contributions by Fritz Eichenberg and Lynd Ward in the United States.

It was not until the late 1940s and early 1950s that innovating concepts began to be explored by the American artists Misch Kohn, Leonard Baskin, and Arthur Deshaies (Deshaies working with lucite engraving). Their use of large-

"There are no formulas which can describe an artist's relationship to his work and material—it differs widely with his philosophy, and temperament and character. My own approach to the woodblock is not a purely mechanical or technical one, it is intimate, highly personal, emotional and sensual.

"The first cut made into the darkened surface of a woodblock, with the point of a steel blade or a burin, releases hidden forces which one can hardly gauge beforehand. The steel locates a spark, a source of light spreading slowly over the face of the block as the design emerges, white against black.

"This to me constitutes the never ending excitement—the suspense, the challenge, the surprise, as the graver and the wood take over, guide your eye and hand, create drama in a wealth of light, shadows and textures.

"Metal, linoleum as synthetic surfaces would never do for me what the living wood can do—each block, with its own inherent character, quality of age and grain, and often with its imperfections, offering a new and different challenge.

"Of all the species I have tried, end grain boxwood, slowly aged and cured, carefully planed and polished, has been the best partner in the game. First it was the famous Turkish boxwood, later Cuban and other Latin-American substitutes, less and less durable and reliable as time went on. Endgrain maple, even side grain Swiss pear and cherry had to fill the gap.

"As for the tools, most of them have remained the same old faithful companions over half a century, given to me as a student in Leipzig, often passed on to my own students later—indestructable if treated with due respect, kept razor sharp on an old Arkansas oil stone. Often an electric drill with a flexible shaft is used for grainy textures or for clearing larger areas.

"Not much else is needed except some stiff black ink, some sympathetic Japanese vellum, and some spoon like thing to rub its back with—gently— and a print is born. That—and good light, good eyes, good music—and a lot of patience."

—Fritz Eichenberg

Opposite:
Fritz Eichenberg
"The Folly of War" 1971
Woodengraving 18" x 11⅞"
Aquarius Press, Baltimore

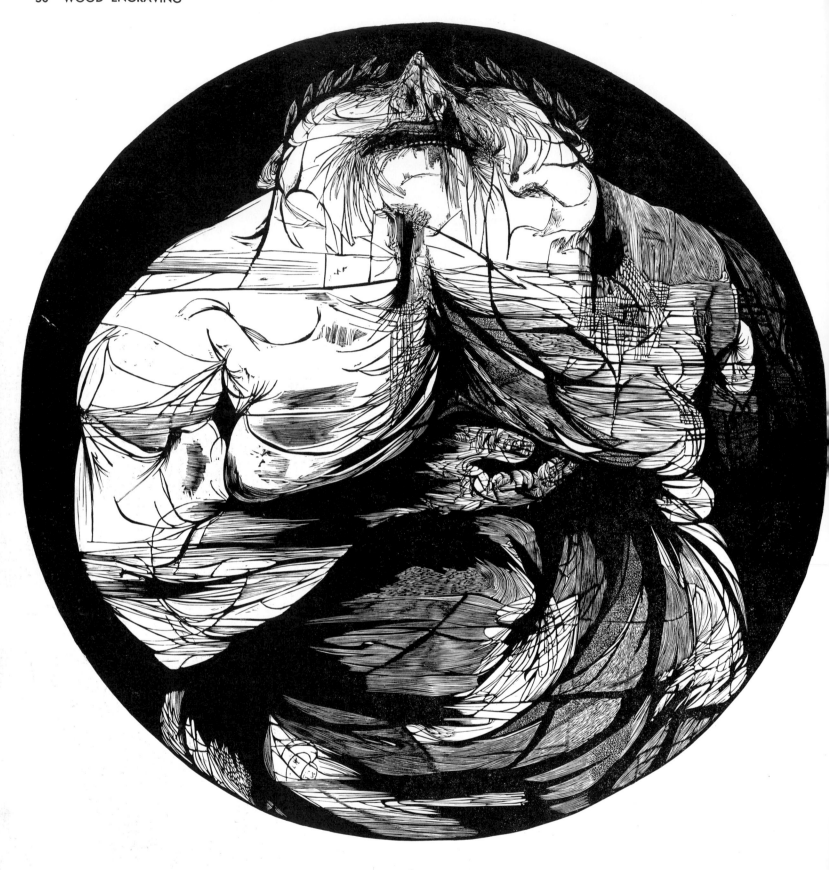

Leonard Baskin
"Death of the Laureate"
Wood engraving 11½" diameter
Collection Ben Sackheim

scale blocks and a freer handling of tools helped to reinstate wood engraving as a medium that complimented contemporary images.

The technique of wood engraving is both demanding and rewarding. The care and patience necessary to plan, cut, and print a wood engraving have deterred many artists from working with this method, but it has attracted a small group of artists who have produced prints of great precision and fine detail and controlled textures. Inevitably, the photo-engraved line cut and half-tone supplanted the wood engraving, and today there are virtually no skilled wood engravers working at their trade.

WOOD

Turkish boxwood, the most desired of all woods, is now very hard to get and quite expensive when available It is usually found as a veneered block, with the top layer of Turkish boxwood and the bottom section of another wood. The next most sought-after wood is South American box-wood, which is about one-half the price of the Turkish variety. Even cheaper is domestic maple, which is one-half the price of the South American boxwood. All these woods are suitable for engraving. The blocks must be made by specialists with precise planing and finishing machinery; because of the many small pieces used to assemble a larger block, the gluing and fitting is a critical operation. Only a few manufacturers remain who still produce blocks of good quality.

DRAWING ON THE BLOCK

All the detail and texture which you desire in your final print must be cut in the block by you. The block offers none of the wood grain, saw marks, or knotholes commonly found in plank grain woodcuts. The wood engraving is done on the end grain of the wood, which offers no variation in resistance to the tools used by the artist.

In general, it is easier to make white lines into a black background than to cut around a black shape on a white background. This simple fact, as true for a woodcut as for a wood-engraving, should be remembered as you prepare your design. The variety of stipples, tones, tints, and textures depends upon the ingenuity of the engraver, but tones based upon white cuts are easier to make than those built up of black lines or dots. If you need cross-hatching, you will find that white line cross-hatching is simple but black line cross-hatching requires cutting out tiny white squares between the lines, a tedious procedure at best.

You may draw directly on the block with pencil or ink to establish the basic areas of the design prior to cutting. If you use pencil, it should not be so hard that it indents the block. These indentations will print as white lines and can ruin a block. Fix the pencil drawing with any good charcoal or pastel fixative so that it doesn't rub off as you work. You can transfer a drawing by using carbon paper If you blacken your block with India ink before you begin it will be necessary to use light colored pencils or white charcoal to transfer

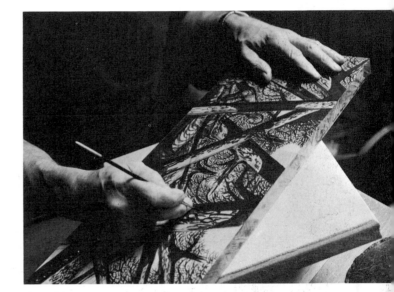

Lynd Ward paints his design directly on an end grain block with india ink in preparation for a wood engraving.

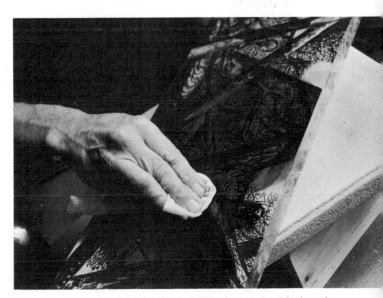

When the india ink has dried Lynd Ward tints the block with red oil color. This will enable him to see exactly where his cut is going.

Lynd Ward
"Pathfinder" 1971
Wood engraving 8" x 22"
Courtesy of the artist

Simplest possible use of capacities of the end grain block using a minimum of engraving tools—only five or six involved.

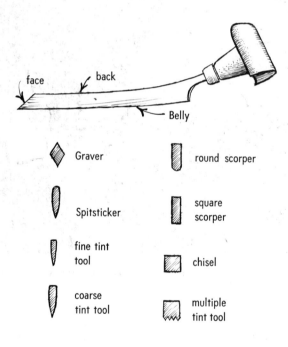

face   back

Belly

◇ Graver   ▯ round scorper

▮ Spitsticker   ▰ square scorper

▮ fine tint tool   ◪ chisel

▮ coarse tint tool ▨ multiple tint tool

WOODENGRAVING TOOLS

your design onto the block. This method allows you to visualize your final result much better than working on the natural color of the wood. Too much fixative swallows up the tracing, however, and a good compromise is to tint the block with a grey or colored ink, then use black pencil or charcoal to outline the design. When this is fixed it will remain visible. If a felt pen is used, fixative will not be necessary.

Do not work out your preliminary sketch so completely that cutting it becomes a mere tracing of your design. Instead, keep your sketch as an indication of what you want and put your effort into the cutting itself, so that it will be fresh and spontaneous. It is important to keep your enthusiasm strong, and repeated tracings and redrawings of a design are boring and tiring. Besides, the textures and tonalities of the wood engraving are difficult to approximate in a sketch, and it is worthless to spend hours indicating something that you can do better by cutting into the wood.

WOOD ENGRAVING TOOLS

The tools used in engraving lines are called gravers or spit stickers, and tools called tint tools are used when tones are built up. The diagram shows a tool and its parts. The spit stickers are normally used for curved lines, but gravers may also be used to cut curves. When you clear out large areas of white, the scorpers or chisels are used in the same way gouges are used for wood-cuts.

To hold the wood-engraving tool, pick it up from the table as shown in the photo. The thumb guides the tool as it is

The engraving tool is held like this, with the thumb along the shaft of the tool.

In order to turn the block easily Lynd Ward has constructed a rotating turntable that swivels at a touch.

being pushed by the palm of the hand. When curves are being cut, the wood is turned, not the tool. To facilitate the turning of the block, a leather sandbag has traditionally been used as a base for the block, although many substitutes can be devised The sandbag is the most efficient support for smooth turning when cutting precise curves, and anyone who wants to do much engraving will find it a worthwhile acquisition.

A large magnifying glass is very helpful when detailed cutting is necessary. The glass should be mounted on a stand in order to free the hands for work.

The curved belly of the engraving tool serves the purpose of keeping the tool away from the block while the line is being cut. If the tool were straight, the belly of the tool would dent the wood at the beginning of the stroke.

When cutting white areas with the scorpers or gouges, be careful to remove the shoulder of wood that is left after the outline has been cut. This edge doesn't show until the block is being printed, and if printed must be cleared away afterward. Use a thin card to protect the edges when you are gouging out white areas. If you do dent the edges of a black area with the belly of the tool, sprinkle a few drops of water on the dented spot. Light a match and hold the block over the flame so that the water steams and the wood is expanded back to its original shape. Minor dents can be removed in this way, but deep bruises are another matter and require plugging.

PRINTING

The technique of printing a wood engraving is similar in principle to that of woodcut printing, but the ink used should be very stiff and the paper should be smooth and fine. Thin, runny ink will clog or fill the fine textures and tiny stipple openings. The roller used should be gelatine or plastic, in perfect condition, and the ink film must be thin and even.

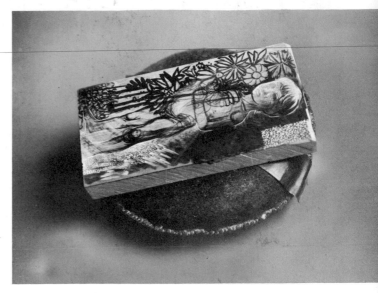

The conventional sandbag is shown here, with a partially cut block, which can turn and tilt as needed. This sandbag is made of felt.

The tool is pushed through the wood, while the block is turned into the cut.

Left: Lynd Ward's press, based on the Washington press, common equipment in the U. S. in the 19th century.

Below: A thin film of stiff ink is rolled over the block with a good roller. An even coat of ink is essential for a fine proof.

The inked block is centered on the bed of the press by Lynd Ward.

Ink should be thoroughly distributed on the roller. When printing with a burnisher, rub carefully over the entire surface of the paper, using even, steady pressure to eliminate streaks and light spots. There must be enough black area for the ink to act as an adhesive and grip the paper, keeping it from slipping. If your block has too much white area and only a small percentage of black line, it may be necessary to print the block in a press. See the previous section on press printing woodcuts for details.

PAPERS FOR WOOD ENGRAVING

The rough, hand-made papers are rarely suited for wood engravings, and then only when the blocks are press-printed. The best prints are taken on smooth, fine paper, such as India paper and thin Japan paper. The machine-made papers that are smooth and soft will yield better results than heavy, hard papers. It may be necessary to dampen some papers, but they should be damp only, not soaked, as some papers disintegrate when too wet. If you print on a damp sheet by hand burnishing, use a dry piece of paper between the burnisher and the damp sheet as a buffer sheet.

The paper is eased onto the block with the assistance of a piece of cardboard. The thin paper tends to sag and the cardboard prevents premature contact with the inked surface.

Finishing touches are added with hand burnishing. Lynd Ward protects the thin paper with a card and uses a Japanese bamboo rice spoon as a rubbing tool.

The lever exerts a downward pressure on the form; because the entire surface is printed at once, great pressure is needed.

Below: When the packing sheets are lifted, the ink shows through the thin paper.

Below: The proof is pulled from the block. The piece of wood in front of the block serves as a guide for the paper in order to keep margins consistent.

Contemporary Relief Methods

THE LUCITE PRINT

The search for new materials to help express the ever-expanding range of esthetic freedom has been a natural outgrowth of the changing image of the print in the last ten or fifteen years. A logical and exciting development has been the artist's awareness of the potential of new materials, developed primarily for industry, that could be used for his own creative use.

Lucite is a material that has been used very individually by a number of artists. Arthur Deshaies, an American printmaker, was one of the first American artists to use the material expansively. He used it for relief engraving and intaglio.

Jack Sonenberg
"Dimensions, 1970 No. 1"
Relief Print, with thread 25" x 21"
Associated American Artists Gallery

The plates are made of newsboard, and covered with an acrylic medium to stiffen them and isolate them from inks and solvents. They will stand up to the printing of large editions. One set of plates is used for color that is rolled onto the surface. All the color is usually printed in one run through the etching press. Another plate is used for blotting ink off the paper, and embossing the paper at the same time. The tonality of the color depends on the different levels in the second plate, and the adjustment of pressure on the press.

It can be cut with engraving tools or the same gouges used for woodcuts. However, the density and hardness of lucite makes it far more resistant than wood. One of the great assets of the material is that it can be purchased in dimensions up to 28″ by 36″, which makes it a highly desirable substitute for the boxwood used in wood engraving, whose largest dimensions are seldom more than 12″ by 20″, because larger sizes would be in danger of breaking. There can be a great deal of freedom in the preparation of the image because the lucite is transparent. A preparatory drawing can be placed under the lucite sheet and used as a clear guide for the artist's cutting.

If a thin film of water-based ink is rolled on the surface and allowed to dry, it will aid the cutting because every cut mark will be clearly visible. Water-based ink is suggested because it can be washed off easily and will leave the surface in its natural state. Tools must be kept very sharp when working the lucite because of the toughness of the material. You must also be careful not to scratch or mar the surface in areas you wish to keep uncut. Lucite is a very sensitive material and responds to the slightest scratches from any sharp tool. A needle or a razor blade can develop interesting areas of texture. An electric drill, a vibro-graver, or any electric tool of this type can be used with great success. The transparency of lucite can also be an assist when the plate is being inked if it is held up to the light to check the build-up of ink before printing a first proof.

The possibilities for drypoint and intaglio printing are many and are discussed under the section on intaglio.

The use of lucite for color printing has distinct advantages. Because lucite is transparent, it is naturally easy to register and to align plates one over the other to check accuracy.

THE CELLOCUT

The cellocut process was developed by Boris Margo, painter, printmaker, and sculptor. It is basically the utilization of a liquid plastic material consisting of sheet celluloid dissolved in acetone.

Solutions of varying consistencies are used to coat any smooth surface such as Masonite, Presdwood, copper, brass, aluminum, or zinc plates. After the liquid has set, it may be worked with etching or woodcut tools. A thicker solution may be applied to form a heavier raised surface. The plates may be printed in relief or intaglio, by hand or with an etching press.

Margo's earliest experiments evolved out of his work with drypoint on celluloid. In the thirties he began to experiment with the celluloid in liquid form and to build up areas with thicker plastic, impressing textures or imbedding materials into the plate itself. Rollers of different degrees of softness and hardness such as gelatine and hard rubber were used in color printing in order to reach recessed and raised surfaces with a wide range of colors.

Boris Margo's inventive work with this medium was a forerunner of the use of collage, assemblage, and acrylic adhesives that took the form of the collagraph in the late fifties and sixties.

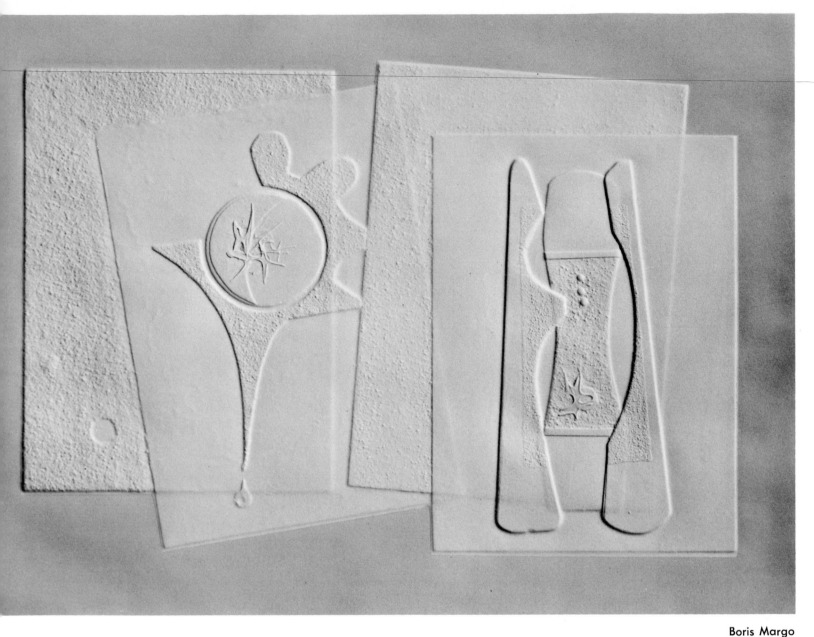

Boris Margo
"Pages from the Book" 1969
Cellocut 20" x 28"
Courtesy of the Artist
Photograph by Arthur Swoger

LINOCUT

The use of linoleum as a craft material and as a means of introducing young children to the print often makes serious artists avoid it. This is unfortunate. Because a material is simple, easily obtained, and easy to cut does not mean that it cannot offer some rather good features. Some excellent work has been done with linoleum by major artists. Matisse and Picasso have used it to great advantage. Matisse was able to produce a sensitive bold line of great fluidity in his *Seated Nude.* Picasso used linoleum for his important series of color reduction prints discussed in the section on that method.

Within the limitations of the medium lie some of its assets. It is very available and therefore inexpensive. The ordinary heavy linoleum of good quality, with canvas backing, is best. It can be purchased in floor-covering stores. Avoid the inlaid or patterned types. A white, light grey, or tan is easiest to use because preparatory drawing with India ink or magic markers is so visible. Prepared blocks can be purchased in art supply stores, but they are much more expensive and their only advantage is that they are mounted on plywood. Mounting on plywood can be done without difficulty

Josef Gielniak
"Improvisation II (Fantaisie sur un theme morbide)" 1959
Linocut 7 1/16" x 9 5/8"
Pratt Graphics Center

if a wood backing is desired. For a large block this might be an advantage. However, if the printing of a linoleum plate is to be exploited by using an etching press, it is best to leave it unmounted. Detailed discussion of these possibilities are included in the intaglio section. The cutting tools used for linoleum can be the same ones used for the woodcut. They must be kept very sharp, although the material is fairly soft and offers little resistance to cutting. However, there is an abrasive material in linoleum that is very destructive to the cutting edge of your tools. You must sharpen your tools frequently. One of the cutting advantages is that linoleum can be cut in any direction without resistance and is sensitive to punctures and scratches so that textural surfaces can be imposed into it. One method of utilizing interesting textures is to place textured material of not too much height such as sand, wire, metal washers, watch parts, and the like on the linoleum, place a piece of smooth cardboard on top of the objects, and run it through an etching press. The impressions of the objects on the linoleum will be sharp and clear.

Though linoleum imposes little of itself as a material, it serves as an easy vehicle for color. The slightly pebbly quality of its surface can lend a very subtle texture.

Printing the Linocut

The linoleum block is printed exactly the same as the woodcut. The use of rollers and the hand rubbing are no different. However, there is more of an advantage in press printing the linoleum relief than in the woodcut. Because the unmounted linoleum is thin and flat, it can be printed in any etching press. Its relief surfaces can be rolled with ink, the paper placed in position, and a light blanket placed over it. It may then be printed with medium pressure in any etching press.

Etching Linoleum

Linoleum may be etched with caustic soda (sodium hydroxide) and printed as either a relief print or an intaglio print. Various resists, such as etching ground, asphaltum, heated paraffin wax or varnish, may be painted on the block and later scratched or incised into. The caustic soda should be used in a saturated solution and, as it is very dangerous, must be handled with care. It can be brushed or swabbed on the linoleum and replenished as it loses its strength. Deep biting takes hours, unfortunately, and this disadvantage is a serious handicap. Sheet linoleum is becoming hard to find in the United States because of the prevalence of the modular squares now in favor for floor coverings.

HAND EMBOSSING THE RELIEF PRINT

Though it may seem that the inkless embossed print or the color and black and white print with areas of embossing is a very contemporary innovation, embossing was used by the Japanese for whole areas of pattern in prints as early as the 18th century. This method was called *gauffrage*. Hand embossing a relief print is done by forcing dampened thick Japanese rice paper into the recessions or cut-away areas in a woodcut, linoleum cut, or any relief print. The areas that are embossed are the negative white areas. It is said that Okumura Masanobu was the first of the ukiyo-e artists to use embossing. Some artists used it to define pattern in garments, and sometimes an object such as a scroll or a headress was embossed. Utamaro used embossing in some of the women's faces of his prints. Harunobu, Buncho and Shunsho also made effective use of embossed areas in their prints. Crude use of embossing was made in England in the early 18th century by J. B. Jackson. French artists in the late 19th century experimented with inkless embossings much like our cast paper prints.

High-relief embossing can be achieved quite effectively with the woodcut or the collage relief print. The print can be designed specifically for embossing alone or can combine embossing with the use of color in the oil base or the water base method. When color is to be used in the print the embossing should be the last operation. The paper is so sensitive to the depressions in the wood that even delicate woodcut strokes, holes, and textures appear strongly embossed.

A heavy Japanese paper takes embossing best because the fibers are pliable and there is less risk from tearing. We have found that Torinoko, Kochi, and Masa papers give excellent results. Dampen the paper slightly by dipping it into water and removing it immediately. Blot it well between dry blotters. The paper should be almost dry. It is also possible to emboss without dampening the paper but there is greater danger from tearing. Place the paper on the block. Use the register frame if other colors have been printed first. Press firmly into the recessions with a curved chrome burnisher used in etching. Take care not to tear the paper. We have found the burnisher works very well because it can be forced into small places and has smooth sides that do not mar the paper. If the point on the burnisher is ground down and dulled there will be no danger of tearing. The Japanese sometimes use the elbow for pressing the paper into the recessions on the block. This method works amazingly well.

COLLAGE RELIEF PRINT

The freedom of today's artist to use a wide range of materials is almost endless since the early collage experiments of the Dadaists, Braque, Picasso, and Schwitters. The new vitality in printmaking owes an obvious debt to this tradition of experimentation and unorthodoxy in visual expression.

The relief print has been very adaptable to new materials and experimental means. "If it can be inked, it can be printed" is the only rule. This rule leaves the relief print open to endless possibilities, including found objects like charred discarded wood, driftwood, intricate printed circuits, crushed tin cans, and container lids. It leaves open the possibility of inking and printing anything from a manhole cover to a weathered door of a barn. During some of our experi-

Relief rolled found objects tooth picks, paper clip, electronic copper disk, clock part. Printed on an etching press.

Relief rolled found objects: razor blade, flat machine part, washer, luggage key, electronic disk, clock gear all printed on an etching press.

Crayon rubbing of manhole cover.

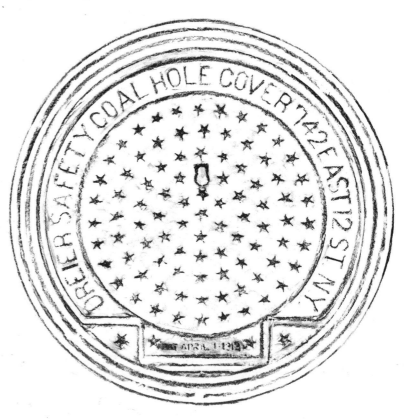

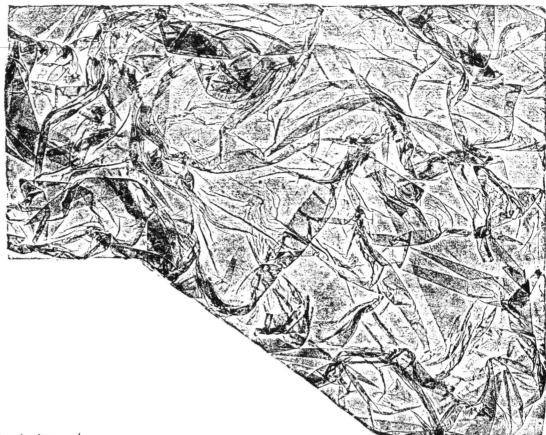

Relief rolled crumpled bond paper gessoed onto a carboard backing.

Below: Relief rolled electronic circuit panel, copper on plastic by Techniques, Inc., Englewood, New Jersey.

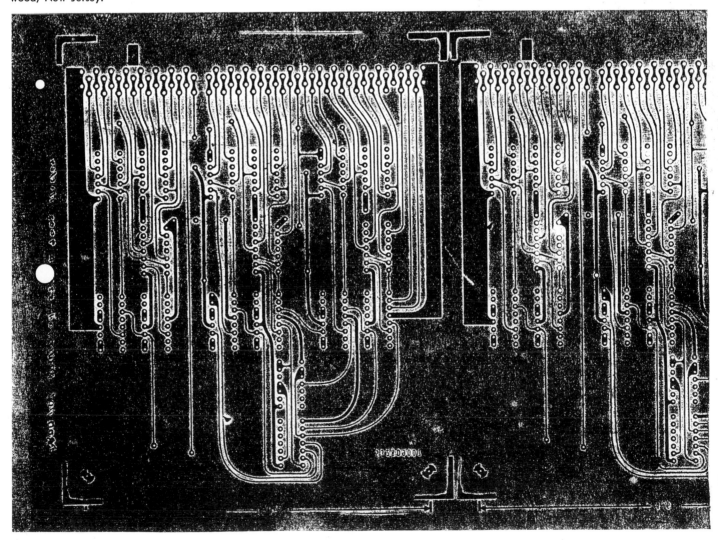

Relief rolled commercial greeting cards.

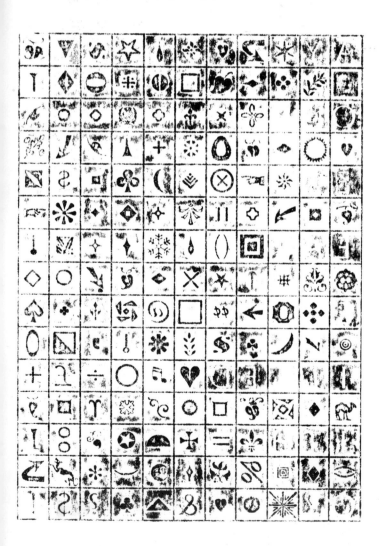

mentation with unorthodox materials, one student inked his own face with a soft roller and printed himself with quite interesting results. The wisest procedure is to gather objects and store them for future use. Seeing the assembled objects together can often give the artist ideas for images. Sometimes transformations such as hammering out metal objects in order to print them more easily is desirable. Some systemizing in the collecting can also be useful. Organic materials such as wood, rocks, slate, and plant forms can be collected, inked, and proofed to see what possibilities may be inherent in each object. Technological materials gathered together can be very suggestive; gaskets, gears, parts of clocks, screening, plastics, machinery, tin, aluminum, or copper that can be cut with a pair of shears can be intriguing in form. Soft materials such as cloth, dust, sand, tubed solder, metal particles, lace, string, oilcloth, or embroidery produce completely different images. These soft materials and organic materials such as grasses and plant forms can be soaked in acrylic liquids and hardened and printed as single units or glued down immediately with Elmer's glue or gesso. The printing of a whole group of objects with great variation in texture and form can develop a rich amount of source material that can be cut out. These images can be manipulated into compositions to explore their possibilities more easily as printed areas than as objects. After the relationships of objects are determined, their silhouettes can be traced on cardboard or Masonite in order to position them, or they can be glued to a board for more permanence during the printing of the edition. Experimentation and inventiveness are the key. Without them the objects merely become prints of themselves without any transformation. Michael Rothenstein, the English printmaker, has used found objects imaginatively in many of his prints.

Printing the Collage Print

The printing procedures for collage prints are not much different from those of the woodcut, except that the collage print, because of its porous and varied surfaces, requires more inking and softer rollers. For very rough surfaces, a soft ink and a soft roller will help to achieve the nuances of surface textures. A fairly absorbent, sensitive paper is also good to use for best results. If the paper is thin, a second sheet may be needed between the print image and the burnisher to keep it from tearing. Often, the use of the hand and fingers is sufficient to print rough surfaces, and a wooden burnisher can be used for smooth areas. If the paper to be used is quite thick, dampening it lightly and blotting it well may help to make it more supple and malleable around uneven surfaces. In all instances care must be taken to keep the paper from tearing.

Hard rubber roller. Printed on an etching press.

Relief rolled traffic sign. Printed on the back of translucent paper through an etching press.

Relief rolled traffic sign printed on the top of paper laid over the embossed metal sign.

Broken glass, inked and printed by rubbing.

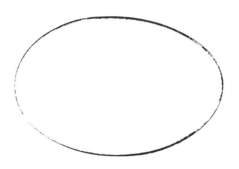

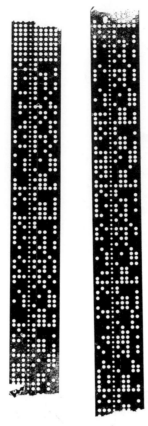

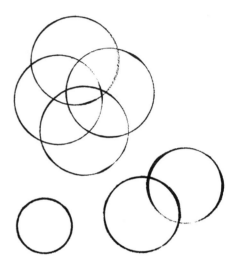

Relief rolled paper computer tapes, printed on an etching press.

Stamped prints made from wooden numbers and a cut cardboard sun shape.

Relief rolled Yugoslavian coins. Printed on an etching press.

Stamped prints made from the bottoms of glass jars of different shapes. The lower group is printed from the inked heads of flat-head wood screws.

Below: Prints made from dried glue and other adhesives; from left to right; Plastic Wood, Ceramic Glue, Liquid Aluminum, Miracle Adhesive, Liquid Solder, Duco Cement, Liquid Steel, and Thermo-grip Glue.

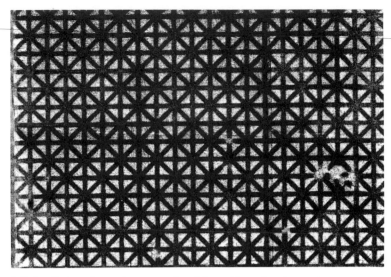

Relief rolled perforated screen printed by rolling directly on the paper laid on top of the screen.

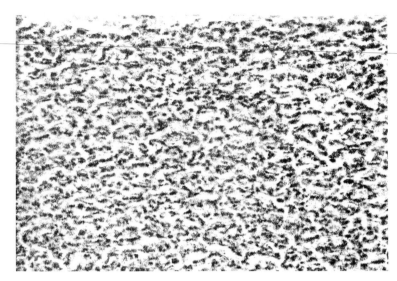

Relief rolled textured glass. Spoon printed.

Relief rolled aluminum perforated screen. Printed on an etching press.

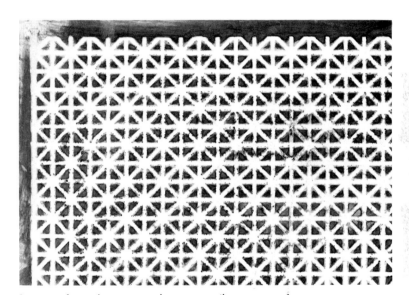

Same perforated screen used as a stencil to protect the paper. Printed with a rag and dilute ink.

Relief rolled wooden french curves. Printed on an etching press.

Relief rolled wooden french curves printed on the top of paper laid over the objects.

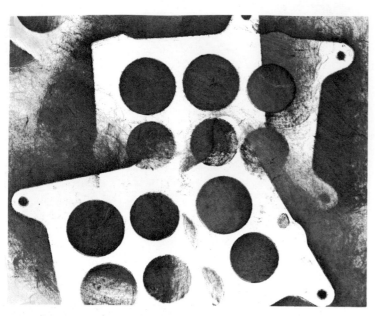

Metal gasket used as a stencil. Dilute ink is applied with a rag.

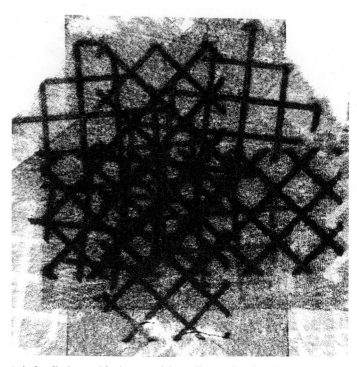

Relief rolled zinc block printed by rolling a hard rubber brayer on top of the paper laid over the block. Four printings with Japanese rice spoon.

Relief rolled directly on to paper using gasket as a stencil to protect the paper.

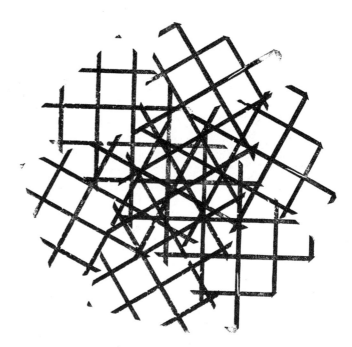

Relief rolled zinc block printed three times by spoon printing.

Relief rolled metal gasket printed on an etching press.

Relief rolled zinc block used as a support for photoengravings. Spoon printed.

CARDBOARD RELIEF PRINT

The flexibility of cardboard, its ease of cutting, and its availability make it an ideal material for a relief print. If two- or three-ply chip board is used, it can be handled very much like wood itself. Sharp tools are needed for cutting. We have found the best tools to be industrial single-edge razor blades, which can be discarded when they are dull. An exacto knife with blades that can be resharpened is suitable for fine detail cutting, though cardboard is not particularly suited for very fine work. The cardboard can be cut into and peeled away very much as wood is cut. Sometimes the lower surface can be inked and printed if that enhances the composition. It is best to cut areas with some angulation away from the edge of the form, just as wood is handled, so that the form does not break away in printing. Textures can be hammered or scratched into the cardboard with a variety of instruments from a dressmaker's wheel to punches and rasps.

A freer use of the cardboard relief can be achieved by cutting all the forms out completely, arranging them on a piece of three-ply cardboard or ⅛" Masonite until the relationships are satisfactory, and then gluing them down with Elmer's glue or gesso or lacquer and coating them to seal the surfaces. Papers of various thickness, in addition to cardboards of different thickness from three-ply chip board to mat board to shirt cardboards used by laundries, can be used. Masking tape also makes a quick, easy material to build up linear structures.

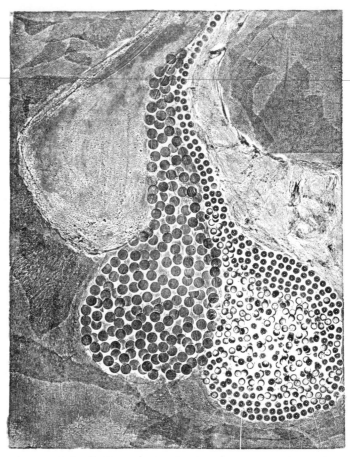

Above: Relief rolled sequins, paper tissues, paper towels, sand in wet gesso on mat board. Printed on an etching press by Kathleen Dixon, Manhattanville College.

Relief rolled cut paper and cardboard, paper toweling on cardboard. Four blocks by R. Fontaine of Pratt Institute, Brooklyn.

Left: Relief rolled towel, fabric, crumpled paper, and paper strips on pebbled mat board. C. Witko, Pratt Institute, Brooklyn.

Seal both the cardboard relief print and the collage print with plastic spray, diluted Elmer's glue, gesso, or lacquer. If this is not carefully done the whole composition will break down during inking and cleaning with solvents after printing. Sometimes the sealing of the surface can become structural if gesso is used undiluted. The brush strokes become integral parts of the form. Cutting cardboard away for some forms and painting the image with gesso to utilize other forms can become a very free way to work. The gesso should be fairly thick if it is to print as a structural image.

The cardboard and the collage prints present unique opportunities to exploit texture and surface. Varied color textures printed over each other can develop the color quality with great richness.

Edmond Casarella
"Blaze of Glory"
Color cardboard cut 13" x 15"
Courtesy of the artist

Printing the Cardboard Relief

Printing the cardboard relief print is not too different from printing the woodcut. Although the surface of the cardboard print must be well sealed, it is still a more absorbent surface than wood and will take a little more ink. The soft rollers suggested for the collage print are very good. Sometimes just hand rubbing without a burnisher is all that is necessary because of the softer color inks and the softer surface of the cardboard relief print.

Cardboard to Repair a Woodcut

The use of cardboard as a relief material can have a dual purpose. It can be used with great individuality as a means of expression on its own, and it can also be used very efficiently in combination with the woodcut to make additional plates or to make corrections. There are times when a key block of some complexity is cut out of wood and additional colors with simpler forms are cut out of cardboard. In such instances, using cardboard for the color areas would be very logical and easy. It also is very helpful to use cardboard to repair an area, by shaving down the wood and inserting cardboard. Mat board or chip board in two or three ply may be used. It is important to glue the areas down securely with Elmer's glue or gesso and to spray the surface with plastic spray or to brush on diluted Elmer's glue or gesso.

WOOD VENEER AND BALSA WOOD COLLAGE PRINT

Wood veneers in a variety of grains can be used very successfully in developing a wood relief collage that can be inked and printed as an ordinary woodcut. The veneers can be glued to any rigid surface, such as ¼" Masonite or ¼" plywood. We have had students glue the veneers with gesso or animal glue to ¼" plywood and after the gluing was completed, proceed to cut and develop both the glued veneer and the plywood upon which it was glued with interesting effects. Balsa wood, used in model building, can also be used particularly well for geometric concepts. The balsa comes in a wide range of strip sizes and thicknesses and is readily available in art supply stores, especially where architecture students trade. The balsa, though very soft, can be cut and gouged after gluing.

MASONITE RELIEF PRINT

Masonite can be used with some success for the relief print. The hard-tempered Masonite works best. There is a soft-tempered kind that is not advisable because it cannot be cut well. When hard-tempered Masonite is used, ordinary woodcutting tools can be manipulated easily enough if they are kept very sharp. One side of the Masonite is very smooth and can be utilized for fairly detailed cutting. The other side has a texture that resembles a weave and can be developed as textural surface however, it can become monotonous. Some artists find Masonite more expressive with color, as

the textural and linear range of the material is certainly less than the potential of the black and white woodcut.

Power tools can be handled with success in enriching the surface and imposing textural qualities on either side. They can also be used on the smooth side to develop linear and structural imagery. Masonite has considerable potential as an intaglio plate.

GESSO OR PLASTER PRINT

A very fast way of working in the relief print is to use plaster as a basic material for the block. When the plaster is semi-dry, it is quite workable with a variety of tools, and images and textures can be developed with remarkable ease. The technique is fairly simple and requires no special skill or equipment.

Place a piece of plexiglas, lucite, ¼" plate glass, formica, or any smooth-surfaced, flat material on a table. Make a frame of 1" by 2" or 1" by 3" lumber and lay it flat on the plexiglas, arranged to fit the size of block that you want to make. You may use masking tape to hold the frame in position.

Use a large mixing bowl or pail to mix enough plaster to cover your plate to a depth of ¾". Add the plaster to the water in a pail large enough to permit stirring. Use ordinary builders' plaster and mix well with a stick. It should be thin enough to pour.

Pour one half of your mixture onto the plexiglas. The smooth surface will make the printing surface of your dried plaster block. When half the mixture has been poured into the frame, put the pail aside and place a piece of aluminum or copper window screening, previously cut to fit your block, on the wet plaster. It should be slightly smaller than the finished block. This mesh will act as a stiffener and internal brace for the plaster and will give it strength and resistance to breaking. When your screening is in place, pour the remaining plaster into the frame. The screening will be sandwiched between the layers of wet plaster. After 20 minutes or so, the plaster will feel hot. It may be removed from the frame at this time. While it is soft, scratch into it or work in whatever manner you choose with nails, needles, screws, and the like. Because plaster dries rather slowly, the time that you have to work on the damp block will vary with the temperature. It would be helpful to brush the smooth surface of the plaster with a coat of India ink. When you scrape or scratch the surface, each mark will be clearly visible. You can work with great speed on the block while it is damp. When plaster is dry it becomes very hard and will yield fine detail and thin lines. If you want to soften the block after it is dry, soak it in water for 5 or 10 minutes to restore some of the qualities of easily cut new plaster.

To make a plaster block, Richard Otreba of Poland constructs a frame of 1" by 2" furring strips arranged around a flat sheet of plexiglas or lucite.

Otreba pours plaster into the form made by the wood strips and the sheet plastic. A piece of screening or wire mesh is placed in the wet plaster to give it strength. Before the plaster has completely hardened it may be scratched or incised easily.

Opposite:
John Ross
"Duomo" 1959
Cardboard relief 29½" x 22¼"
Collection Cincinnati Museum

Arthur Deshaies
"Cycle of a Large Sea: Unbeing myself" 1961
Plaster relief engraving 54" x 36¾"
Brooklyn Museum

If you have overcut an area or want to fill some lines, add new plaster with a palette knife, let it harden, and sand it smooth with fine sandpaper.

Before printing the plaster block, seal the surface by spraying with a few coats of clear lacquer. This seal will make the block easier to clean and will toughen the surface for the brayer and the inking. The printing should be accomplished by hand rubbing only. Any press printing will probably split the brittle plaster and crack it beyond repair.

GLUE PRINT

Certain adhesives and glues that dry to a hard consistency and do not dissolve in the solvents used to clean oil-based inks may be used as textures or linear images. They include Plastic Wood, Miracle Adhesive, Liquid Steel, Liquid Aluminum, Duco Cement, wood putty, polymer acrylic gesso, modelling paste, and many other products.

THE STAMPED PRINT

Many surfaces may be inked and printed. Bottle caps, wine corks, jar bottoms, machine parts, wooden numbers and sign-makers letters, and other found objects can be printed but are too bulky or awkward to be glued in position on a base board. Make a cardboard or oak-tag position sheet, cut holes in it where you want to print a particular shape, and use this position sheet as a guide for printing, directly on the finished print, whatever shape you choose. Simply stamp the shape onto the paper, using adequate pressure and a few blotters or newsprint sheets under the paper to act as a cushion. Repeat patterns can be attained quickly and with little trouble by using stamped shapes.

You may cut simple forms into Ruby erasers and even Art Gum erasers. These make wonderful little stamps, and repeats are easy with them. You can quickly make a forest by cutting two or three trees from erasers or small wood or cardboard pieces. These stamps may be inked with rollers, with conventional stamp pads, or by rolling out color onto a slab, pressing the shape into the color, and then stamping it onto your print.

THE MONOPRINT

Materials

Printing ink, oil colors, water colors, brushes, rags, sponge, sticks, metal tools, cardboard squares, rollers, medium-weight paper for stencils, any non-absorbent material such as glass, lucite, formica, masonite, rice paper or any fairly absorbent paper, mineral spirits, rubbing tools.

The monoprint is exactly what the word indicates. It is a one-print method. An image is made on a nonabsorbent surface, such as glass, with inks or paints and transferred onto a piece of fairly absorbent paper by placing the sheet of paper on the prepared surface and rubbing the back with the hand or a rubbing tool. The monoprint is a unique image and cannot be duplicated, nor can an edition be made as in other printmaking medias. Because the image cannot be reprinted, it is not considered a print image and is most often barred from print exhibitions. However, as it does produce very unusual results, somewhere between the print and painting, it deserves a place in this section. It is also a good way to quickly realize the idea of the printed image, the reversal of the image and the rubbing of a relief block.

Anyone who has cleaned off a painter's palette of many colors knows that in the process of cleaning off the palette with a palette knife very beautiful color qualities take shape.

A three-dimensional assemblage of cast plaster impressions from Antonio Frasconi's inked wood cuts.

Below: A number of small wood blocks are cast in plaster, making embossed impressions, forming a single unit by Antonio Frasconi.

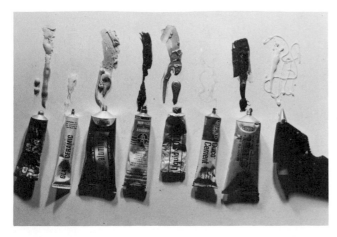

Adhesives, cement, and glues that harden when dry. They may be inked and printed. Included are materials available in most hardware stores, such as plastic wood, Duco cement, liquid steel, and aluminum. The device at the right is a heat-operated glue gun. See page 64 for print of these adhesives.

If at that moment a piece of rice paper were dropped onto the palette and rubbed with the hand or a rubbing tool, a close duplication of the palette image would be transferred to the paper. The monoprint can be as free as that, color strewn on a nonabsorbent surface and drawn into with stick or sharp tool or manipulated with a rag, or mineral spirits used to help move the colors around and create blending effects.

The monoprint can also be approached in a very painterly manner with the image painted in numerous colors directly on the smooth surface with a variety of brushes and then printed. If necessary a sketch can be prepared on paper and used as a guide by slipping it under a piece of glass and the color applied with brushes or rags or rollers on the glass surface. This method can allow a number of prints to be printed with some controlled uniformity. Printing paper can also be held in position by being taped to the smooth surface of glass or other material while color is applied and printed in two or three sequential printings that allow overprinting effects. The taping will insure accurate registry.

Rollers can be used to roll a single color or many colors onto the printing surface, and an image can be drawn into the inked area with sticks, metal tools, or cardboard cards.

Cut or torn paper shapes can also be placed on the rolled ink surface to combine the monoprint with a stencil print.

Another very interesting use of the monoprint is to combine it with a partially worked plate. An etching plate, lithograph plate or stone, or woodcut can be developed to a certain point, after which painted or drawn material can be added to the plate or stone. It can then be run through the etching or lithograph press or, if wood is used, rubbed by hand to produce the softness of a painted image with the qualities of the print.

Michael Mazur paints directly on an etching plate with ink and turps and combines cut plates and embossing to produce unique images.

Michael Mazur
"Artist-Model and Studio View" 1968
Cut plate monoprint 15⅞" x 31¾"
Terry Dintenfass Gallery, New York

THE INTAGLIO PRINT

INTRODUCTION AND HISTORY

The beginnings of the intaglio process can be traced to the work of 15th-century European craftsmen in metal. Engraving on metal by goldsmiths and armourers was a flourishing art long before the first engravings were printed on paper. Goldsmiths were highly respected, and most of the early engravers who began to experiment with printing on paper had been apprenticed in goldsmiths' workshops. Engraving on paper may very well have evolved out of a need to record a design engraved on a piece of armour or a decorative gold receptacle. According to Hind, the earliest dated print on paper is one from 1446 by an anonymous German engraver known as the Master of 1446, who did a series of *The Passion of Christ*. The first engraver on metal known by name was Martin Schongauer, the gifted German artist whose strong and expressive line and delicate shadings through a network of cross-hatching characterized his work.

In Italy, the art of engraving developed more directly out of the classic ideals of the Renaissance. One of the earliest Italian engravers was a goldsmith named Maso Finiguerra, who worked in silver and gold in a manner called *niello*. In niello work the metal was engraved in line, and the lines were filled with a black substance that gave a strong light-and-dark quality to the metal similar to a printed line engraving. Hind discounts the possibility that the very first prints on paper were made from these niello designs, as scarcely any niello prints go back as far as 1450. He feels it was more likely that niellists began taking impressions of their work on paper after observing the already existing practice among engravers.

Other artists began to engrave in metal specifically for printing. Two methods of working, the *Fine Manner* and the *Broad Manner*, evolved in Florence. The *Fine Manner* used much fine gradation and cross-hatching, and the *Broad Manner* used a freer kind of pen drawing with wide shading. The engraving of Antonio Pollauiolo, *The Battle of the Naked Men*, developed a more personal style. Andrea Mantegna, who produced a great number of engravings, seems to have been an early developer of the atelier system of producing his work, with craftsmen doing most of the engraving. This

Martin Schongauer
"Death of the Virgin" ca. 1471
Engraving 10⅟₁₆" x 6¹¹⁄₁₆"
Metropolitan Museum of Art
Harris Brisbane Dick Fund 1940

75

Jacques Callot
The Strappado (from The Miseries
and Disasters of War) 1633
Etching 2¾" x 7⅜"
Collection of the authors

achieved additional tints by hand coloring the paper or even the canvas he sometimes used instead of paper. The tinting was done either before or after the impression was made.

After Rembrandt and Seghers, an entire school of portraiture developed in the Netherlands, the etchings of Van Dyck being most noteworthy.

In France the work of Jacques Callot in the 17th century was varied and compelling. His interest ran from direct portraits and military plates to studies of beggars, the *commedia dell'arte* and a unique series, *Miseries of War*. These are a group of small plates showing peaceful villages occupied by tiny figures involved in the horrors of war. This series is probably one of the first statements of protest in the print. Callot's technical achievements were notable in his use of the swelled line in etching and of successive bitings.

After the 18th century there were fewer noteworthy artists working with etching, except for Francisco Goya in Spain, Hogarth in England with engraving and etching, and Tiepolo, Canaletto, and Piranesi in Italy. The visionary work of Goya and his incredible skill with the newly developed aquatint method to enhance his powerful satiric fantasies is carefully studied by students of etching and sought by collectors.

The *Desastres de la Guerra*, Goya's biting reflection on the French occupation of Spain, is one of the great commentaries of all time on the horrors of war and man's inhumanity to man. His *Caprichos* were fanciful, courageous satires of court life and attacked the corrupt court of Charles IV and the Inquisition.

The 19th century, with its obsession with perfection, brought only a steady decline in etching as a creative medium. Great technical proficiency became more and more an end rather than a means.

Later, the artists who developed a new awareness for the beauty of the medium through the artist's own creative exploration of the plate and the printing helped to implement an etching renaissance. One such was Meryon, in France. Towards the end of the century, Whistler, Ensor, and Munch began to use etchings with bold imagination.

The development of the intaglio process in the years since the end of World War II has been almost limitless in inventiveness of image and exploration of technique. The early impetus of Stanley William Hayter's Atelier 17, in Paris before World War II, in New York City during the war, and back in Paris in the post-war years, played a leading role in technical experimentation and the development of unique methods for the use of color. The creative use of the intaglio process in France, England, Germany, Yugoslavia, Poland, and the United States owes much to the heritage of Atelier 17.

INTAGLIO TECHNIQUES

The general term *intaglio* (from the Italian *itagliare*, which means to engrave, carve, or cut) covers a multitude of processes, including engraving, etching, drypoint, aquatint, soft ground, lift ground, mezzotint, and collagraph, as well as a variety of associated techniques. The incised line in the plate holds the ink while the surface is wiped clean. Only the line prints when dampened paper is placed on the plate and both are run through the etching press, with enough pressure to force the paper into the lines.

In an *engraving*, the line is cut into the plate, usually copper or zinc, with a hard steel burin, pushed into the plate by the hand. In *etching*, the line is bitten into the plate with acid wherever the artist has drawn through an acid-proof ground, usually made of wax, lacquer, or asphaltum.

In an *aquatint*, tones are bitten into the plate after the surface has been covered with many tiny droplets of rosin or lacquer. The acid bites the areas around these droplets, producing a tonal effect, which deepens as the plate is left in the acid until the desired tone is achieved.

A *drypoint* line is scratched into the plate with a sharpened needle. In this case the burr of metal thrown up by the point of the tool catches more ink than the line itself. The resulting print makes a rich rough line unlike the crisp hard line of the engraving or etching.

The *soft-ground etching* is made from a plate covered with a ground to which vaseline or tallow has been added. As this ground never really hardens when dry, a variety of textures may be pressed into it, which may be bitten into the plate and then inked and printed.

A *lift-ground etching* requires a clean plate that receives a drawing or painting made with a water soluble ink. A thin coating of liquid wax ground is applied over the entire surface of the drawn plate and the water-soluble ink is soaked off, exposing the plate only where the drawn image has been placed. These lines may be bitten in acid and the plate inked and printed.

A *mezzotint* is made by repeatedly pressing a curved, serrated mezzotint rocker over the surface of a copper plate until it has received many thousands of tiny little indentations from this tool. This procedure is extremely time-consuming, but plates made this way yield rich velvety blacks that can be obtained in no other way. After the entire surface of the plate has been roughened, scrapers and burnishers are employed to achieve tones of grey and white. Mezzotints do not produce large editions because the plates wear out quickly.

A *collagraph* is essentially a print from a collage plate made from a variety of materials which have been firmly glued to a base plate, usually cardboard, hard board, aluminum or other such material. This collage plate is inked by the intaglio method, leaving the recessions or indentations to hold the ink and therefore print when run through the press with dampened paper.

If an uninked plate is run through the press into dampened paper, the resulting impression will be an *embossing*, in which the recessed lines in the plate cause a raised line in the print. If an intaglio plate has the ink rolled onto the surface only, the incised lines will print white, slightly embossed on a solid background. All of these variations are used extensively by contemporary printmakers.

CONCEPT AND IMAGERY

The incised line of the etching plate yields a raised line of ink in the impression that has a crisp, intense, and forceful

A plate chopper used to cut zinc and copper etching plates at Indiana University.

A small plate cutter at Pratt Graphic Art Center in Manhattan.

Below: A zinc plate is cut to size by Herman Zaage at the New School for Social Research in New York City. The foot treadle operates the cutting blade.

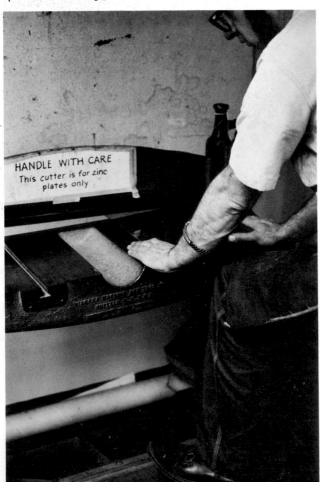

character. This quality has been appreciated by artists who are fine draftsmen and is one of the reasons why some artist-printmakers so love the etching process. The great pressure of the etching press achieves a closer conjunction between the paper and the plate than that of any other graphic process. The plate will show lines of the most sensitive and delicate nature, satisfying the most precise draftsmen over the centuries in which etchings have been made. The medium is also particularly flexible, and changes can be made with relatively minor effort by scraping out those lines that need revision, allowing for repeated redrawing of difficult passages without discarding the rest of the image.

It is possible to ink a single etching plate in many colors to create a color print. It is also possible to print several plates, each inked in different colors, one after the other, in register, on the same impression. There are a number of other ways to create color prints with the intaglio method, but it is easier to achieve color prints by the other graphic techniques, such as screen printing, lithography, and relief printmaking. The time consumed in inking, wiping, and printing an intaglio plate in colors is considerable, and if color is the prime concern you should consider other methods. However, if you want to combine the unique quality of the drawn image and the embossed line with color you may find the intaglio techniques well worth mastering. Many artists use several techniques to achieve color in their prints, such as combining intaglio processes with screen printing or lithography. In most cases the intaglio plates should be printed last to retain the embossment of the lines.

THE PLATE

Zinc and copper are the metals most often used for intaglio plates, with aluminum a distant third because of its brittle quality. As the price of zinc is about one-quarter that of copper, students and beginning printmakers frequently choose the lower-priced metal for their experiments in etching. Brass is occasionally substituted for copper, it bites slowly and very cleanly, and is less expensive than copper. Dutch mordant is used for biting.

Copper is the preferred metal to use for engravings, because of its even texture, uniform ductility, and good printing qualities. It wipes to give a brilliant proof, resists corrosion, and may be steel plated to pull large editions. It is quite expensive, however, and students will find it cheaper to work on photoengraver's zinc. The zinc made today is quite hard, approaching the hardness of copper, because of the alloy structure of the metal. It is more brittle than copper, however, and is not as nice to engrave. It wipes with a slightly muddy effect, and the molecular character of the material makes a brilliant proof more difficult to achieve than with a copper plate. It is a good choice, however, for the beginner. Aluminum and magnesium are poor for engraving because of their brittle texture and should be used only when nothing else is available. Steel has been used for engravings for centuries, and it is still used today in the Bureau of Printing and Engraving in Washington, D.C., to make the engravings for postage stamps. The steel must be soft enough to be cut by the point of the burin. The surface of the plate must be covered with wax or grease when it is stored, or it will rust very quickly. It is not easy to polish a rusted steel plate without weakening fine lines.

When you buy zinc or copper, try to get it directly from the manufacturer or from the supplier who services photo-engraving shops. If you buy it from the art materials supplier you will pay a premium price. The plates come in a variety of sizes, such as 15" by 18", 18" by 20", 20" by 24", 18" by 36", and any variation from these stock sizes involves a cutting and handling charge which can double the per-square-inch price of the basic metal. As the metal is quite easy to cut, a considerable saving can be made by buying the larger sizes and larger quantities of plates. A crate of ten plates can weigh quite a bit, and shipping charges should be ascertained before ordering from a distant supplier.

Cutting Plates

The easiest way to cut a plate, either zinc or copper, is to use a commercial plate chopper, which will be found in every photoengravers shop. Many schools are purchasing this piece of equipment, and if you do a lot of etching on small plates you will appreciate the convenience of the large treadle-operated chopper. A smaller hand-operated model is also in use, but a better buy would be a larger used foot-operated machine, available in larger cities from suppliers to the photoengravers trade. Where floor space is limited, the smaller models may be mounted on a table.

Cutting with a Draw Tool

The most common method of cutting plates is to score them with a draw tool, available from most etching supply houses (see list of suppliers at the end of this book). The draw tool is used as shown. The plate is scored about a dozen times, at first with slight pressure, then with increasing pressure until the groove measures about ⅓ the thickness of the plate. Use a steel T-square or straightedge as a guide and to prevent slipping, at least until the groove is well established, it may be necessary to clamp the straightedge with C clamps on a very large plate. When the groove is deep enough, turn the plate face down along the edge of a table and bend the protruding edge down. If a straight bend appears, the plate will break evenly when it is worked back and forth a couple of times. If the plate simply curves slightly it has not been scored deeply enough, and you must score it further with the draw tool in order to deepen the groove. Most students hate to use this tool because it tends to slip when the groove is first being established.

Cutting with Power Tools

You can cut plates with a carbide-tipped circular saw, but this requires some familiarity with machine tools. We consider this operation dangerous and even more difficult for a beginner to master than a draw tool.

It is possible to score a plate for breaking with a scraper or heavy burin, but this method requires a strong grip and is a last-choice operation to be done only in an emergency.

Cutting a zinc plate with a draw tool requires repeated cuts in the same groove. A steel straightedge is required and it may be clamped in position, if necessary.

After the groove has been deepened sufficiently, the plate will break if it is turned over the edge of a table and bent down and up several times. Do not scratch the surface of the zinc.

The plate should break cleanly along the scored line.

Irregular Shapes

To break a plate into an irregular or indented shape you may use a strong solution of nitric acid to cut through the plate. Paint a solid coat of liquid ground or asphaltum over the plate, scratch the shape on the plate with a blunted needle, allowing about ⅛" space extra all around, then put the plate into the nitric acid. It will take about two hours in a 3 to 1 or 4 to 1 solution (3 parts water to 1 part nitric acid; see the section on acids) to cut through the plate. You may then bevel the edges with a file or scraper.

Plates may be cut into unusual shapes with a jigsaw or a coping saw. The zinc is soft and cuts easily, while copper needs more time and effort to shape. An acetylene torch will cut through a metal plate in seconds, leaving a molten irregular edge that has a rich textural quality. The propane and butane gas torches used for soldering will not cut fast enough for general use, but they may be helpful when you don't need sharp cutting. Soldered wires and shapes will print well if they are firmly attached to the base plate. Rolf Nesch has used these materials with great distinction.

The easiest way to obtain irregular shapes for intaglio prints is to cut cardboard or paper shapes and to glue them onto the plate with polymer latex gesso. See our description of this technique under "collagraph".

Beveling the Plate

The zinc or copper plate must have its edges beveled to prevent the sharp edge of the plate from cutting through the paper or the blanket. The edge should be angled as shown, which may be accomplished in several ways. You may use files to make the bevel, starting with a coarse file and finishing with a fine file such as a mill bastard. A scraper will work very well. If the scraper makes little ridges or corrugations in the edge, change the angle of cut slightly to reduce them. A patented device used for forming soft metals may also be used. It takes a little longer but produces a very smooth, even bevel. If you start with files and finish with this patented tool, available at Sears, you can make a very smooth edge. Sandpapers and a burnisher, as well as engraver's charcoal, may also be used to smooth the bevel.

The corners of the plate should be rounded to remove sharp points that could catch the wiping tarletan rag or cut your hand if you hand-wipe the plate. All the edges of the plate, including the bottom edges, should be rounded.

Thin plates need no beveling, as the edges are not high enough to cut the paper. Thick cardboard, masonite, and linoleum plates should be beveled to ease the roller over the thick material and prevent the plate from slipping as it is printed. Make sure that the press rollers are adjusted for these extra-thick plates.

LINE ENGRAVING

The technique of engraving with a burin produces a line of crisp, clean edges and a precise character. Areas that require tonality must be built up by a series of closely spaced lines that appear as a tone when enough of them have been

The plate should be beveled. One method is to use the scraper to remove the metal. This is a quick and relatively easy chore.

A file may be used to complete the beveling job. In this case a mill bastard is finishing the edge. For rougher work a coarse file is helpful.

engraved. The characteristic swelled line of the engraving, which is thin at the beginning of the stroke and then swells to full strength as the tool bites more deeply, has been highly regarded by artists of earlier years for several reasons. It is capable of yielding a wide variety of effects ranging from delicate to powerful, and engraved plates will produce large editions. As a matter of fact, when etching started to supplant engraving, the early etchers such as Callot used a special tool called the *echoppe* to simulate the engraved line by the process of etching. By rotating this tool in his fingers the artist could start with a thin line and then increase the thickness as the line was drawn.

Line engravings are usually made in copper or zinc, and most engravers prefer copper because of its even texture and ductility. Both metals will yield good prints, although copper wipes to a more brilliant white and, because it is harder than zinc, will produce many more prints. When it is steel-faced it may be printed for hundreds, even thousands, of impressions, a fact dealers have known for many years.

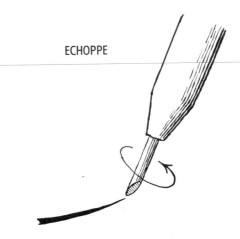

ECHOPPE

Phillippe Mohlitz
"Le Pendu"
Engraving
Fitch-Febvrel Gallery, New York

The burin forces up a sliver of metal or burr. The incised groove is sharp and clean and prints well, for long editions.

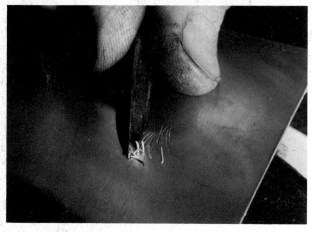

The burr is removed with a very sharp scraper. A dull scraper will scratch the plate. Remove burr as you engrave each line or group of lines. It is very sharp and will cut your hand if not removed.

A multiple tint tool places a series of lines into the plate by the dry point method, i.e., scratching the plate.

Engraving Tools

The basic engraving tool is the burin, a shaft of very hard steel, rectangular in section, which is sharpened at an angle of about 40°. This tool is picked up as shown in the photo. The thumb and the forefinger guide the tool, while the basic forward thrust comes through the palm of the hand. It is important to remember that the plate is pushed into the tool as much as the tool is pushed into the plate. This technique reduces the possibility of slips and gives greater control of the line being engraved. When cutting long sweeping curves, the hand that holds the tool actually moves very little while the other hand pushes the plate into the tool.

Start the line by raising the handle of the burin slightly until the point is driven into the metal. Then lower the handle until it is almost touching the plate. When the plate is pushed into the burin a long sliver of metal will be forced out by the point of the tool. All burrs and raised points of metal should be carefully removed with a very sharp scraper. If these points are not removed, they are hazardous because of their sharpness and will present a problem when the plate is being inked and wiped. They are particularly sharp when the burin is taken out of the line suddenly. If the scraper has not been honed to a very keen edge, it will scratch the plate and cause unpleasant grey streaks where you have used it. These streaks must be removed with engraver's charcoal or a burnisher, which proves that dull tools will always cause trouble. Remember to use the scraper all over the plate. Check thoroughly before printing to avoid painful cuts when hand wiping.

Multiple-cut tools may be used to create tones and textures. These should be sharpened to a very keen edge for metal engraving. The very fine multiples (65 lines or more to the inch) will produce soft greys and blacks.

Frequently an etching will need certain lines strengthened and intensified. Instead of regrounding and re-biting the plate to correct a few lines it will be quicker to use a burin to engrave the lines a little deeper. Remember that an engraved line will print as a very sharp black and may stand out from its etched neighbors with unexpected strength. Be discreet in your use of this technique.

LINE ETCHING

The artist who relies upon fluency of drawing for the realization of his images will find that the etched line offers tremendous advantages over a line drawn with pen and ink. While a pen may occasionally run dry, the etching needle needs no ink to complete its stroke. The needle will not sputter or drip if it is twisted or if its direction is changed suddenly. The thickness of a line may be increased while you are drawing with needles by using a wider point or by leaving the plate in the acid for a longer period of time in order to deepen and widen the line.

Tones and textures are easy to get with aquatint and soft-ground techniques, and these can be used to enhance the line work or to add shapes and tonal areas to the image. An etched line can vary from the faintest scratch to a deep black stroke ⅛″ wide. Even wider lines may be obtained by using multiple strokes or by the lift-ground process.

Jacek Gaj
"Dance" 1965
Etching
Pratt Graphics Center

It is easy to draw through a wax ground with a needle, so easy, in fact, that this process is normally learned first when you are approaching the intaglio technique. It is more difficult to control a drypoint line and far more difficult to achieve success with line engraving. A variety of tools have been used to draw through the ground. Almost anything that will remove the ground will suffice as an etching needle. To make a dark area with lines alone will require many lines close together, usually cross-hatched and often bitten in the acid in several applications of cross-hatching. Rembrandt has used this process with power and sensitivity, and his prints may be studied with great reward to the beginning etcher. If lines that are closely spaced are left too long in the acid, they will fuse together and eventually lose their individual character. Dense blacks are achieved only through multiple biting of many cross-hatchings, with each series of lines bitten properly.

Materials

Zinc or copper photoengraver's plates
Needles (old dental tools are good)
Hard ground and roller *or*
Liquid ground and 1" or 2" flat brush
Nitric acid and glass storage bottles
Plastic tray for acid (large enough for plate)
A glass measuring cup for preparing acid solutions
Mineral spirits (such as benzine or varnoline for diluting and cleaning the ground)
A watch or a clock for timing the bite
A triangular scraper (for removing errors)
A curved burnisher (for burnishing and polishing errors and lightening aquatints)

ETCHING GROUNDS

Liquid Grounds

The acid-resistant covering that protects the plate is called ground. There are many formulas for making grounds, and many different types are available for purchase. Only those grounds that use chemicals available today will be discussed. The exotic chemicals of past ages are difficult to obtain; there is little advantage in knowing a formula that specifies the use of "Rosin of Tyre" if you can't find it.

The most commonly used ground is a liquid ground, painted on the plate with a wide, flat, soft brush. Although several companies manufacture this type, it is easy to make a large batch and bottle it for future use. The ingredients are easily obtainable.

2 parts asphaltum
2 parts beeswax
1 part rosin (powdered)

All ingredients are dissolved in varnoline or benzine of low volatility. Although heating hastens the process, the penetrating odor requires excellent ventilation; and the danger presented by a pot full of hot ground, which is quite inflammable,

Liquid ground should be flowed onto the plate with a wide soft brush. The ground should drain to a thin even coat, when it can be placed on the hot plate for a minute to speed drying. Do not overheat the ground, or it will false bite.

makes it prudent to recommend the slower but safer method, without heat. Asphaltum is usually obtained in a liquid state and is usually added last to the mixture of rosin and wax. As the rosin is hardest and slowest to dissolve, it is placed in benzine or varnoline first and allowed to dissolve, with occasional stirring. The beeswax is added next, along with more varnoline. The usual procedure is to make the ground somewhat thicker than required and then to add solvent to each batch as you use it. Good ground will take an amazing amount of solvent without being over-thinned. A little heat will speed the drying process after the ground is on the plate.

Several commercial grounds made with ether or chloroform as a solvent are available. These dry very quickly and are not brushed on but poured over the tilted plate. The plate is then twirled or spun quickly in order to spread the ground rapidly over the entire surface. It takes only a few seconds to cover the plate. When these grounds are dry they are very slick and hard and may be handled quite a bit without damage. Such a ground may be used as a stop-out varnish because it dries so quickly. As it tends to feather or bleed, however, you must be careful with it. The cost of commercial grounds is very high, and most artists will find that making their own ground will be much cheaper.

Asphaltum, thinned with varnolene or mineral spirits may be used as the ground if the work to be done doesn't have fine lines. Asphaltum will flake off if it is too thin and is no substitute for a good liquid ground. However it is an excellent ground for very long deep biting and when cutting through a plate.

To apply a hard ball ground, the plate should be heated on the hot plate until the ground melts and may be spread evenly with a hard roller. This roller is made of hard linoleum. Hard rubber may be used if the plate is not too hot. Soft rubber and gelatine are not suitable for this work.

Hard Ground

Hard ground is more difficult to make than liquid ground because it must be heated to melt the ingredients together. The ingredients are the same as for the liquid ground but omit the solvent. As several companies sell good hard ground (called ball ground because it looks like a dark ball about the size of a golf ball) you can buy it quite easily. Webers, Cronite, and Graphic Chemical all have hard ground at reasonable prices.

The etching plate must be heated on an electric or gas hotplate to melt the ground sufficiently to spread it easily. Do not overheat it, or the wax will bubble, smoke, and burn. The ground may be rolled over the warm plate to a smooth, even, transparent coat. A roller of hard rubber may be used if the plate is not allowed to become too hot. A linoleum roller is very handy, but hard to find. Leather rollers are still available from Craftool or Rembrandt Graphic Arts Co., although expensive. Soft rubber or gelatine rollers should not be used to spread hard grounds because they will melt or be deformed by the heat.

I have seen dabbers used so skillfully to apply a ball ground that the wax appeared to be absolutely even over the entire plate. The plate should be warmed just enough to melt the ground, then rapidly worked over with short, dabbing strokes. The heat will distribute the wax over the surface. A dabber may be made easily from a piece of umbrella cloth or fine silk, some cotton, and a 3"-diameter disk cut from two or three pieces of cardboard.

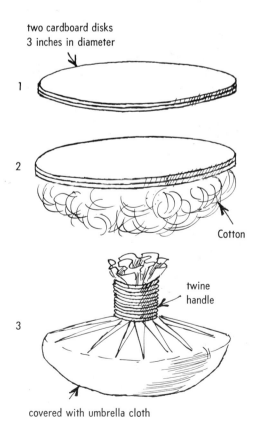

two cardboard disks 3 inches in diameter

1

2

Cotton

3

twine handle

covered with umbrella cloth

MAKING A DABBER

A plate is smoked using an overhead rack made from wire coat hangers to support the zinc. The rack is hung from the ceiling on wires.

A card is used to draw into a soft-ground. The edge will pick off the ground where it touches the plate, and these lines may be bitten in the acid.

Below: To obtain a line drawing in soft-ground, place a piece of textured paper under your drawing next to the soft-grounded surface.

Very Hard Liquid Ground

A very hard, thin, transparent, durable liquid ground may be made by diluting Heims Steel Etching Ground with an equal quantity of lacquer thinner. This ground, which ordinarily dries too quickly to brush out evenly, will dry a little more slowly when mixed with the lacquer thinner. Mix only enough for each separate use. To find where the basic ground is available, see the list of suppliers at the end of the book.

All liquid grounds should be applied with a wide soft brush to a tilted plate, which lets the ground flow across the plate and drain to a thin even coat. Placing the plate on a heater, for a few seconds only, will hasten the drying process.

Staging Ink Ground

A hard, tough ground may be made by using staging ink, a commercially prepared compound sold by photoengravers' supply houses, such as H. Pitman. It is brushed evenly over the plate, then heated to about 250° or 300° F., over an electric hotplate. It may be removed with mineral spirits.

Smoking the Ground

Occasionally it is helpful to transfer your drawing onto a blackened plate, in order to see the drawing better and to see the lines as you open them with the needle. The color of most grounds is close to that of copper, and it is not easy to see what you have drawn when you use copper.

The traditional method of blackening a plate is to smoke it with the carbon deposit of a candle or taper. The plate must be warmed to soften the ground so that the carbon will color it completely and not simply remain on the surface. Use a small hand vise to grip the edge of the plate, cushioning the jaws of the vise with a few pieces of cardboard to prevent scratches. Warm the plate over a hotplate or a gas burner, but don't cause the ground to bubble or smoke. Light a taper or candle that will smoke and pass the candle under the plate, grounded side to the flame. You may use a wick and a glass jar containing kerosene, grease, or vaseline. Move the flame constantly, and don't touch the ground with the wick. The carbon deposited on the ground should fuse with it and form a solid black coat that will not rub off. Your needle will now make lines that are plainly visible. An overhead support made of wire coat hangers will enable you to smoke large plates with ease.

Stop-Out Varnish

Any acid-resisting compound that dries quickly may be used as a coating to prevent certain areas from further etching in the acid solution. Quick-drying ether or chloroform-based grounds may be used. Hard ground is always handy, and when length of drying time is not too important a factor, it makes a suitable stop-out. Asphaltum is frequently used, as it is kept in every etcher's shop. Commercial stop-out varnish is usually alcohol-based, with rosin and coloring dissolved in it.

When it is necessary to bite the plate very deeply, you may protect unbitten areas of the plate by covering them with Contact paper. This is a plastic sheet with an adhesive backing. The plastic resists the acid.

Soft Ground

A soft ground, even when dry, remains soft and sensitive to pressure. Different textures may be impressed into it, and these textures may be bitten by the acid into the plate. You make soft ground by adding vaseline to liquid hard ground and mixing thoroughly. About one part vaseline to three parts ground by volume is correct, depending upon the softness desired. Other materials, such as tallow or lard, may be mixed with hard ground. In such recipes you should add more of the soft material to the liquid ground, up to equal volumes of each. Vaseline is more easily obtainable at any drug store, and its composition is more dependable than either tallow or lard.

Soft ground should be applied by a wide smooth brush to a very thin even film. The sensitivity of the ground changes as it thickens, and an irregular ground will give uncertain textures.

A paste soft ground made by Weber's is available in supply stores in the New York area and is very easy to apply. Heat the plate moderately, dab a few spots of paste onto the plate, and roll it out to a thin even film with a moderately soft roller. Do not use a plastic or gelatin roller on the warm plate, because the heat will injure the roller.

Soft-Ground Techniques

The classic method of working in soft ground is to draw through a thin sheet of textured paper, such as pastel paper or thin watercolor paper, onto a plate that has been covered with soft ground. As this ground remains sensitive to the touch even after it is dry, the plate must be handled with care. A fingerprint will be bitten, and other slight scratches and bruises will show. Make a bridge from a piece of thin plywood, as shown, to keep your hand away from the surface as you draw. The textured surface of the paper will pick up the soft ground from the plate. If you use a hard pencil or ballpoint pen, the line will be relatively thin, but if you use a blunt stick or the curved end of a burnisher the line will be fairly wide. The line will have the characteristic pebbly texture of the paper after the plate has been bitten in the acid. You may tape your sketch, which can be on thin tracing paper, to the table in position over the grounded plate. Then various papers of different textures can be slipped between the sketch and the plate to get a variety of textures in the lines.

You can use fabrics and materials of different weaves and textures by placing them on the plate in the desired position on the soft ground. Run the plate through the press, with pressure somewhat less than used for printing. Put a piece of waxed paper or newsprint on top of the fabric to protect your blankets from the soft ground, which may be forced through the porous fabric. You can use corduroy, burlap, denim, lace, linen, and other fabrics, as well as pieces of paper, cardboard, gasket material, cork, string, or

When using soft-ground it is wise to employ a "bridge" to raise your hand away from the sensitive surface. Draw with heavy pressure to make sure that the paper will press down into the ground and remove it from the plate.

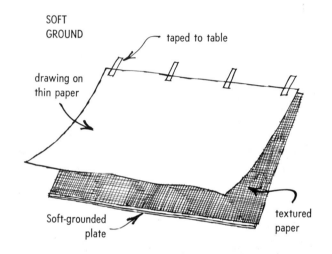

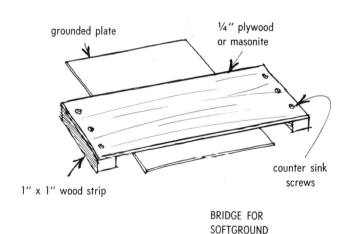

BRIDGE FOR SOFTGROUND

Below: You may use pencils, sticks, or any other kind of stylus as a drawing instrument.

When you check your plate be sure that the textured paper has been forced through the soft-ground, exposing the metal. Varying the pressure will give different weights to the lines. Increasing the length of the bite in the acid will also darken the lines.

Textured fabrics may be pressed into a soft-grounded plate with a hard rubber roller.

Grasses and plants may be impressed into a soft-ground. Here they have been run through the etching press, with the pressure somewhat reduced from printing pressure. Protect your blankets with waxed paper or smooth newsprint.

Below: When the grass and plants have been removed, their impression has been forced into the soft-ground. The plate should be bitten in acid without delay because the surface is receptive to all sorts of pressure and accidental smudges easily occur.

any other found items. You may touch the ground with any object to make an impression of that object's shape in the soft ground. If you don't want certain areas to bite, stop them out with ground, asphaltum, or varnish before you immerse the plate in the acid. It is possible to use the point of a needle in the same way as you would when working on a hard ground. The line will be sharp and clean after biting. In fact, the soft ground is very useful when you are reworking a plate that has already been bitten. The soft ground clings to the irregularities of the etched plate better than the normal hard ground and prevents foul biting around the edges of deeply bitten lines.

AQUATINT

The process of aquatint should be mastered by every printmaker who intends to do serious work in etching. The wide variety of greys, ranging from delicate, light washes to rich, deep blacks are indispensible to an artist who needs tonality in his work. The principle of aquatint is simple. A fine mist of acid-resistant tiny droplets or particles of acid-resistant material is dusted or sprayed over the zinc or copper plate. When this mist is fixed to the surface it should cover about 40% of the area. Place the plate in a weak solution of nitric acid. The usual proportions range from 1 part of nitric acid in 8 parts of water to 1 part acid in 12 parts of water. The design is put on the plate by protecting those parts that are to appear white with an acid-resisting ground or stop-out. The acid will attack the unprotected portions of the plate and not the tiny spots that are covered by the droplets. The darkness of the tone is increased by leaving the plate in the acid solution for longer periods.

Below: The typical white dots where the acid has been resisted shows clearly in this enlargement of a print by John Ross. A coarse spray paint was used. The black lines are through a soft ground, the white lines are acrylic polymer gesso.

The Rosin Dust Method—Hand Applied

Finely ground rosin may be dusted over the plate from a small cloth bag that is shaken or tapped from a short distance above the plate. This dusting should be done in a draft-free place and practiced until a fairly even dusting of rosin can be applied to the plate. The bags can be made from several layers of fine nylon stockings or fine broadcloth. You should be able to control the quantities of rosin powder by flicking the bag with your fingers.

The fineness of the powder will affect the texture of the aquatint tone. If the powder is coarse, the larger particles of rosin will cause larger white dots to appear in the finished print. When a coarse tone is needed you may have to crush lump rosin with a mortar and pestle to the right consistency. The prepared powdered rosin is always ground to very fine powder. It will be helpful to have several bags of rosin of varying degrees of coarseness at hand for a wide latitude of textures in the tones.

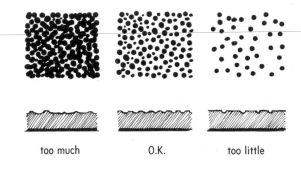

too much   O.K.   too little

AQUATINT COVERAGE

Francisco Goya
"Disparate Furioso" (No. 6 Los Proverbios)
Etching and Aquatint 8½" x 12¼"
Collection Jacob Landau

To make an aquatint bag, place few spoonfuls of rosin powder on a square of porous cloth.

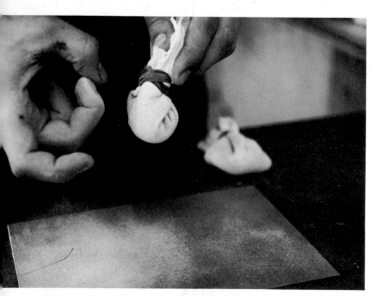

Fold up the corners of the cloth square and tie with string or a rubber band. Different degrees of coarseness can be kept in separate bags. The coarser grind will require a coarser mesh fabric.

Flick the aquatint bag with your finger to force the powder through the mesh of the cloth. Experiment in a place free of drafts or sudden breezes. An even misting of rosin powder is essential.

Top, right: An aquatint box, operated by compressed air to blow rosin particles into the air. The shelf on which plates are placed is visible through the glazed front. Indiana University.

Bottom, right: Aquatint chamber at Cooper Union, New York City. An electric fan blows the rosin particles into the air.

Rosin Dust Method—Dust Boxes

The best control over an aquatint tone is obtained by a dust box, which can be constructed in several ways, each of which requires a ledge or open shelf near the bottom of the box upon which to place the plate. The principle of the box is to contain a cloud of rosin dust, which will settle evenly over the plate. This cloud of rosin can be raised with a hand bellows or a motor-driven fan. The plate is not placed on the shelf immediately, but only after the heavier particles of rosin are allowed to settle. The finer particles will float longer in the air in the box and drop more slowly to the bottom. This process allows great control over the evenness of the tone.

INSTRUCTION *of* PUFF PUFF MACHINE:
- make sure that there is no plate in the box
- close the box.
- turn on the machine for 20 seconds.
- turn OFF the machine.
- open the draw and put the plate on paper
- close the box
- let the rosin settle for 1½ minutes
- remove the plate carefully and close the box.

Moo

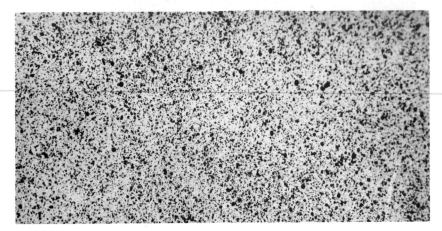

The rosin particles darken to an amber color when they are hot enough to fuse to the plate. The plate should be heated just enough to cause the rosin to adhere to it. Too much heat will melt the rosin into an impervious coat that the acid cannot evenly penetrate. *Above, right:* The proper amount of particles for an aquatint should cover about 40% of the surface of the plate. This coverage is from a can of pressure-spray enamel.

Below: A zinc plate, bitten in fresh 8-1 nitric acid, yields tones as shown in this test proof. Paint spray was used for the aquatint.

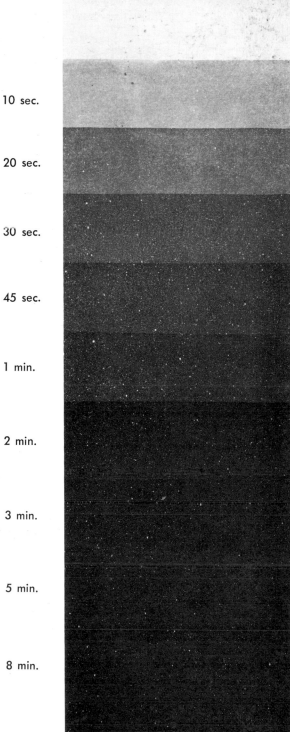

10 sec.

20 sec.

30 sec.

45 sec.

1 min.

2 min.

3 min.

5 min.

8 min.

15 min.

Another method for agitating the rosin powder is to revolve the entire box on a pivot, placing the plate on its shelf when the larger pieces of rosin have settled. The disadvantage of this method is that the large plates in use today make the revolvable box a very cumbersome affair. A simpler solution would seem to be found in the bellows or fan-operated box.

In each case a window made of plastic, plexiglas, or glass is necessary to enable you to view the plate to check the quantity of dust that has settled on it. The plate must be removed when it is properly covered.

All rosin-dust aquatints must be adhered to the plate by heating. A hotplate that can reach a temperature hot enough to melt rosin, 300° to 400° F., must be used. Electric heat is safer than a gas flame, but either type will work. The rosin will turn to an amber color when it is hot enough to stick to the plate. By constantly turning the plate you can keep the rosin from burning or melting into a solid layer. It must be evenly heated. Viewing the plate from the edge will enable you to judge the color of the rosin more exactly. You should wear heavy gloves when handling heated plates. If the aquatint powder has not adhered firmly to the plate, it will float off when placed in the nitric acid, and the tone will be spoiled.

The Paint Spray Aquatint

A very rapid method of obtaining an aquatint is to spray the plate with a fine mist of enamel paint from a pressurized paint can. With a little practice this procedure can be made practically foolproof. It is particularly useful when light and middle-value grey tones are needed. Start spraying off to the side of the plate to be sure the spray is working well, then spray the plate, and stop spraying only after the plate has been passed. Work back and forth in a regular pattern, holding the can about 12″ to 14″ away from the plate surface. Experiment with various brands of paint until you find one that sprays a mist fine enough to suit you. Some brands will spray little drops, which will cause coarse white speckles in your printed tone. Do not use spray cans when they are nearly empty, as they tend to sputter and spatter irregular drops.

The advantage of spray paint is that it dries almost instantly and does not have to be heated. The disadvantages are that the spray is smelly and the fumes may be dangerous. A very long bite in the acid may wash off the particles of paint, so that the deeper black tones may require a heated rosin aquatint. Only your own experiments will determine what best suits your requirements.

Stopping Out Aquatints

You may use hard ground or stop-out varnish to stop out those parts of an aquatinted plate that are not to be bitten. The plate is normally covered completely with the dust or spray before the design is painted on top, although it is possible to paint the design first and apply the dust or spray later. The possibility of ruining a complicated drawing with a poorly applied aquatint is always present and heat needed in a rosin aquatint may melt the ground. Therefore, it is prudent to do the aquatinting first. All parts that are to appear white must be covered with ground or varnish before the biting. A light grey tone can be bitten into a zinc plate in 10 seconds if it is placed in 8:1 nitric acid solution. The longer you leave the plate in the acid, the darker the tone gets. After 3 minutes in the acid the tone is quite dark (about 85% of black), and it gets darker very slowly, taking 10 or more minutes to develop into a rich, dark value. If you have covered too much of the plate with particles of rosin or paint, it may never develop a really deep tone.

Quick-drying grounds, such as ether or alcohol-based grounds, are not suitable for delicate linear stop-outs because they tend to feather or spread when applied to the aquatint plate. Any acid-resisting varnish will work, if you understand how to use it. In general, weak acids and slow biting are better because they allow for careful control, but the artist may want to use strong acid for a rough accidental effect and then develop the image from there.

In general zinc plates are so much softer than copper that they yield far fewer prints, particularly in the case of aquatints. You will find that zinc aquatints will start to weaken and the prints become lighter and lighter after only 20 to 50 impressions. If you need long editions, use copper plates, bitten in ferric chloride or Dutch mordant, and steel-face them. With this process, a very thin coating of chromium is electrolytically deposited over the entire surface of the copper plate. This coating is very hard and resists wear better than the copper. It may be renewed several times to prolong the life of valuable plates.

Sandpaper Aquatints

A grey tone may be obtained by using sandpaper instead of rosin or paint, although the quality of the tone may not be as fine or even. The procedure is simple. Place a thin coat of hard ground over a plate and let it dry. Put the plate face up on the bed of your etching press, cover the plate with a piece of medium sandpaper, and run it through the press with the pressure reduced. It may be necessary to run the plate and sandpaper through several times in different positions to assure an even tone. The particles of sand puncture the ground, allowing the acid to bite the plate in those

When an aquatint is bitten correctly the texture is even. The outside of these shapes was impressed into soft-ground and bitten very deeply. The center left area is aquatint; the right side is soft-ground texture.

points. Technically the effect is the reverse of the rosin aquatint, but the tones look similar to the eye. The stopping-out procedures are the same as before. A drypoint quality can be achieved by placing the sandpaper over a clean plate without ground and running it through the press.

White Effects and Soft Edges on Aquatints

You may use a grease or wax crayon to draw directly on the aquatinted plate before it is bitten, in order to get a soft white line. Press hard enough to deposit the wax or grease on the plate, where it acts as a resist to the acid. Melted rosin, which is quite hard and durable, is better than spray paint, which is delicate and easily damaged. The best crayons are soft litho crayons, children's wax crayons, craypas, or even wax candles. You can soften hard edges this way, too. If you want aquatint to fade gradually into a white background, fine sandpaper may be used to soften the edge.

Flour of Sulphur Method

For delicate wash effects, the flour of sulphur method is very easy and produces soft, pale tones. You need only olive oil and precipitated sulphur powder, called flour of sulphur, which you may keep in an old saltshaker. Use the olive oil as a paint, placing it directly on the surface of the plate where you want the tone. Shake the sulphur powder into the oil, blow off the powder where it has fallen on undesired places, and then let the plate sit for a few hours. The sulphur will bite into the plate, but to a very shallow depth, which may wear rapidly but produces delicate soft tones of grey.

LIFT-GROUND PROCESS

This process enables you to use the intaglio plate for the liveliest, most autographic brushed line or mass that you can produce. It is a direct process; if you paint a black line on a plate, you get a black line on the print. The design is brushed on with a water-soluble paint. There are several formulas that work well. Picasso used a solution of sugar melted in boiling water, colored it with a tube of black gouache or watercolor, and finally added gamboge, a photoengraver's compound, that dissolves readily in water. Other usable formulas are as follows:

> 10 parts Karo syrup
> 2 parts black India ink
> 1 part powdered soap
> 1 part powdered gum arabic

Another formula for lift ground is:

> 10 parts simple syrup (1 part
> sugar to 5 parts water
> boiled to a syrup)
> 3 parts black poster color
> 2 parts detergent
> (gum arabic is optional)

The use of poster paint alone is inadvisable because the binders in the paint do not dissolve as completely as you would

Peter Milton
"October Piece" 1970
Lift ground etching 17¾" x 23⅞"
Courtesy of the artist
Photo Eric Pollitzer

sugar must be removed in the latter case or the whole area will later lift.

"I make the sugar-ink by dissolving enough sugar in heated India ink to make a heavyish syrup when it cools, and I then dilute it to workable consistency by adding more ink. In low humidity conditions a few drops of glycol antifreeze retards drying and improves the handling of the ink. I use a Hunt #107 hawk quill and #104 mapping points, with the point often touched up and refined with polishing paper as a sharpener. The point must be cleaned often to keep the ink flowing freely.

"When the drawing is finished the plate is covered with an extremely dilute (benzine) hard-ground using Peterdi's formula. The ground must be even, and I have found a bubble level useful in leveling the plate to even the settling of the liquid. I use a 2″ white bristle brush. If there is any streaking of the liquid it will be due to the ground's not being dilute enough. It should be very gratifying to know that one has many chances to get the ground perfect. If after drying the ground seems too thick (will not lift well), too thin (will false bite), too uneven, or too rough with impurities, the plate can be flooded with benzine and cleaned with a very soft absorbent material without injuring the drawing. I usually try 5-8 times before I am satisfied.

"The plate is then placed in a tray of hot water, just hot enough to be uncomfortable to the hand, and left until the water has cooled to room temperature. The sugar in the ink reacts with the water and swells, so that the ink softens; the ground over it loosens and may be rubbed away by hand. The plate is methodically and vigorously rubbed until the metal is. exposed at every point that there was a sugar-ink mark. There is no mark so delicate that it shouldn't lift if everything has gone right.

"I etch the plate in the manner normal for copper, with Dutch mordant and many stopping-out steps, using rosin/alcohol/methyl violet dye as the stop-out varnish. Any mark or shape too broad to hold ink well during the printing can be strengthened. Since a heated aquatint is likely to foul the ground, I either spray on a rosin/alcohol solution through an atomizer or use a commercial paint spray, such as Krylon flat-black enamel.

"Later I add much straight engraving with the burin to refine the image, and it is at this stage that the figures take on their rather photographic quality. I do not use photo-engraving aids and, while this is impractical, it is curiously satisfying. I do use photographs extensively, but only to draw from. In *October Piece* I spent around 3-4 months on the pre-acid drawing stage and 2-3 months on the post-acid engraving.

"It must be said that this approach as I am using it is probably as antithetical as can be conceived to the more-or-less contemporary printmaking concepts which emphasize openness to materials and to the medium itself. As much as anyone, I would hate to see such procedures as I have just outlined lead us back to the kind of frozen tedium that afflicted printmaking for so many years before its present health."

The etched line of Kathe Kollwitz is revealed by the glistening of the ink as it lies on the paper.

The checkerboard effect is caused by a parallel line roulette, used in two directions at right angles to each other. Print by Ross.

Below: The central texture is caused by a parallel roulette on top of a fabric-textured soft-ground tone.

ing is reversed as it is transferred, then restored when it is printed from the plate.

ETCHING NEEDLES AND ROULETTES

Any point that will remove the ground will enable you to etch the resultant line in acid. Old dental tools are good, if resharpened to suit your hand. Commercially made etching needles, with a steel point set in a wooden, pencil-like handle, are also practical, if expensive. You can sharpen a nail, if you wish, as long as you can draw fluently with it. However, an overly sharp point may catch in the metal and stick. Because the line will not bite if all the wax is not removed from the line, a very light touch is somewhat dangerous.

Various roulette wheels are made in order to produce a variety of tones and patterns in the plate. They can provide regular patterns, usually numbered according to the number of lines or dots per inch that are incised into the drum, and irregular patterns, which are usually handmade. Roulettes are expensive but very helpful when different textures and tones are needed. They can be used to cut directly into the metal of the plate, when the tones will print dark from the burr produced by the tiny metal edges. Roulettes may be used with ground, and the textures will be bitten deeply and permanently into the plate by the acid. Linear roulettes will produce continuous parallel lines if the tool is rolled back and forth without slipping or skidding.

Old phonograph needles, pins stuck into erasers, sticks, punches, and all sorts of implements have been used to make lines or textures in etching, and you will have to decide which points best serve your purpose.

ACIDS

Nitric (For Etching Zinc and Copper)

One of the most useful acids is nitric; it will etch either zinc or copper. When purchased in technical grade, it is very strong and quite dangerous and should be handled with care. It is not necessary to buy the chemically pure acid for etching. It is mixed with water to various dilutions; the stronger solutions, such as 4 parts water to one part nitric, usually used for deep biting or strong line work and the weak solutions, such as 8 or 12 parts water to one part nitric, usually used for aquatints and fine lines.

When diluting acid, always put the water into the container first, then add the acid. Use a glass measuring cup and work slowly and carefully. Never leave acid where it can accidentally be knocked over. Put it away in a locked cabinet when you are not using it.

Zinc plates will release white bubbles of hydrogen gas in nitric acid, which will indicate the strength of the acid. Intense bubbling shows a fresh, strong acid and faint bubbling results from weak or exhausted acid. Nitric acid biting into zinc produces a rugged, irregular line if the plate is left too long in the acid. It is advisable to keep a bottle of ammonia handy, in case of acid splashed on clothing, to neutralize the action of the acid with the base. Because a drop of acid will

.eat a hole in clothing very rapidly, work aprons or old clothes are essential in the shop.

Dutch Mordant (For Etching Copper)

The standard formula for Dutch mordant, for etching copper, is:

Hydrochloric acid	10%
Potassium chlorate	2%
Water	88%

Dissolve the potassium chlorate in water first, then add the hydrochloric acid. This acid, used for copper plates, bites slowly and is wonderful for fine lines and aquatints because it is easy to control the depth of the bite. As no bubbles are produced, careful observation of the solution's action is necessary. Dutch mordant is favored by artists who want good control over even, close tones and who want no accidental effects or textures. Be sure to label all your acid solutions clearly. The mordant turns greenish-blue after its first use and is easy to identify but should be labeled as a matter of policy of good housekeeping. Proper organization is essential to success in most endeavors, and printmaking demands all the organizational skill you can muster.

Ferric Chloride (For Etching Copper)

Ferric chloride (iron perchloride) acid, long used by commercial photoengravers, is able to bite copper plates with precision and is useful for fine work and aquatints. It bites very slowly, and plates should be turned face down in the solution to allow the precipitate to fall out of the lines, where it would eventually clog them if left to accumulate. This method prevents visual observation while the plate is biting and mandates an accurate timing procedure, which some artists resent, and therefore they reject the acid. It is usually diluted with equal amounts of water to make a reddish-brown solution. If you can establish a reliable timing chart, ferric chloride should be extremely useful.

Aluminum Etch

While aluminum is too soft for general work, it is cheaper than zinc or copper, and some beginning students may find it helpful for experimental work in elementary techniques. An acid to etch aluminum can be made by mixing the following chemicals into ten parts of warm water: one part potassium dichlorate, one part sulphuric acid and one and one-half parts of hydrochloric acid. All these chemicals are mixed by weight, not volume.

Acid Trays

For plates up to 30" by 24" it is possible to buy photo trays made of a white plastic material that successfully resists acids. These trays are readily available and are not expensive. Black rubber photographic trays may also be used, but they disintegrate in time and are not as durable as the white plastic. Stainless steel trays are best of all because they are

An irregular roulette with a carbide tip will roughen the surface of a plate into a deep black, if desired. The tone produced is close to a mezzotint black in effect.

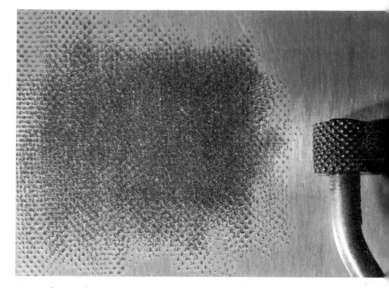

A regular roulette produces a more mechanical tone than the irregular tip. They are made in a number of patterns and sizes.

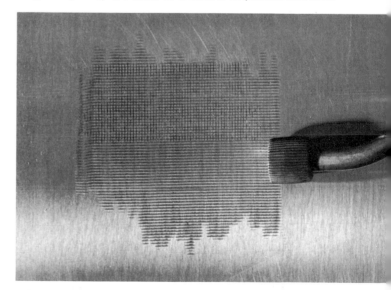

A lining roulette will make parallel lines that form an even tone. They may be cross-hatched by holding the tool at a right angle to the first set of lines.

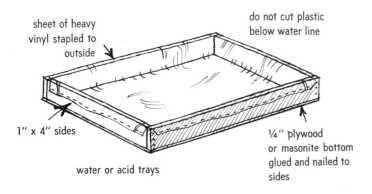

sheet of heavy vinyl stapled to outside

do not cut plastic below water line

1" x 4" sides

¼" plywood or masonite bottom glued and nailed to sides

water or acid trays

CHEAP LARGE WATER OR ACID TRAY

By squeezing the bulb, you can induce fluids to flow from the large storage container to the smaller can. This type of siphon is very useful in the graphic workshop for draining acid trays and transferring liquids without spillage.

Below: The plate should be eased into the acid tray. It should be lifted on end every minute or so in order to remove gas bubbles. Do not brush a soft-ground to remove bubbles.

strong and unbreakable, but they are quite expensive. For larger plates you may have to order custom-made plastic trays from a photo supply house. Lacquer thinner will dissolve some photographic trays, and care must be taken to test the tray first in order to avoid softening the surface when you use this solvent.

It is easy to make trays from pieces of 1" by 4" pine, with a bottom of ¼" plywood or ¼" hardboard. While it is possible to waterproof this type of tray with tapes and varnishes, the easiest way to make it usable is to line the inside of the tray with vinyl or plastic sheeting, folded up over the sides and stapled to the outside of the 1" by 4" framework. This lining will make the tray suitable for water and all acids, and any size desired may be constructed quickly and cheaply. The plastic sheeting may be replaced rapidly, as it tends to develop pinholes and tears, particularly if the plates have sharp edges. We have used many trays of this type and find them easy to maintain and inexpensive.

Emptying Acid Trays

The most convenient way to drain acid from a tray is from a spigot built into the bottom. This type of tray is very expensive, however, and few artists can afford them. A useful substitute is a hand-pumped siphon that operates on gravity, once the siphoning process has been started. Most of the siphons are available from automobile accessory stores and were designed to siphon gasoline and similar fluids. They are made from white plastic, which is acid-proof, and have ¼"-diameter plastic hoses. They will drain a gallon of liquid in about 5 minutes, which is the major disadvantage of the method, because the time involved seems excessively long when you are cleaning up the workshop. However, there is no danger of spilling the acid, which is important enough to make the wait worthwhile. The siphon can also be used to transfer varnoline, lacquer thinner, and other fluids from one container to another.

Small quantities of acid can be poured into a funnel set in the mouth of the container. Plastic containers are useful but occasionally develop leaks, and glass bottles are breakable but never leak. Acid bottles should have plastic caps or ground-glass stoppers. Metal caps will soon corrode through from the fumes in the bottle.

Biting the Plate

Plates should be eased into the acid bath to avoid splashing or spilling the solution. A hooked dental tool makes a convenient implement with which to hold the plate while it is being immersed in the acid. Be careful not to scratch the ground. Examine the plate after a few moments to see if the lines are all biting correctly, or if any areas are false-biting. A false bite will occur in a section of plate where the ground has been bruised or damaged in a way hard to detect. Remove the plate promptly and stop out the offending areas with a stop-out varnish, such as rosin dissolved in alcohol, shellac, or even liquid hard ground.

If the acid is nitric, gas bubbles will soon form in the lines. Bubbles should be removed by lifting one edge of the plate out of the acid with a hook and letting all the acid drain off the surface. Then replace the plate in the solution. Bubbles should be removed regularly to avoid an irregular, ragged line, unless this effect is desired. The traditional turkey feather to remove bubbles is still used, and as long as it does not scratch the ground is a helpful tool, though somewhat inefficient. With soft grounds, it is not possible to brush the plate with anything because of the danger of scratching the ground. These plates must be lifted and drained.

Drawing on the Immersed Plate

If certain lines are not biting properly, it is possible to work on the plate while it is still in the acid bath. You must remember that the longer the lines bite, the deeper and darker they get. This means that all delicate work should be done last and heavier lines should be needled in as soon as possible. Francis Seymour Haden, a 19th century English etcher, frequently worked on his plates while they were still in the acid. Good needles will corrode rapidly with this treatment, but resharpened dental tools will work admirably for this process.

Deep Biting

For relief etching where two thirds of the thickness of the plate must be removed, nitric acid is the strongest mordant and therefore the fastest. Because of the heat generated by the acid in removing large quantities of metal, it is wise to have a second tray containing cold water alongside the acid tray. When the plate becomes warm, slide it into the water for a minute or two to cool it. If the plate becomes too warm, the ground will become soft and, as the biting increases in vigor with heat, the whole process may escalate out of control and the plate be ruined by false biting and unwanted corrosion. Acid quickly loses its strength when deep biting of large areas is necessary, and the solution must be replenished frequently. Have plenty of ventilation for this procedure because the fumes are noxious. If much biting is done it should be in an area that has mechanical ventilation, with an outside vent. As the fumes are corrosive, most metal nearby will soon rust unless lacquered or otherwise protected.

Plates from photoengravers' supply houses are usually back-coated to protect the reverse side. Scratches and nicks are frequent, however, and if not protected will soon become very deep and, in rare cases, bitten through the plate. Check the backs of the plates being bitten deeply and retouch scratches with asphaltum or stop-out varnish.

DRYPOINT

Although this process may be the simplest in theory, it is quite difficult to control the drypoint technique when you need delicate drawing and even tonalities. The idea of using a sharp hard steel point to scratch into the plate is very appealing because it seems so simple and basic. However, etching is actually easier for the beginner to master, while the drypoint requires a high degree of skill. The burr of metal

When space is at a premium, water and acid trays may be stacked one above the other. Water must be on top, acid underneath. This setup is from the Graphic Art USA Exhibit in Belgrade, Yugoslavia, 1965. Trays have built-in spigots for easy draining.

Vented acid chamber in the studio of Rudy Pozzatti, Bloomington, Indiana. Note black siphon on left wall for draining solutions back into containers.

The single dry point needle scratches the plate, throwing up burr on one or both sides of the line, depending upon the angle of cut. The angle shown produces a double burr.

When inked, the dry point burr traps and holds a large amount of ink, printing the velvety black line so prized by dry point connoisseurs.

that is raised by the point actually holds more ink and prints with more effect than the incised line itself, which is usually quite shallow and holds little ink. When the burr is new, the print has rich, dark blacks; but when the burr starts to break off and wear down, the blacks get weaker and greyer until the plate has lost much of its character and vigor. A drypoint on zinc will yield only 25 or 30 impressions. Copper will furnish about double that number and, when steel-faced, may yield from 100 to 200 decent impressions. Hardened steel, carbide tips, and diamond points are all suitable for making drypoints. Lovis Cornith, Jacques Villon, and Max Beckmann have produced striking prints with this method.

CORRECTING ERRORS

Scraping, Burnishing, and Polishing

It is almost inevitable that some lines or tones will need to be eliminated or reduced in value. The scraper, a three-sided wedge of hardened steel, is the tool usually used for this job. It should be kept very sharp on a fine india or hard arkansas stone, and the steel shaft can be wrapped with masking tape to protect your fingers. Scrapers come in many sizes and shapes and are virtually indispensable to the etcher. Some methods, such as the mezzotint, rely exclusively on the scraper for the development of the image, while almost all techniques have some need for this useful tool. It can remove amounts of zinc or copper by scraping, and it acts as an eraser.

Lovis Corinth
"Selbstbildnis"
Drypoint 7¾" x 6⅛"
Metropolitan Museum of Art
Gift of Mr. and Bruno Adriani 1959

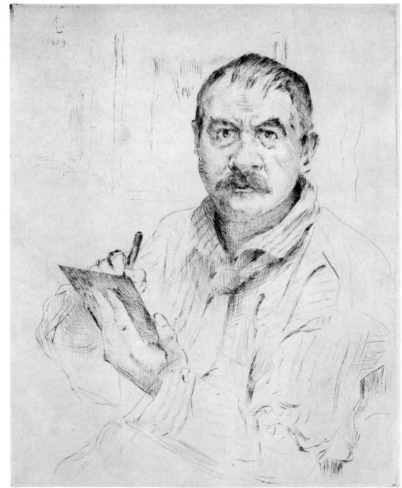

When working over a large area, use enough pressure and keep changing the angle of cut, in order to avoid building up ridges or "drifts," which are minute corrugations in the surface of the plate. A dull tool will add scratches instead of removing them, so keep the scraper sharp. The edge does the cutting; and as there are usually three edges to each tool, you can remove a lot of metal in a short time. You must scrape over an area and not just along a thin line or the scraped indentation will print as a grey smudge.

After the scraping is finished, the surface of the plate will have to be smoothed further, with fine sandpaper, such as 0000 or finer. This surface, in turn, would print as a smoky grey tone and will have to be burnished and charcoaled for a smooth polish. It may be necessary to use jeweler's rouge for the final polishing if a brilliant white is desired. Engraver's charcoal, made from hard maple, is usually used with water to increase its efficiency. A few drops sprinkled on the area to be polished will be sufficient. Without water, charcoal does not cut as well.

Repoussage

If the plate has been scraped to such an extent that the surface is simply too low to print properly, it may be necessary to force the metal back to the original level from the back of the plate. This raising, called *repoussage*, may be done in several ways.

Mark the back of the plate with crayon or chalk outlining the area to be raised, using two pieces of wood fastened together as a caliper. You must have a smooth metal sheet as an anvil upon which to place the plate, face down. With a ball-peen hammer, hammer the back of the plate to force the metal up to the level of the printing surface. Hammer gently at first. The surface may then be sanded and polished until it is smooth and even again.

It is possible to glue paper shims on the back of the plate, in position, under the scraped area. Run the plate and shims through the etching press several times with enough pressure to force the metal up to required level. In fact, whichever method you use to force the metal to the correct level, it is a good idea to glue paper shims on the back of the plate to prevent the scraped area from being pushed down again by repeated printings under strong pressure.

SCRAPER

masking tape

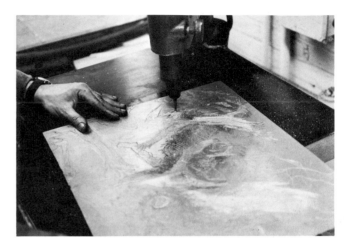

Al Blaustein uses a photoengraver's router to remove unwanted lines from a zinc plate. The router is locked into position and the plate is tilted slightly to control the depth of cut. Pratt Institute, Brooklyn.

Minor scratches may be removed by polishing the plate with engraver's charcoal and water.

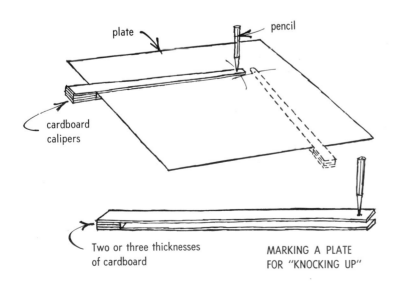

plate

pencil

cardboard calipers

Two or three thicknesses of cardboard

MARKING A PLATE FOR "KNOCKING UP"

PAPER

Etchings are printed into damp paper because the fibers must be soft and pliant in order to be pressed into the incisions and indentations of the metal plate. The ability of the paper to withstand the abuse of printing, dampening, pressure, and stretching without tearing or discoloring is of primary importance. Most highly prized papers are made of all rags, with little sizing, long fibers, and no chemical residue. Good papers come from Europe and Japan, with France, Italy, and Germany still the prime producers of rag base papers suitable for intaglio printing.

Proof Paper

Good proof impressions can be taken on index paper, cover stock, Basingwerk, or other papers that will not disintegrate when they are dampened. It is possible to use newsprint for a rough proof, but it is so soft that it tears easily and of course it is extremely perishable. For a finished proof it is wise to use the paper on which you will print the entire edition, in order to judge the tonal values exactly as they appear in a final print. Proof papers need not be 100% rag because you are not concerned with the permanency of the proof, until the image is complete enough to warrant preservation.

Dampening Paper

Many papers may be soaked directly in a tray of water, then rolled between clean blotters until the surface moisture has been absorbed. A hard-rubber roller, plastic roller, or wooden rolling pin may be used to blot the excess moisture. Most papers need only a few minutes in the water bath to be ready to use. For proving plates and for small editions this method is satisfactory, but because rolling the paper between blotters is time consuming it is faster to prepare paper in advance when larger editions are needed.

The day before you print you can prepare a stack of paper, 20 or more sheets, by dampening every other sheet with a moist sponge. Stack the sheets together and wrap them in vinyl or oilcloth, and the moisture will be distributed evenly throughout the stack in 24 hours. Make sure the sides are covered or they will dry first. The amount of water needed depends on the absorbency of the particular paper, which can be determined only by experience. Some notes on popular papers follow.

The paper must be soaked in water to soften the fibers. Many papers can be completely immersed and left to soak. This should be done before you start the inking and wiping process.

Domestic Papers

Strathmore makes an all-rag paper suitable for etchings, called Artist's paper. It is expensive but strong and fine. Acme Index and Beckett cover papers have a rag content and print well for inexpensive papers. Tweedweave, Alexandra, Pastelle, Hammermill, and Tuscan are machine-made papers of fair quality, suitable for proofs and student work.

Imported Papers

Rives, light and heavy, is a standard paper, all rag, good quality, and suitable for many plates.

Rives BFK, a heavy, fine paper, is available in many sizes.

It is a very useful paper for etchings, collagraphs, and lithographs and has become one of the most respected papers made.

Arches text, available in buff and white, both laid and wove, is a rag paper used extensively in this country and Europe. It is good for small plates and plates that are not too deeply bitten.

Arches cover is a fine, heavy, sensitive paper useful for collagraphs, etchings, and lithos. The buff color is very handsome.

Basingwerk, made in three weights, is a useful paper for proofs and for some editions. It is inexpensive and practical.

Fabriano Classico, in various weights up to 300 lb., is a watercolor paper. The heavier paper is very strong and suitable for embossing, collagraphs, and deeply bitten plates. The deckle edge is worth saving. An expensive sheet.

Copperplate is a fine paper, but it can not be soaked as it falls apart if too wet. Should be dampened by blotters only and handled carefully.

Fabriano text and cover is available in many beautiful colors and is one of the few colored papers that may be used for etching. It is not an all-rag sheet.

German etching paper is a good, large white sheet, moderately expensive and fairly useful.

Italia is white, strong, good for etching, collagraphs and general intaglio printing. A paper well liked by many printmakers, it is moderately expensive.

J. Barcham Green watercolor paper is a nice sheet, good sized and well made. It is a standard paper in England and deservedly so.

Millbourn is available in many weights, and the heavier sheets are a joy to hold and very expensive to buy. Use it for special plates.

Murillo is a light buff color, very heavy, marvelous for collagraphs and extraordinarily sensitive for black-and-white etchings. If this paper were made in white it would be one of the most popular sheets around.

Umbria is a good, useful paper in a medium size sheet.

Kochi, a Japanese paper, is suitable for etching if not soaked.

Dampening Trays

For small sheets of paper the standard size photo-trays made of white plastic are suitable. Larger sheets may need a tray made to fit. The construction may follow the directions for acid trays, using 1″ by 4″ lumber and a plywood or pressed wood bottom, covered with a sheet of heavy vinyl. The most convenient tray has a spigot built in to allow easy drainage. Paper left in trays will form slime and mildew after a few days. The odor generated from this mess can be highly unpleasant, so keep your water trays clean by regular rinsing. A few drops of household bleach added to the water will keep mold to a minimum.

ETCHING INK

The chemical components of etching ink are very simple, and it is relatively easy to make your own. Linseed oil, the

Used army-surplus mixer used for mixing pigment and plate oil in ink manufacture at Indiana University.

Inking the etched plate with a cardboard squeegee is a fast, efficient method for normally bitten plates.

basic ingredient, is added to powdered pigment, and this mixture makes etching ink. There are several brands of ink commercially available, some very inexpensive and of good quality. It is usually sold in 1-pound cans, and the waxed-paper lid should be carefully replaced on the ink before the lid is put on the can after each use. It is more important to put the paper disc on the ink, with no air bubbles underneath, than to put the metal lid on the can. If the ink hardens over, it is messy and wasteful to skim off the top to reach the fresh ink underneath. If you make your own ink, it should be preserved in cans or jars with a similar paper disc as a seal against air.

There are several black pigments available that will make good ink, such as bone black, Frankfort black, vine black, lamp black, ivory black, and drop black. They can be mixed together to exploit the best characteristics of each. One pigment does not have all the qualities essential to good ink, such as intensity and strength of color, even texture, and easy wiping. Mars black is normally not suitable for etching ink. The addition of umber or ochre or blue will make the ink take on warm or cool tones as it is wiped. Mix the dry powdered pigments first with a palette knife, then add a small quantity of plate oil, which is thickened linseed oil. A grinding muller is used for small quantities of ink, with an old litho stone or a glass or marble slab as a grinding surface.

Rudy Pozzatti, of Indiana University, suggests the following ink formulas:

For general printing	3 parts vine black
	1 part bone black
For printing drypoints	4 to 6 parts vine black
	1 part bone black
For printing engravings	2 parts vine black
	1 part bone black

When very large quantities of ink are needed, some schools use power mixers to combine the pigment and oil. The University of Indiana has a used dough-mixing machine in which it mixes the basic ingredients. Power mixers are economically feasible only when hundreds of pounds of ink are needed, to offset the initial cost of the equipment.

The thickened linseed oil that must be used in ink-making can be purchased as plate oil or be made by boiling raw linseed oil until it thickens. Linseed oil may also be thickened by lighting a match to the surface and burning off excess fluids, a smelly and somewhat dangerous procedure. If the oil is not thickened, the ink made from it is difficult to wipe and prints weakly. Most printers buy their ink from reputable manufacturers.

Inking the Plate

The ink must be forced into the etched or engraved lines, the surface wiped clean, and the plate printed onto dampened paper through the etching press. There are several methods of applying the ink.

Inking with Cards

A very quick and easy way to ink a plate, and to accomplish a good part of the wiping, is to use small matboard or chipboard rectangles of cardboard, about 3″ by 4″, as small squeegees, to push the ink over the surface of the plate and into the lines. The edges of the cards must be cut straight and smooth. A good papercutter will be the most useful tool for cutting. Cut the boards into long strips 3″ or 4″ wide, then cut one or two strips at a time into the rectangles that you need. The inking is very fast and the first wiping even faster with these cards. You will save a great amount of tarletan or crinoline by the use of the cards because most of the excess ink will be removed before you start the rag-wiping. The disposable cards are made from scrap pieces of matboard. A rubber window-cleaning squeegee is handy. It can be cleaned with a rag and used instead of cards.

Inking with a Roller

Small paint rollers, 3″ to 6″ in length, are good for distributing the ink over the plate and for getting the ink into the lines. Mohair and short-nap rollers are easiest to clean and are preferred, but almost any nap is usable. The problem comes when you have to clean the roller after you have used it. If it isn't cleaned it soon hardens into a rocklike cylinder and is more trouble to clean than it's worth.

Inking with a Dabber

Rolled scraps of blanket felt make good dabbers, useful for pushing ink into the incised lines of an etching plate. The felt strip should be from 5″ to 8″ in width and 20 or more inches in length. Roll it tightly, and use string, masking tape, or rubber bands to hold it in place. Cut the ends smooth with a hacksaw or sharp knife, and keep cutting new felt as the ends harden. Dried ink is a distinct handicap to the dabber, which is useful mainly for small plates or for spots that have been missed with the card or roller. Leather dabbers are used, too, and they are easier to clean and to keep soft and supple. They are made somewhat differently than felt dabbers, being filled with cotton waste or an old soft rag and then tied with string into a shape that makes a good handle.

Inking the etched plate with a pad of crinoline. Atelier Desjobert, Paris.

Inking is accomplished in this intaglio print workshop with a roller.

Below: Inking the etched plate with a dabber made of old etching felts. This procedure is useful for very deeply bitten plates.

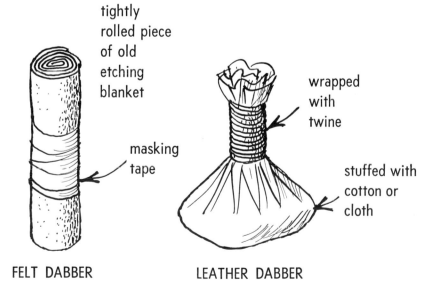

tightly rolled piece of old etching blanket

masking tape

FELT DABBER

wrapped with twine

stuffed with cotton or cloth

LEATHER DABBER

Custom-made hotplate built in on level with table top. Indiana University.

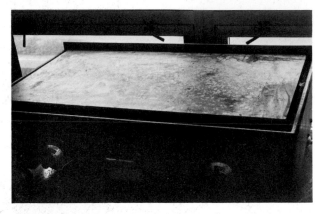

Commercial restaurant hotplate that has been found serviceable by Indiana University.

Inexpensive two-burner electric hotplate with open grid surface. This type heats the plate quickly but does not retain heat long. Indiana University.

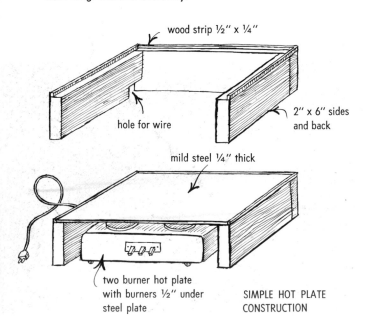

wood strip ½" x ¼"

hole for wire

2" x 6" sides and back

mild steel ¼" thick

two burner hot plate with burners ½" under steel plate

SIMPLE HOT PLATE CONSTRUCTION

Gloves

When you are inking large plates or printing a big edition it is helpful to wear cotton work gloves; the problem of inky hands is ever present in the workshop, and gloves keep at least part of the ink away. The hardware store sells cotton work gloves with knit cuffs, and these are best. Rubber or vinyl gloves make your hands sweat and are uncomfortable after a few prints. The gauntlet type of glove is too awkward. Leather gloves are good if you have an old pair that you won't mind soiling. The gloves must be removed for hand wiping and for paper handling.

Hotplates

The hotplate is essential in the etcher's studio, not only for fusing rosin aquatints to the plate but for warming those plates that need very rich and full printing to bring out their best characteristics. Most professional etching printers rarely use the hotplate in printing plates, however, because it may cause more problems than it solves. In general, ink at room temperature, if wiped when fresh and not left to dry out, will yield good prints, particularly from plates that are normally bitten and not worn. Problems that arise from use of the hotplate are these:

1. If the plate is overheated it may bake the ink into the finer lines, causing them to print faintly.

2. The plate will develop a buckle in the center if it is heated too much. Sometimes this fault comes out when the plate is cooled, but sometimes it does not.

3. If the plate is printed when it is too hot, it may dry the paper somewhat and cause spotty effects. The heat dries the paper quickly, in any case, so that multiple-plate color printing is difficult to register when the second plates are being printed.

However, it is undeniable that slight warming does enrich a weak plate and enhance tonality. Learn to be judicious in your printing, and use the hotplate with care. It certainly is necessary in a cold workshop.

The best hotplates are made commercially, usually for restaurant kitchens where quantity frying is done, but these are very expensive unless purchased from a dealer in used kitchen equipment. A good hotplate can be made from a two-burner electric heater of excellent quality. Arrange a piece of ¼"-thick steel plate on a frame of wood or angle-iron so that the electric heater can slide underneath and almost touch the underside of the steel plate. You can shim up the heater with asbestos or other fire-resistant material. The area of the steel plate should be large enough to accommodate your larger plates and should have a flush top surface with no screws or nails sticking up to damage your plates.

Although many older workshops had gas-flame hotplates (even wood charcoal has been used) it seems silly, these days, to tolerate the dangers of an open flame in such a promising place for a fire as a printmaker's workshop. We have used the kitchen gas range when speed and high heat was desirable, but it is more prudent to rely on electric heat and check the wiring frequently!

Wiping the Plate

The initial wiping of the inked plate should be done with tarletan or crinoline, which is somewhat like starched cheese-cloth. It should be balled into a mass that fits the hand comfortably. You can wipe, with light pressure, in a circular manner or in one direction after another. The purpose of wiping is to remove most of the ink from the surface of the plate while still leaving it in the etched lines. At a certain point, when the design is visible but somewhat hazy or smoky, the rag wiping should be stopped. If the plate is overwiped the lines will be weak or broken and tonal values will be dry or light. A little oil of cloves added to the ink beforehand will prevent quick drying and lengthen the time you can spend on the wiping.

After wiping with the cards, crinoline or tarletan rag is used to wipe, in a circular motion with little pressure. When the image is fairly clear, but still a little smoky or hazy, stop wiping with the rag. Too much rag wiping will weaken the lines.

Hand Wiping

At the point when the etching design is still slightly blurred, the hand wiping should start. If too much ink still remains on the plate, it will not wipe clean, as it should after a few strokes with the edge of the palm. Use the side of your palm, and wipe quickly, with very light pressure, over the surface of the plate. Copper wipes faster than zinc. Plates with large amounts of white area are more difficult to wipe than darker, more tonal plates, because more ink must be removed from the surface. Wipe thoroughly, removing all the smears and surface blurs. Wipe your hand frequently on a cloth or on some newspaper kept nearby. You cannot clean wipe a plate with dirty hands. Work quickly and efficiently. If you wait too long before printing the plate the ink will start to dry and the print will be weak and pale.

The hand wipe is accomplished with a light, fast stroke, using the side of the palm. A few strokes in one spot should brighten the area and wipe the surface clean.

Below: The paper wipe, if used, will polish the surface even more than the hand, and will give a more brilliant plate tone. Some plates need paper wiping more than others. To keep rich aquatint tones, use a minimum of paper wiping.

Paper Wiping

With some plates, newsprint or pages from old telephone books can be used to wipe the ink from the surface, instead of hand wiping. The paper polishes the metal and makes for a brilliant print with whiter whites than the hand can produce. Too much paper wiping, however, will overwipe the plate. In general, aquatint tones will be richer if hand wiped only. Those areas of the plate which are white or very light can be lightly paper-wiped just before printing. Do not use paper towels or tissues to wipe because they are too absorbent and pull too much ink from the etched lines. Wiping plates is somewhat tricky and a little practice is necessary to achieve good results. However, no magic touch is necessary. We have taught students to ink, wipe, and print plates in a professional manner in a very short time. Roughly bitten plates, collagraphs, and materials other than copper or zinc are more difficult to print, however, and some experience is desirable to get the best results from printing these kinds of plates. Don't forget to wipe the edges of your plate, too. The plate must now be printed promptly.

PREPARING TO PRINT

Placing the Plate on the Bed

The bed of the press should be run out to one side of the press. Put clean newsprint on the bed to keep your impres-

which will print etchings if they are not too deeply bitten. Do not leave blankets in the press overnight. They get damp from contact with the printing paper and can rust the rollers and the bed with continued contact. Hang the blankets over a wooden bar or roll them up and put them away. The blankets should be cut to the width of the roller and somewhat shorter than the length of the bed. They should be aligned carefully to square with the bed. Crooked blankets will get caught in the press and the corners will be cut or torn, a common sight in print workshops with many beginning printmakers. Some workshops demand that each student provide his own blankets!

THE ETCHING PRESS

So many presses are being made at this time that we have prepared a chart showing the manufacturer's name and address, the size of press he makes, the cost, and other information and comments that seem appropriate. Used presses are scarce, although they should be coming on the market as the total quantity of presses increases. Old ungeared presses turn up now and then, but they should be checked for worn bearings or bushings. Beds tend to warp, too, and should be checked with a straightedge. Warps of more than $\frac{1}{16}''$ in the center may cause trouble.

The basic etching press is a steel or Benelux bed, which passes between two steel rollers. There are usually guides to keep the bed from moving out of position or from falling off the end of the press. Small presses may be ungeared, but presses with beds wider than 18'' should be geared. Chain-drive presses are very common because they can have high gear ratios, making possible the easy printing of deeply bitten plates, which need great pressure. Planetary-gear presses are good but require more physical effort than the worm-gear presses. Some of the better presses are made by Charles Brand, Graphic Chemical, Rembrandt Graphic Arts, Meeker-McFee, Glen Alps, American French Tool Co., and Wilfred Kimber. Check with the manufacturer for the latest prices; they have been going up constantly over the past few years.

Motorized presses are made by many companies because of the demand for large presses. It is a difficult job to print large plates by hand unless the gearing system is very efficient. Our own press is a 30'' by 50'' motorized Brand that has worked well for five years. Micrometer gauges are a big help when plates of different thicknesses are to be printed or when blankets are frequently changed. They are essential in a school or workshop with many students.. Without micrometers the adjusting screws have to be changed by trial and error, which results in a ruined print now and then. Pressure can also be adjusted by adding or removing blankets. A slight increase in pressure can be obtained by adding a blotter or two on top of the blankets before running the press.

PRINTING THE PLATE

The best prints are pulled from a freshly inked and wiped plate. Ink starts to dry in a few minutes, and nothing should be allowed to interfere with the printing cycle once it has been started. Run the plate through the press once. If the pressure has been properly set, one printing should be enough. Every time you double-print a plate (pass it through the press twice) you run the risk of a double image or a blurred print because of the slight shifting of the paper. It will shift if the lines are not deeply bitten or if the paper dries and shrinks a little from contact with a warm plate. If you must adjust the pressure do it quickly so that the paper does not dry in the blankets. Loss of humidity causes the paper to shrink. Remove the proof by lifting the edge with paper picks. Pull the proof slowly enough to prevent tearing of the soft paper. Too much pressure will cause the print to be mashed into the plate, sometimes so tightly that it is impossible to save the print. If the plate curls, the pressure is too great. Run it through the press face down to straighten it out.

Run the plate, paper, and blankets through the press, once. The pressure should be enough to force the paper into all the etched lines, pulling the ink out of them and making the print, or proof, or impression from the plate.

Drying the Print

The usual methods of drying prints are simple but very important. A buckled or curled print will never fit properly in a mat or a frame. If you have excess margin on your paper you may tape the damp proof to a plywood board or a wall, using 1½"-wide gummed paper tape around all four edges. You may also staple the edges, about ¼" from the edge, placing the staples no more than 2" or 3" apart. The paper must be trimmed after the print is dry, which usually takes a day or less.

If you do not want to trim the paper or if you have a large number of prints to dry you can put them between blotters, with clean newsprint next to the fresh ink. Place transite or asbestos boards on top of every couple of prints to keep the weight on the prints. The blotters and newsprint should be changed every day until the prints are thoroughly dry. Drying can take from 2 to 5 days, depending on the thickness of the paper and the humidity of your studio. If you take prints out too soon they will buckle afterwards. The blotter method keeps the maximum embossment of the impression. The tape and the staple methods force the paper to shrink, flattening a good deal of the embossment. Remove the staples with the tip of a curved burnisher when the print is dry.

Typical plate-cleaning box, filled with sawdust saturated with varsol, varnoline, mineral spirits, or other low-volatility cleaning solvent. Indiana University.

Cleaning and Storing the Plate

Clean the plate with mineral spirits, varnoline, sub-turps or, if it is very dirty, with lacquer thinner. Coat the plate with asphaltum, heavy grease, or hard ground to keep it from rusting. If you are going to store the plate for a long time wrap it in wax paper first, then in newspaper or brown wrapping paper. Do not leave newsprint paper in prolonged contact with the plate, as the acid inherent in the paper will corrode the plate.

Intaglio Color Printing

ONE-PLATE METHOD

An etching plate may be inked with several colors by applying the ink with cards or small dabbers to certain areas. The cards can wipe the areas fairly well without too much merging of the colors, but when the final wiping is accomplished a certain amount of blending and mixing of colors is inevitable. Wipe the lighter colors first and use a separate piece of tarletan for each color. When you come to the final wiping use clean pieces of newsprint or, if you are wiping with your hand, be careful to keep the darker colors from contaminating the lighter colors. It is possible to print somewhat consistent editions, although precisely similar impressions are virtually impossible with this method.

THE CUT-PLATE METHOD

If you cut a zinc, copper or collage plate with a jigsaw into sections, somewhat like a puzzle, each section can be inked and wiped with a different color etching ink, the parts put back together, and the reassembled plate printed. The plate may be cut into pieces by deep biting in the acid bath. This way success in printing a uniform edition is much more likely because the colors have much less chance of contact with each other. Frequently, however, there is a white line around many of the forms because the cut removes metal and these cuts can not hold ink; they therefore print with a white "river" or "thread." If this white line is utilized as part of the image, it can enhance the print.

Plates may be cut into pieces with a high-temperature cutting torch, acid, saws, thinner plates with tin-snips, or scissors. Cardboard or masonite plates can be cut with knives, razor blades, jeweler's saws, or jigsaws. Of course these plates can also be inked by the relief process as well as the intaglio method by using rollers or brayers and letterpress ink.

STENCIL COLOR PRINTING
ON A SINGLE PLATE

Color can be placed on an etching plate prior to printing by the stencil process, using cut paper or sheet metal as the stencils. In this process the color shapes must be planned

in advance and cut from acetate or an ink-resistant paper, such as tag or an oiled heavy bond paper. The shapes should be somewhat larger than actually wanted because the thickness of the paper hinders the roller from contact with the plate along the edge of the shape. A soft rubber or plastic roller can be used to roll the color on the plate. The procedure works best when executed in the following manner.

Cut the apertures in the stencil, using a razor blade or sharp knife. If you need overlapping colors, you must have separate stencils for each color. This practice is somewhat dangerous because the first color stenciled on the plate may be disturbed by the next stencil. Do not attempt too complicated a color-overlapping scheme. When your stencils are cut, mix the stencil color, using letterpress ink or etching color made less viscous than normal by the addition of linseed oil. The viscosity of the stenciled color must be less than that of the ink used for the intaglio lines in the plate. Now ink and wipe the plate with the basic etching ink, of normal or thick viscosity. Place the plate, face up, on a sheet of newsprint (acetate or glass is suitable) and position your first stencil over your inked etching plate. If you are printing an edition, you can tape the stencils in position and mark the position of the plate. On a separate inking slab, using a soft rubber or plastic roller, roll out a thin even film of the color to be stenciled on the plate. The roller should be large enough to cover the entire shape at one pass to avoid streaks. Be careful not to pull up the stencil, as it will tend to adhere to the ink on the roller. The ink deposit should be as perfect as possible to avoid having to go back and roll again. The first roll usually pulls up some intaglio color, which is transferred to the roller where it can contaminate the stencil color or be deposited back on the etching plate in the next pass of the roller. The plate may now be printed, in the usual manner, in the etching press. Because of the time involved in the inking process, it will be helpful to add oil of cloves to the etching ink to retard drying.

It is possible to add color to an etching impression that has dried. The stencil method may be used; but because the color will lie on top of the intaglio ink, it should be a thin transparent film unless it is to remain as a surface color, sitting on top of the intaglio impression. The stencil is placed directly on top of the paper and the color rolled on with soft rubber or plastic rollers. You may use water-based color for this technique, and as it sinks down into the paper and is naturally transparent it often works quite well. If too much color is deposited on the print, blot it off with clean newsprint.

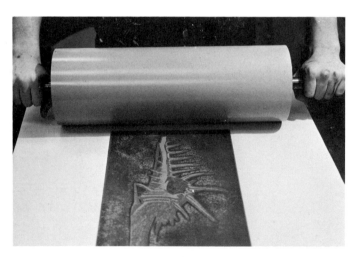

An etched plate which has been inked and wiped by the intaglio process is about to have its surface covered with a thin film of relief ink from a large composition roller. This roller should be large enough to cover the entire plate in one roll.

SURFACE ROLLING

A surface color of letterpress ink may be rolled over an intaglio plate immediately prior to printing. The intaglio lines will stand out on top of the background color with clarity. The background film of ink must be thin and even, and a large roller, in perfect condition, is best for this purpose. Try to place the color on the plate with the least number of rolls to avoid pulling too much ink from the intaglio lines, weakening them and contaminating the color.

MULTIPLE-PLATE METHOD

To print intaglio plates in register is complicated by the fact that the dampened paper stretches as moisture is added. When printing two or more plates the shrinkage that occurs as the paper dries out causes problems in registering subsequent plates. Do not plan a register that will require precision that cannot be easily obtained by whatever method you employ. In general, color registry in the intaglio processes is not so accurate as that obtained in other procedures, such as silk screen, woodcut, and lithography. For this reason, many artists make mixed-media prints, trying to get the advantages of several processes in their images.

When you print from two or more plates in sequence, it is easier if the plates are of similar size and can be placed into a thin cardboard or heavy acetate mat taped to the bed of the etching press. This guide ensures that each plate is placed in precisely the same place each time. Cut the apertures carefully, avoiding making the opening too large, which would cause a shifting of the plates. The paper should have two straight sides and can easily be positioned by using folded masking-tape register tabs. Strapping tape, made of fibres, will make excellent register tabs. It is only necessary to have three tabs, two on one side and one on another side. Time is the enemy in this process, as the paper tends to dry out after the first printing while the second plate is being inked. If both plates are inked before printing, the ink on the first plate tends to dry. An efficient work setup makes the difference in color work! It is quite feasible to print an intaglio plate with several other colors on top of the first impression so that all the colors fuse and blend together in less than an hour. If the paper is kept damp between printings, the shrinkage will be minimized.

A rather primitive method of registering two plates consists of pulling a proof of the first plate, leaving the paper face up on a table, then placing the second plate, face down, directly over the impression of the first plate. The only difficulty with this method comes when you attempt to turn the plate and paper over in order to print it on the etching press. It takes good pressure with your hands to keep the paper from shifting as it is flipped over in contact with the plate. The process is useful for proofs and trying out various color combinations. Edition printing requires fixing the position of the plates with the mat method previously described.

COLOR BY TRANSFER FROM A ROLLER TO AN INTAGLIO PLATE

You can transfer the design from any relief plate, such as a half-tone or a line photoengraving or a linoleum-cut block by taking the inked relief design on to the surface of a clean large plastic or composition roller in perfect condition. This image in turn, may be rolled over the surface of an inked intaglio plate, causing a combination of both images. The accompanying diagram indicates a procedure to keep the plates in proper register. The key to this process is the roller, which must be large enough to contain the entire image on its circumference. The guide strips can be made of

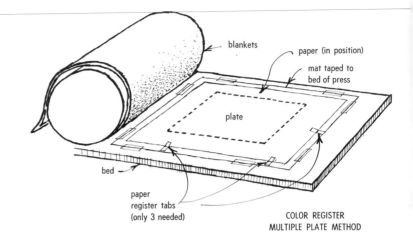

COLOR REGISTER
MULTIPLE PLATE METHOD

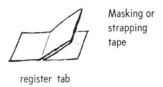

register tab

Masking or strapping tape

SCREEN PRINTING REGISTER TABS

rollers for relief color blocks

Mark the roller at the point where printing starts

direction of roller

A

A

color relief block

color relief block

guide for large roller

intaglio plate

"A" equals circumference of large roller

COLOR REGISTER SYSTEM

To create multicolor prints from a combination of relief blocks and an intaglio plate, the intaglio plate should be inked and wiped first. Use oil of cloves in the ink to retard the drying time. Next ink the surface of the relief blocks with small brayers, using letterpress ink of less viscosity than the intaglio ink. Place the blocks and plate in the sequence shown, making sure that circumference of the large roller is adequate to carry the complete image. Mark the edge of the large roller at the point where the blocks start to print. At each complete turn of the roller the point where the next block should be placed will be clearly evident. Mark this point on your table so that the blocks will align properly in each printing cycle. As you roll the roller over each block, the color will be picked up on the roller and transferred to the intaglio plate at the end of the cycle. This plate should be printed promptly in the etching press, using dampened paper.

1" by 2" lumber stock, except when you use thick relief blocks, such as woodcuts, which may require 2" by 2" stock. The roller must be cleaned after each printing cycle. The etching plate must be inked and wiped each time, and in most cases, it must be cleaned, too, between inkings. Some remarkable juxtapositions of images are possible with this method.

MULTILEVEL COLOR INTAGLIO PRINTING

Stanley William Hayter has developed methods of printing which depend on varying levels in the plate, which can be inked with soft rollers and inks of different viscosities. These processes have enabled many artists to exploit textures and rhythms not obtainable by any other means. The method requires large rollers of varying hardnesses. The softest rollers will be pressed into the deepest levels, while the hardest rollers will touch only the highest levels of the plate.

The intaglio plate can be inked and wiped with the normal etching ink, of heavy viscosity, as the first step in the process. A large, soft roller is inked with an even film of medium-viscosity ink, such as letterpress ink without alteration or dilution. This roller is passed over the plate with heavy pressure, to ink the deepest surfaces of the plate. The lower viscosity of this ink prevents it from sucking up the intaglio ink. Now a harder roller is inked with an ink of even less viscosity than before. This roller touches only the higher relief surfaces of the plate and does not penetrate to the lower levels. To make the ink less viscous or sticky, add a little linseed oil to the letterpress ink. The colors must be chosen so that the last color on the plate will not be contaminated by the prior color. The plate now can be printed in the etching press, by the usual method. Further information on color printing appears in the section on collagraphs.

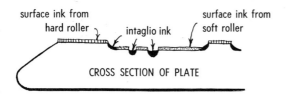

surface ink from hard roller

intaglio ink

surface ink from soft roller

CROSS SECTION OF PLATE

CHINE COLLÉ

Chine Collé is another method for obtaining color in an etching through the use of colored paper collage. In this process, differently colored papers glued to the printing paper allow the artist to use flat color areas without two-plate printing. The colored paper can be cut or torn into shapes that will make a permanent part of the image. The pressure of the etching press will laminate the etching paper and the colored paper together with an adhesive such as dilute library paste or potato starch. When the etching plate is printed with intaglio methods, the lines and tones of the etched plate will print on top of the pasted paper forms.

Colored papers that may be used include Moriki, Mingei, Tsujuko, and Toyogami from Japan. Fabriano text from Italy and domestic papers that do not fade in the light are best. Scores of beautifully colored tissue papers that fade very rapidly are tempting to use but have almost no permanence. If you evaluate these colored papers as you would oil pigments and apply the same standards of stability, you will avoid the cheap dyed papers that are not designed to last. There are many buffs, off-white, and grey sheets that are color-fast, subtle, and quite suitable for chine collé work.

To complete a print in this process, after your etched plate has been brought to the desired state (it may be aquatint, soft-ground, lift-ground, dry point, and so on), you must decide on the areas to be colored. Design it on tracing paper or thin bond paper. Choose your colored paper and trace or score the shape of the area onto its back surface. Cut or tear the shapes to the proper size. These pieces should be dampened between blotters or newsprint until they are uniformly moist, with no surface water or drops showing. Dampening may take several hours, the time depending on the paper used. Your etching plate may be inked and wiped in the normal manner. Use a few drops of oil of cloves (Eugenol) in the ink to retard the drying process. Now turn all your damp pieces of colored paper, face down, on a clean newsprint, and brush a thin even coat of dilute library paste or thin potato starch over the back of the pieces. The wiped etching plate is placed on the bed of the press, the colored paper is placed face down, (glued side up), in position, on the plate; the printing paper, dampened in the usual manner, is put over all, with adequate margins, and then the plate is printed in the usual manner.

The ink will be printed on top of the pieces of colored paper, and the color will appear underneath your network of lines and tones, glued in position on the backing paper.

Misch Kohn
"Ornate Figure"
Chine collé and lift ground etching 34¼" x 17¾"
Weyhe Gallery

CHINE COLLÉ PROCESS

inked and wiped intaglio plate on press bed

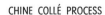

colored paper in position on top of intaglio plate. Glue side up

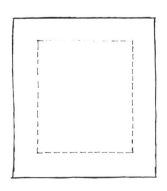

Dampened rag paper over all

The Collagraph

DEVELOPMENT

A new printmaking technique, most frequently called the collagraph, has been appearing in exhibitions with great regularity in the last few years. The collagraph, as generally defined, is a print of a collage of a wide variety of materials glued together on masonite, cardboard, or a metal plate. Any fairly rigid material such as lucite or plexiglass can be used. The collagraph differs from the cardboard relief print in that it is printed as an intaglio plate or as a combined intaglio and relief plate. The word *collagraph* should not be confused with the term *collotype*. A collotype is a mechanical printing process developed in the late 19th century that uses a photo gelatin process for reproduction.

Various terms have been used for the medium, such as collage intaglio, collage print, collagraph or collagraphy. We prefer the term *collagraph*, as coined by Glen Alps, because it seems to describe the technique best. The derivation of the word tells much about it. The word *collagraph* stems from the Greek term *colla*, meaning glue, or the French *coller*, to glue, and from the English word *graphic* pertaining

Glen Alps
"Three Chickens" 1958
Collagraph, 22½" x 33½"
Courtesy of the artist
Photograph Whitie Marten

Rolf Nesch
"Toy" 1965 (Plate)
Metal collage plate 22⅜" x 16½"
Collection Walter Bareiss

to written or drawn material. The main function of any descriptive word is to clarify a process for the general public. As long as artists remain individualists they will use a variety of terms for similar processes.

The historical evolvement of the collagraph would be difficult to trace. As early as the late 19th century, prints have appeared that indicate that adhesives were applied to copper or zinc plates and then inked and printed.

The innovating experiments with collage and assemblage by the early 20th-century French artists, such as Picasso, Matisse, and Gris, did much to open the way for the later printmaker's use of unorthodox materials. This freedom of concept and use of materials had a direct influence on many contemporary printmakers. Rolf Nesch, the Norwegian printmaker, was one of the first artists to use an assembled plate in the 1930s. His material was primarily metal, and his work is described as a metal collage with some forms soldered in place and other forms cut and assembled unadhered for printing.

The collagraph seems to have evolved directly from the concepts of Nesch, with the addition of more flexible materials. Numerous artists have developed personal methods from this approach. Glen Alps, printmaker and professor at the University of Washington in Seattle, was an early innovator with the collagraph. His experiments with collage intaglio with his students led him to a creative use of the medium. He was the first to use the term *collagraph* as a means to describe the technique. James Steg, a professor at Newcomb College of Tulane University in New Orleans and Dean Meeker, at the University of Wisconsin, have developed personal statements through the collagraph.

Our own development of the collagraph grew out of our use of the cardboard and paper relief print. For a number of years in the 1950s we found the flexibility of cardboard an excellent vehicle for large color prints. We glued various thicknesses and textures of cardboard and paper on either cardboard or Masonite for our images. Sometimes we used a three-ply chip board and cut into it with X-acto knives and razor blades, much as the woodcut is cut. We glued a variety of materials such as textured papers, cloth, lace, metal objects, and sand to the relief plates to develop surface variations. The tonal nuances were interesting and rewarding. Later, as we began to work with etching, we felt the need to use the intaglio in a more flexible manner. When John Ross was artist in residence in 1964 with the United States Information Agency exhibition "Graphic Arts USA" in Romania, he began to experiment with plates made out of cardboard, paper, and cloth and any found objects that would print and relate to the image. The response to the experimental medium by Romanian artists was very enthusiastic, as their use of the print had been most often traditional in concept.

The intaglio plate is developed through the subtractive procedure of acid biting the image into copper or zinc. It

Opposite:
John Ross
"Vertical Forces" 1967
Color collagraph 21½" x 14"

A collagraph, with a sand texture yielding a deep black at top. A hex nut gives its distinctive form to the center area. Other forms are cut cardboad, paper, and sheet metal glued into the plate.

Below: An antique coin was imbedded into a mat board plate and its embossed forms catch the ink and print. Print by Ross.

can be a long, painstaking process. Its scope is tremendous, the range of tonal development unique. The collagraph does not displace the etching image but introduces possibilities for a different kind of statement through the variety of materials available and the ease and flexibility in developing a collage plate.

RELATING IMAGE TO MATERIALS AND TECHNIQUES

The actual assembly and creation of a collage plate is physically simple, but it has its pitfalls. The major cliche to avoid is an overdependence on the material. It is easy to become trapped by the rich quality of surface and texture that comes from the simplest piece of cloth, tarletan, or lace glued down on a firm surface, then inked, wiped, and printed as an intaglio. The same entrapment awaits the artist in his first use of soft-ground etching. The materials impressed in their natural state can begin to dominate the artist instead of being used by him as a vehicle towards expressing a personal statement.

There are numerous helpful suggestions that we can make at this point. If the artist has some experience with etching and knows the tonalities possible through the use of aquatint, soft-ground textures, and wiping, he will feel more secure and will be able to plan and visualize in relation to a past body of experiences. If the artist has done some work with relief methods, in color and black-and-white, through relief etching, woodcut, or collage relief, he will be able to use the medium as a combination of intaglio and relief in a more inventive and personal way.

Materials for the Collagraph

The materials suggested here are easily available to anyone, and the items are inexpensive. These materials we have found particularly useful. You will add other things relating to the needs of your own expression.

Two and three-ply cardboard and chipboard, thin cardboard such as used by laundries in packaging shirts.

⅛″ to ¼″ tempered Masonite, 2-ply cardboard or zinc plates, heavy acetate, or lucite to be used as bases for gluing.

Paper (for cutting images, not printing) in an endless variety of thickness and texture from heavy watercolor paper to thin tissue paper to paper doilies.

Cloth in all textures from fine silk to burlap.

Novelty fabrics, such as lace, rick rack, cloth tapes, or embroidered fabrics.

Wire, metal screening, metal washers, a wide variety of hardware store items that are meaningful to your image.

Found objects, such as gaskets, bottle caps, coins, or old container lids, sometimes with relief lettering. The range is wide open as long as the object is printable.

Sandpaper, from fine to rough, beach and builder's sand, coffee grounds, metal filings, sawdust, even cat litter has been used. Crushed walnut shells have also been used to hold black tones by Glen Alps in some of his prints.

Used photoengraving plates, paper mat plates.

Acrylic gesso and Elmer's glue for gluing, polymer medium, sobo modeling paste, clear plastic spray can.

Razor blades (industrial, single-edge may be purchased cheaply in boxes of 100 in discount drug stores).

Single-edge razor-blade holder, available in most hardware stores.

X-acto knives with interchangeable small blades, excellent for fine work.

Large and small scissors.

Scoring tools such as nail punches, wheels, and rasps.

Brushes of all sizes.

Palette and painting knives.

ASSEMBLING THE PLATE

The actual procedure for assembling a plate is dictated in part by the methods most comfortable for the artist. If he is used to working freely without thinking out the images, he will no doubt feel at home with assembling his materials and immediately cutting and arranging them in a spontaneous way, as he would approach the creation of a collage. Very often it is difficult to predict the actual tonalities of the collage materials before they are printed. However, soft pencil, charcoal, colored pencils, and pastels can indicate directions for the artist to follow. He may feel more secure if a finished sketch to size, tonality, and color is prepared. It is impossible to prescribe the best method. The artist has to determine it through his choice of image.

One way to understand the full potential of the medium is to prepare an experimental plate with a great variety of materials, objects, and methods.

Take a piece of ⅛" tempered Masonite or cardboard at least 12" by 15" and, with either Elmer's glue or gesso, adhere a variety of materials to it. Coat the surface of the plate well with glue where the piece of paper, cardboard, cloth, or object is to be placed, as well as the back of the material. After pressing it into place, be sure it is well secured with no edges or areas lifting. If the material or object is difficult to manage, use weights to hold it down. If cardboard or some similar thick material is being cut into a form to be glued in position, bevel the edges so that it will be easier to print.

When cloths, lace, string, or thin materials such as paper or tissues are used, glue the top surfaces too, in order to lock them in position more securely.

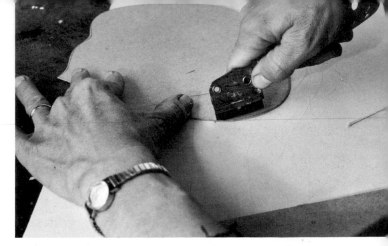

Cutting cardboard for a paper relief plate or a collagraph requires fresh razor blades and a good blade holder.

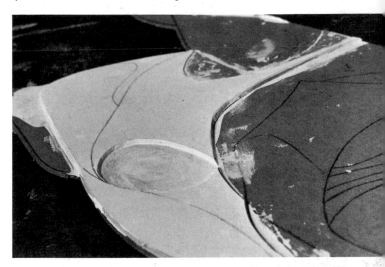

Cut the edges at a bevel to facilitate printing. Polymer acrylic gesso is used as the glue and the sealant.

Larger pieces may have to be weighted during the gluing process. The edges should be firmly glued and sealed.

Below: Both sides should be glued. The gesso is very resilient and will not crack, even under pressure. It is waterproof when dry.

Other materials, fabrics, paper, buttons, coins, and such may be glued to the base board.

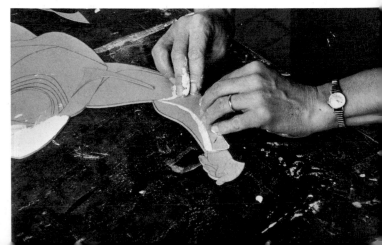

Twine, sandpaper, coarse sand, cardboard, and bitten zinc plate etchings are included in this section of a plate.

An old coin, cut paper, and an aquatint etching make up this part of a collagraph.

Acrylic polymer gesso was sponged on top of a lightly aquatinted tone. The deep black lines have been bitten through soft ground. Print by Ross.

If particles such as sand, coffee grounds, sawdust, or crushed walnut shells are being used, coat the surface of the plate well with Elmer's glue or gesso and sprinkle the material into the wet adhesive. After it is dry, apply a coat of gesso or glue to the surface.

Cut into the cardboard, Masonite, or acetate, or lucite plate to see the potential of incised lines.

If many varying textured materials are used, you will learn how they wipe and produce a variety of tonalities when printed. Cloth that varies from fine silk to burlap will produce different tonalities. Papers such as watercolor or charcoal or etching paper will give similar results. Oilcloth will wipe very clean, giving an almost white quality. Smooth papers will give very light tonalities. Sandpaper, sand, sawdust, coffee grounds, carborundum, cat litter, or crushed walnut shells will all hold a large amount of ink and print quite black.

If the cardboard or Masonite is not large enough for all these materials, make more than one experimental plate.

Another plate could contain pure gesso, Elmer's glue, polymer, or any similar material. These materials can be used like paint with both stiff and soft-bristled brushes to give variety to the line or mass. Allow the material to dry well and then spray it with a liquid plastic to make wiping easier. Allow the plate to dry very well before printing.

If Masonite is used as a base, be sure to bevel the sides of the plate well with a file just as a metal plate is beveled, to ease printing and to avoid sharp plate marks in the blankets.

In an ordinary etching press such as the Brand press, it is wise not to build the plate up higher than two to three thicknesses of matboard or the height of Masonite and one cardboard without special matrixes and devices or the use

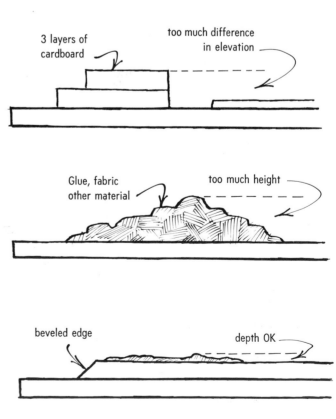

COLLAGRAPH THICKNESS

Clare Romano
"On the Grass"
Color collagraph 10¼" x 30¾"
Collection Museum of Modern Art, New York
One cardboard plate cut into six segments, inked separately with 9 colors in in-
taglio and relief, reassembled on the press and printed in one run through the press.

John Ross
"Quadros XII" 1969
Color collagraph 20" x 20"
Collection New Jersey State Museum
Two plates are used for this print,
each one inked in five or six colors.
The second plate is printed in reg-
ister on top of the first impression
while the ink and paper are still
wet.

Rolf Nesch
"Toy" 1965
Metal collage print 22⁹/₁₆" x 16½"
Collection Walter Bareiss

of a direct drive press. It is unwise to try to run thick objects or single raised objects of more than these heights through the press.

INKING THE COLLAGRAPH

Before any inking is done, be very sure all the materials are adhered very well to the plate. You may spray it with a clear plastic spray to facilitate wiping. The inking process is essentially the same as used in inking an etching plate. Any previous experience in etching is extremely useful.

We have found small 2″ by 3″ or 2½″ by 2½″ squares of matboard very useful in inking a collagraph plate. They are easily made and can be used and discarded at will. The sharp corners are very good for forcing the ink into small areas and corners. The flat edge can pull and push the ink and also force it into textured areas. This method is very good for plates with large raised areas and textured areas.

Felt daubers are often used by etchers for inking. However, the daubers get very stiff from dry ink, and perpetual trimming of the end is necessary to keep it supple. Sometimes a stiff stipple brush is very good for a low-relief, very textured plate. Our students have used toothbrushes and nailbrushes for inking.

We find black Cronite ink very adequate for the collagraph because it is a fairly soft ink and easily wiped. Graphic Chemical makes a superior ink that is fairly stiff. With a mixing knife, mix about a teaspoon of plate oil with an area of ink about 6″ in diameter on a slab. Both Cronite and Graphic Chemical ink often require the addition of plate oil to insure easy wiping. A few drops of oil of cloves is a necessary addition to the ink to retard drying when inking becomes a lengthy process.

Put a generous amount of ink all over the plate. Spread the ink with the cardboards until every tiny area is covered. Use fresh cardboards whenever they become soft. Scrape all the excess ink off the plate and put it back into the can. Continue until only a moderate amount of ink is left on the plate.

Have two pieces of tarletan about 15″ by 30″ ready for wiping. One tarletan with a deposit of ink already on it should function as the dirty tarletan, and the other should be fairly clean, for clean wiping.

Many etchers have rather rigid rules about how the tarletan should be used. We prefer to leave procedures flexible. Arrange the dirty tarletan in a rather loose ball with a flat side for wiping. The dirty tarletan provides a preliminary clean-up for the plate. Press it into small areas and deep textures to remove excess ink. Use its flat side for broad areas until much of the excess ink is removed. Now use the clean tarletan to wipe the surface well until the textures on the plate are easily seen. Some hand wiping is now desirable to bring out structures on the plate. Wipe with the fleshy underpart of the palm, using broad strokes. Wipe the palm frequently with a clean cloth to make the wiping effective. If very light tones are desired in some areas, or on raised surfaces, use a small piece of newsprint paper, ordinary newspaper, or paper toweling held flat to gently wipe over the surfaces to produce a lighter quality. Change the paper frequently to insure clean wiping.

The basic inking starts with the thick plate ink applied all over the plate with small squares of cut matboard.

Paper wiping helps to polish the areas that must be especially well cleaned.

In deep recessons a stiff stencil brush helps to spread the viscous plate ink.

The raised areas of the collagraph plate are rolled with brayers inked with an ink of less viscosity than the plate ink used for the base color.

The plate ink is wiped with a pad of tarletan or crinoline. This process removes most of the ink from the surface areas. Gloves help to keep hands clean.

Clare Romano prepares a segmented collagraph plate by placing the inked pieces of thin cardboard into position.

The hand wipe brings up the rich textural detail. Light, fast strokes with the edge of the palm work well.

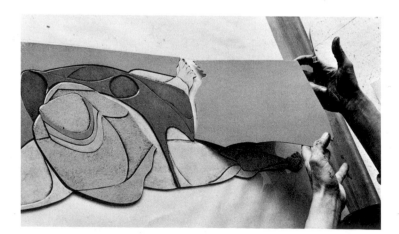

The final piece of the cut plate is put in place; sometimes tweezers or pins are necessary to keep the freshly inked segments from smearing.

PAPER DAMPENING

For proving, an inexpensive paper like index or basingwerk is adequate. Soak the paper from 5 to 15 minutes, depending on its weight. A lighter paper will need less time. A tray of water to soak the paper is necessary. After soaking, hold the paper over the water tray with 2"-square paper or metal grippers to keep the paper clean. An artist we know uses plastic-coated wallet-size calendars that are printer's rejects for this purpose. They work beautifully because they repell water. Thin metal strips can also be used. Allow all the excess water to drip back into the tray. When occasional drops drain off, the paper is easier to blot and will not be too wet for printing. Roll the top blotter with a large hard rubber roller or a rolling pin to help the blotters absorb the water. Murillo, a buff paper of fairly heavy quality made by Fabriano of Italy, is excellent. Italia and Rives BFK and German Etching are white papers that produce fine results. All these papers are excellent for edition work. The choice of weight and color and texture of the paper to be used will be determined by the depth of the plate, color used.

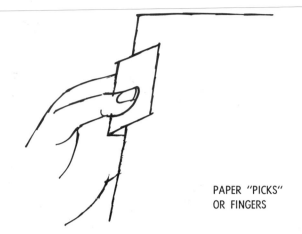

PAPER "PICKS"
OR FINGERS

PRINTING

Procedures in printing a collagraph are very varied. So much depends on the height of the plate and the materials used. When the collagraph is printed in one color in an ordinary etching press, certain controls should be observed so that the bed and the roller are not damaged. The plate should generally not have more than $\frac{1}{8}$" variation in height from the top of the printing surface to the lower printing surface.

Set the press for the desired pressure, which must be determined by experimentation. Place a sheet of clean newsprint on the press bed to keep it clean. Place the inked plate on the newsprint paper. Place a 1" sheet of foam rubber over the plate to absorb impressions from raised objects. Use another blanket over the foam rubber. An inexpensive dark grey, unwoven wool about $\frac{1}{4}$" thick is a good second blanket. Smooth the blankets to be sure they are sitting well on the plate and begin to engage the roller over the plate. You will be able to get the feel of the proper pressure by the ease with which the roller travels over the plate. If it is too tight, reduce the pressure. If it feels too loose, tighten it. After rolling it through at the proper pressure, pull the paper off the plate slowly to be sure no areas are adhering to the plate. If excess ink appears on the proof, blot it with a clean piece of newsprint by rubbing your palm over the surface of the newsprint paper. Examine the print to see how to proceed. Write down the pressure used for printing, and the blankets used. Keep an accurate note so that all the same conditions may be attained in the next proving.

Excess moisture is removed by placing the paper between two clean blotters and pressing the sheets together with a rolling pin.

Drying Print

The easiest way to insure a collagraph's drying flat is to staple it to a homosote board or wall and allow it to stretch flat as it dries. Place staples 1½" apart to insure even drying. However, as stretching inevitably means the loss of a great deal of the depth of the embossing, you may allow the print to dry on a flat blotter for one half to one hour depending on the room temperature. Then pin or staple it to a wall in a semi-dry state. In this way much of the embossing is retained. A more dependable way to hold all the depth in the embossing is to dry the prints flat between clean white flat blotters, about one inch larger than the print. Lay them on a clean large flat surface, and place about two blotters between successive prints. Place a medium weight, the size of the blotters on top of the pile. A piece of masonite or plywood is a good choice. Allow the prints to dry overnight. Replace the blotters with dry clean blotters and repeat again overnight. After 48 hours the prints should be dry and the paper flat with all the embossing just as it was printed.

Another excellent way to dry prints flat is to stack the prints between sheets of ⅛" asbestos board. Warrington Colescott finds this method very efficient because the asbestos does not absorb moisture. However, care should be taken not to breathe the dust when cutting asbestos because it is very harmful.

Clean Up

By the time you are working with the collagraph you should have had some experience with woodcut and etching. The clean-up is the same. The plate must be cleaned thoroughly of all the ink and wiped dry. Slabs, mixing knives, and inking counter should be left clean and neat for next day's printing.

PRINTING PROBLEMS AND REMEDIES

Problem: Ink runs on print, large deposits of ink around forms.

Remedy: Pressure is too great, and too much ink has been left in lines or between forms. Ink may also contain too much oil. Reduce pressure, wipe cleaner, add more pigment to ink, and reduce amount of plate oil.

Problem: Paper sticking to plate or tearing.

Remedy: Pressure may be too great, also ink may be too stiff; add plate oil. Ink may be drying on plate because of long inking time; add a few drops of oil of cloves in addition to plate oil; reduce inking time. Carefully and slowly remove print from plate to avoid tearing, avoid over-dampening paper.

Problem: Uneven printing because of varying heights.

Remedy: If there are different levels on the plate and some areas are not printing well, foam-rubber blankets can be cut to fit into low areas to improve overall pressure. Sometimes dampened blotters placed between the printing paper and foam rubber blankets help to achieve uniform printing.

Problem: Wrinkles in paper as plate is printed.

Remedy: Blankets may be too stiff from deposits of sizing. Paper may be too wet or unevenly dampened, or paper may be of improper weight, probably too thin. Wash blankets often in detergent solution for wool to keep them soft. Try other papers.

Problem: White areas around forms, uneven inking.

Remedy: Pressure may be too little, increase pressure;

Stanley William Hayter
"Danae"
Color Intaglio 22¹⁵⁄₁₆" x 16⅝"
Collection Manhattanville College

plate may not be inked enough; blankets may need washing;
forms may not be beveled enough for paper to make contact.

MULTICOLOR COLLAGRAPH

The flexibility of the collagraph lends itself to a very ex-
pansive use of color. Its potential for multicolor work on
one plate is excellent. Because the method is an additive
one, the necessary variety of levels for printing can be more
easily achieved than with acid biting into metal. The creative
use of one plate in multicolor printing has been extensively
explored by William Hayter and many of the artists who
worked closly with him in Atelier 17 in Paris in the thirties,
New York City in the forties, and back in Paris in the
fifties and sixties. Hayter's book, "New Ways of Gravure,"
is useful for artists who wish to deal extensively with one-

plate color printing. Hayter's methods utilize the deeply bitten plate as a way to use color on different levels. His experiments with inks of varying viscosities and rollers of different hardness and softness are among the most important aspects of his technique. See our description of the Hayter method of multicolor printing in the intaglio section.

We will attempt to explain some of our methods and the methods of other artists using color in the collagraph so that the artist using color in one-plate printing can have as many resources as possible at his disposal.

Inking of Plate as Combined Intaglio and Relief

Any intaglio plate has the potential of being inked as a combination intaglio and relief plate. Even a simple line-bite etching with moderate bite can be inked in the recessions with one color, with a second color rolled on the surface with a gelatin, plastic, or hard-rubber roller, depending on the nature of the image. Without much difficulty a two-color etching is achieved.

The first color or base color, inked in the intaglio method, can be applied in the same manner described under "Inking the Plate" in the intaglio section. The choice of color for the base color is limited only by the etching colors on hand. Some colors need the application of plate oil to make wiping easier. The addition of a few drops of oil of cloves to the color will keep it from drying, and we use it for both the base colors and the relief colors. The wiping will depend on the color and the image. Because the etching ink is of heavy viscosity it will remain in the recessions. After the base color is wiped, a soft plastic roller can be used to add another color of medium viscosity such as letterpress ink to some surface areas as well as to recessions. The lower viscosity of this ink prevents it from pulling up the intaglio ink. Where still other colors are desired for other relief areas, small rollers can be used to add color or the relief areas can be wiped clean and color added with small rollers to produce the greater clarity of a single color. A hard roller with ink of even lesser viscosity will allow deposits of ink on high relief and not in recessions. In order to make the ink less viscous or sticky, add a little plate oil to the ink until the desired consistency is found. The more small rollers you have on hand to provide variation in hardness and softness, from gelatin to soft plastic to hard rubber, the more flexibility there will be in the use of color. Sometimes the rollers can be used to remove color from certain areas in a plate so that a color applied to the clean area can sing out clearly and brilliantly.

In some complicated color procedures a stencil of commercial frisket paper or acetate sheets can be used to mask out certain areas on a plate to ease inking. One student used a stencil very successfully to ink only certain areas in a complicated plate that was to be inkless embossing except for a few areas.

Printing the Color Collagraph

The length of time required for inking depends on the complexity of the plate. The less time it takes to ink the plate the better. If a plate takes more than one hour there is a danger that the ink will dry and not print in dry areas. Place the plate on a large sheet of acetate to protect the press bed. Guide marks for placing the plate can be scored in the acetate or marked on a piece of newsprint paper under the acetate. Guides for paper can be designated on the press bed with masking tape. Acetate is useful because it can be easily wiped clean of ink. Take the paper out of the water, blot it, and so on, as described earlier in the intaglio section, and place it on the plate. Place a piece of newsprint paper over the etching paper to absorb moisture and to keep the blankets dry. Add necessary blankets, adjust pressure, and roll the plate through.

If there are metal objects incorporated in the plate, it is wise to use a piece of 1½″ or 2″ foam rubber next to the plate and then one of the dark grey blankets over the foam rubber. This padding will protect the more expensive white woven felt blankets and keep them in reserve for printing more evenly surfaced collagraphs or etchings.

After the plate has been fully developed and proved, and an edition is desired, we have found the preparation of a *printing procedure diagram* of invaluable assistance for

Clare Romano
"Zagreb Night" 1966
Color collagraph 22″ x 26¼″
and etching

future printing. Like many other contemporary printmakers, we do not print our editions immediately after completing a plate. We often will print 10 or 12 of an edition and then go on to new work. We return to finishing the edition when printing time is more available or the demand for a given print requires printing. To construct a printing procedure diagram, we pull a newsprint impression of every plate after the finished print has been pulled. The residue remaining on the plate is sufficient to give us the basic structure of the image with a good indication of color areas for future reference. We then key areas of the print to the rollers used, write out color mixing recipes for difficult colors to mix, general wiping procedures, press pressure, number of blankets used, type and order of placement on the plate, and paper used. All our rollers are numbered for easy keying because rollers of different softness and hardness are needed for the various surfaces. Our total roller count runs close to 90 at this writing. Relief color can be saved for re-use or easier mixing by tightly wrapping it in wax paper packets, and intaglio color in large quantities can be stored in cans. If these procedures are kept uniform, the general printing quality of an edition is easily sustained even with long periods of time between printings.

Cut Plate Printing

In some color printing the best and most versatile solution for the use of many colors, especially if great clarity and brilliance is desired, is to cut the plate apart. With cardboard or Masonite plates, this is very easy and with metal plates a power jigsaw produces very good results. The plates can be cut very precisely, inked separately, then reassembled for printing on the bed of the press and run through in one operation.

Collagraph and Etching Combination

At various times we have combined the traditionally bitten, engraved, or drypoint metal plates with the collagraph plates. We have used etching-gauge zinc and copper and sheet copper and lithograph zinc depending upon the purpose.

Our combination of methods has met our need to combine a delicacy of line and tone with the freedom of the collagraph. The metal plates can be glued into the collage with gesso or other strong adhesives or printed separately as an assembled plate. Particular care must be given to inking a plate with such a combination because the wiping needs of each plate differ.

Photoengraving cuts may also be combined successfully into a plate. We have achieved the best results when the cuts were assembled into the plate without gluing. The cuts print more clearly when rolled as relief plates with hard rollers and thin applications of relief ink.

Photoengraving cuts discarded by photoengraving companies can sometimes be an interesting addition to an image if there is a conceptual reason for their inclusion. Like many mechanical devices they can be overused and become very cliché if not thoughtfully incorporated in an image. They often appear as part of the assemblage of materials in the prints of Clare Romano.

A half-tone relief plate has been inked with a brayer and placed into an intgalio wiped collagraph by Clare Romano.

THE DIMENSIONAL PRINT

INTRODUCTION

The very nature of the intaglio print, even in its traditional form, includes an element of dimensionality because the ink in the recessed line of the plate prints with a raised or embossed quality on the paper.

Eighteenth-century Japanese woodcuts utilized embossing that gave the print a dimensional structure in some areas. Inkless embossing was occasionally experimented with in 19th-century French prints. Two interesting examples of this period appeared in a 1971 exhibition of "L'Estampe Originale" at the Gallery of Modern Art, New York City, in the work of Alexandre Charpentier in *The Girl with a Violin,* a color embossed lithograph, and in Pierre Roche's *Algae,* a color gypso graph.

The new concept of dimension in the print goes far beyond the building of dimensionality through depositing ink. In the hands of today's experimental artist, the print comes very close to being sculpture.

In France, Pierre Courtin's deep engravings in zinc produce prints that are like bas reliefs cast in paper. The Swiss artist Jean Edouard Augsburger prints simple abstract forms in deep relief on very thick, specially made linen fiber paper. The inkless embossed prints of Omar Rayo, the embossed lithographs of Angelo Savelli, who sometimes cuts out areas as part of the structural design, and the prints of Michael Ponce de Leon, who has used cast paper in numerous prints, demonstrate definite dimensionality by some American artists in the early 1960s.

The dimensional prints of today are varied and inventive. To define what the dimensional print should be is really impossible. The purist might require that the dimensionality be intrinsic to the printing operation, as in a molded paper print. For our purposes it is far more interesting to assume that any print that attains some form of dimensionality in its surface should be classified as a three-dimensional print. Such prints include the printing of an image on a three-dimensional surface; a two-dimensional print that has been cut, torn, punctured, or constructed to achieve some degree of dimensionality; the use of transluscent or transparent

Jean Edouard Augsburger
"Untitled" 1970
Deep intaglio & relief 16⅞" x 21¼"
International Graphic Arts Society

surfaces with printed images in construction or overlaying each other; the use of vacuum form printing; and many other techniques.

The extensive printing variations possible in screen printing and lithographic printing have opened up rich possibilities for nontraditional printmaking materials. The very fact that screen printing and lithographic printing are used extensively in commercial printing and packaging makes their potential interesting for the artist who wishes to use dimensional concepts in his work. The simple stencil process of screen printing and the flexibility of lithography allow for a full use of photographic techniques. Screen printing is especially adaptable for printing on hard surfaces such as plastics, glass, and metallic materials. Vacuum-form printing combined with screen printing images becomes a very compatible printing combination because of the flexibility of the screen printing process provided by vinyl inks for printing on plastics. Photographic techniques and commercial printing processes can become creative tools in the hands of the artist.

Robert Rauschenberg has explored kinetic possibilities in the use of moving, overlapping plexiglas shapes with printed images, and on occasion he has incorporated the use of light. Joe Tilson and Tom Wesselman have used vacuum-form printing. Alan D'Arcangelo, Larry Rivers, and Herbert Bayer have used printed dimensional surfaces to achieve a wide variety of imaginative images. Other artists have used mirror reflections, lights, and kinetics in their works.

Grant H. Tittle
"Reflective Colorwheel"
Photo silk screen
24" x 17"
Courtesy of the artist

Below:
Herbert Bayer
"Untitled" 1970
Three dimensional chromed
steel and screen
printed plastic
21½" x 12" x 3½"
Marlborough Graphics

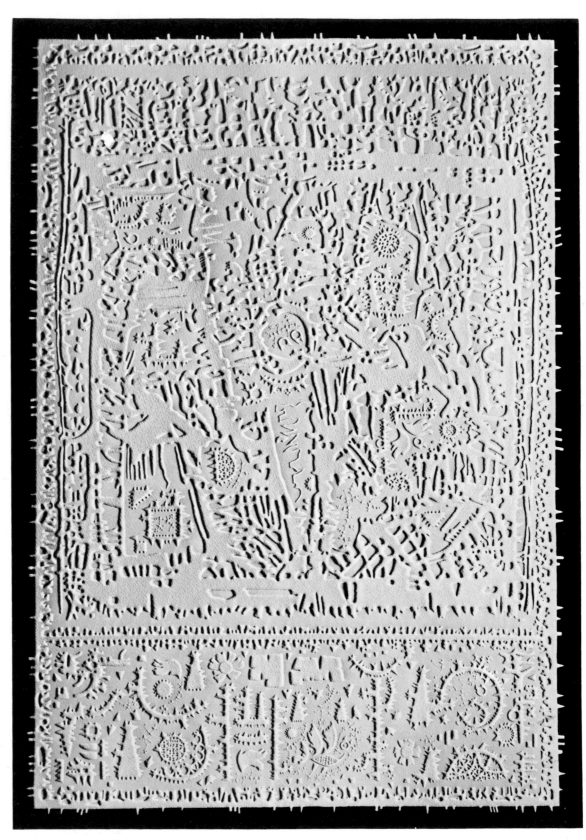

Marjan Pogacnik
"Addio Giardino"
Relief print and embossing 25⅜" x 17½"

UNINKED EMBOSSING FROM
AN ETCHING PRESS

Almost any deeply bitten intaglio plate will produce an embossing that is quite legible if it is run through the press, uninked, into dampened paper. As the paper must retain all the impressions and the indentations, it should be heavy enough to stretch without tearing and should be permanent. Rag pulp makes the best paper for embossing, such as Arches 300 lb., Classico 300 lb., Murillo, and the like. Many artists put two or three sheets together when printing very deeply bitten plates. Special papers can be made to take extremely deep plates. Some artists, such as Michael Ponce de Leon, have special sheets handmade from ¼″ to ½″ thick. Although tremendous pressure can be obtained in an etching press, a few printmakers find it necessary to supplement the press by hand-burnishing the dampened paper into the plate to capture all the embossment possible. Omar Rayo creates his embossed prints by supplementing press printing with the hand-burnishing technique. The paper must not be stapled or taped to a board, or the consequent shrinking would pull out some of the embossing. The prints should not be flattened under heavy weights for the same reason. Most embossed prints are dried in the open or under light blotters. They should be kept scrupulously clean because the slightest smear or mark will deface the image.

Frames for embossings should have inserts to keep the glass from touching the print. If mats are used they should be of adequate thickness to protect the print from the glass. Most embossings look best when displayed with side lighting in order to bring out the shadows on one side of the image. Intense front lighting can obscure the dimensionality of the image.

A unique sheet of paper, custom made by Howell for Michael Ponce de Leon for one of his deeply bitten intaglio plates. The paper has built-in strings for lifting and handling. It is about one half inch thick and is of pure cotton rag fibers.

Below: Two flat keys, uninked, into damped paper yield a deeply embossed print by Doris Seidler.

LEAD INTAGLIO PRINTS

Lead intaglio prints by Louise Nevelson employ innovative methods to produce prints in high relief that are similar to lead bas reliefs except that the relief surface is created on an etching press and not through casting. An original modular matrix is made of thin sheets of wood glued together as a collage. A positive and negative plastic mold is made from the wood collage, and a piece of lead foil is laid between the molds of each modular form. The molds are then rolled through an etching press, creating deep embossing in the lead. The relief is made more pronounced by hand embossing before the lead impressions are removed from the molds. Each modular unit is then given a patina by hand polishing.

A template is used to guide the gluing of each lead relief module onto Fabriano paper with epoxy.

CAST PAPER PRINT

An interesting method resulting in high relief impressions is the cast paper print made from pulp paper. Though a

Louise Nevelson
"Night Sound, 1971"
Lead intaglio 30" x 25"
Printed by Sergio Tosi, Milan
Pace Editions, Inc., New York City
Photograph Ferdinand Boesch

Michael Ponce de Leon
"Countertrust" 1965
Collage Intaglio print 27" x 28"
Courtesy of the artist
Photograph by Arthur Swoger

number of artists have experimented with this technique that employs latex and plaster molds, Michael Ponce de Leon was an early innovator and has used the method rather consistently in the last few years.

Latex Mold

David Finkbeiner has recently made some cast paper impressions that are noteworthy. In the print illustrated, a found object, an automotive part, was adhered with rubber cement to an etching plate. The undercuts, where object and plate met, were filled with clay to make casting easier. After spraying the object with silicone, liquid latex was poured and brushed out over the object and the plate in about six

The plastic sheet is clamped tightly into position.

The electric heating element is rolled over the plastic sheeting to soften it.

Below: The softened plastic is lowered onto baseboard and the vacuum pump sucks the air out, forcing the plastic to conform to the shape of the objects on the baseboard.

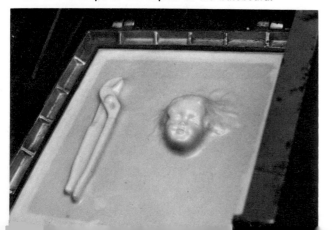

The plastic sheet should be cut to the size of the frame that will clamp it into position.

The Vacuum-Forming Machine

The machine we used is an Audo-Vac, model LV, at Pratt Institute in Brooklyn. It uses a 220-volt electrical heating element that functions like a small oven, heating the plastic to 500° F. The machine is switched on for several minutes before operations start to allow the heating elements to warm up and the compressor to build up pressure to approximately 25 pounds. The objects to be formed are placed on the baseboard, which is covered with many small holes, 1/16" or less in diameter. The plastic sheet is clamped in the frame and then lowered to about 5" or 6" above the baseboard. The heating element is now rolled directly over the plastic sheet, with the elements about 6" above it. After 10 seconds or less, the plastic will first sag, then stretch tight. It will wrinkle a second time and is then ready for forming. The temperature is critical. If it is too hot, the plastic may be drawn so thin that it will break. If too cool, it will not be sensitive enough to follow the contours of the object. Only a series of timed tests will determine the proper heat for your plastic sheet.

The Forming Operation

When the plastic has reached the proper temperature, lower the framed plastic until it has covered your objects and is resting on the baseboard. Turn on the vacuum pump, which will suck the air out through the holes in the baseboard. Air pressure will force the soft plastic down over the objects until it has been molded to their shapes. It may be necessary to turn the vacuum off and on again a few times to cool the plastic until it hardens into the shape of the object. Now raise the frame and the newly formed plastic sheet. Some objects may be stuck into the molded plastic. Remove the plastic from the frame and pry the objects out with a screwdriver or a stick. If the plastic is still soft the objects can be removed more easily than if it has cooled into a hardened state. When the plastic has been overheated it conforms very closely to the shape of the object, which sometimes presents a problem with undercut items that become completely wrapped in plastic.

Printing the Plastic Sheets

If color is to be applied to the plastic it must be applied before the plastic is molded. It is almost impossible to print on the dimensional surface after it has been shaped. The easiest way to put color on the plastic sheet is by the screen print process, using heat-resistant inks such as Colonial's Vacuum Forming Inks, series 7200, or Naz-Dar's Plasti-Vac gloss ink, 700-000 series. Advance also makes an ink suitable for vacuum forming called Multi-Vac Plastic Forming Colors (PAB series). A wide range of colors is available from each manufacturer.

Editions can be printed with uniform results if each step of the process is accurately timed and repeated.

Section IV

SCREEN PRINTING

ᑐDUCTION AND HISTORY

ᐟ of Chinese and
ʒt of all printing
.ly a stencil method
hold the stencil de-
to the paper. Stencil
highly developed tech-
acy and complexity were
waterproof papers. Free-
. linear areas were held to-
or human hair glued between
etimes the silk threads or hairs
s in a regular grid, so fine that
ated on silk with delicate water-
lines of the grid were never visible.
this mesh-like weave may have sug-
as a printing vehicle.
stencil developed as both fine art and
Japanese artists and artisans used it to
ures and screens and to print fabrics for
.ation.
craftsmen adopted the more utilitarian aspects
. In northern Europe stencils were used to color
rds and religious pictures printed from wood-
adually the craft began to be used to enhance furni-
brics, and wallpaper. In 17th-century England stencils
sed to apply flocking to wallpaper. In France stenciled
paper enjoyed great popularity under the inventive de-
opment of Jean Papillon. Oiled-paper stencils and thin
etal stencils were often used to produce intricate designs.
Homes in New England in the late 18th and early 19th century were filled with stenciled papers, walls, textiles, and furnishings.

Precisely where and when the transition from the open stencil process to the use of silk to hold more intricate stencils occurred would be difficult to establish. The earliest documentation of a patent for a silk-screen process is the record of one awarded to Samuel Simon of Manchester, England, in 1907. Simon's patent covered a screen, but he

Ed Ruscha
"Sin"
Screen print 13" x 21½"
Multiples, Inc.

did not use a squeegee. He employed a bristle brush similar to that used in stenciling to distribute the paint. Improvements and developments spread fairly rapidly in spite of early secretiveness about the new process. The silk screen had obvious commercial application and soon began to be used for general printing purposes, posters, displays, and advertising. Its applied use as decoration was almost endless. Furniture, lampshades, rugs, glassware, plastics, leather, toys, and textiles were all easy areas for exploitation. Although the process had strong roots in the stencil tradition of the Orient, where it was used for fine as well as applied art, in the United States and Western Europe it developed only as a commercial process until the early 1930s. Under the leadership of Anthony Velonis, in 1936, a number of artists interested in the aesthetic potential of the medium formed a group to promote the screen print as a means of expression for painters and printmakers. The WPA of New York City permitted the group to form an art project to explore the creative aspects of the medium. Museums and critics began to show interest in silk screen, and Carl Zigrosser, well-known art historian and former prints and drawings curator at the Philadelphia Museum of Art, helped to coin the word *serigraph*, a term widely employed to identify the new prints and to remove them from the onus of commercialism that had developed around the term *silk screen*. "Seri" is from the Latin word meaning silk, and "graph" from the Greek *graphos*, meaning to draw or write.

In spite of these confused early developments, the screen print process as a medium for the serious artist has at last come into its own. The use of the medium as a vehicle for fine artists during the WPA period no doubt helped to estab-

its
sc
fu
it
co
me

sta
the
sub

lish it as an important esthetic process. However, the last
five or six years have seen a more inventive use of the screen
print and a fuller exploitation of the commercial developments of the process applied to serious esthetic statements.
The Pop and Op movements helped to establish this direction.
Photographic processes deftly and creatively used by Andy
Warhol, Robert Rauschenberg, and Larry Rivers have opened
a whole new means of expression. The optical artist finds the

Larry Rivers
"Girlie" 1970
Screen print and collage 29⅞" x 18⅛"
Marlborough Graphics

pre
be
trol
larg
scre
setu
equ
basi
lowi
wor
T
sque
or p
instr
do-it
men

Fram
2
strai
1
A
rugat
S
G
stron
Cl

Silk
Si
tions

Baseb
Or
same
size o
flat.
Tw
screw
board
2"
used
Wi
¼"

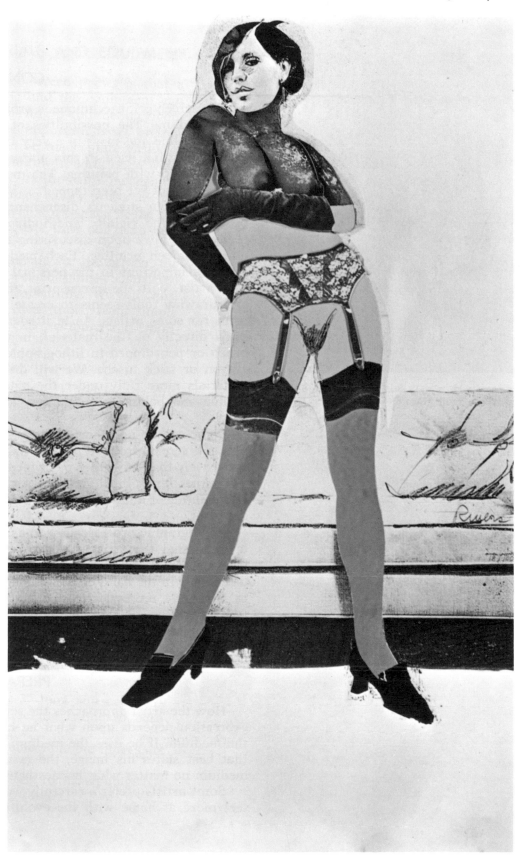

To stretch silk over a frame, allow an inch or so extra of silk all around, then start stapling in the center of one side, with two or three staples.

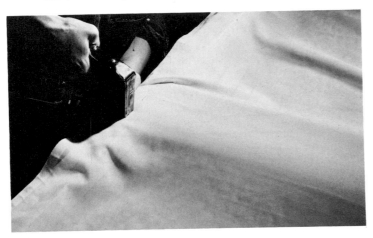

Now staple three or four staples on the opposite side, pulling the silk tight with your fingers.

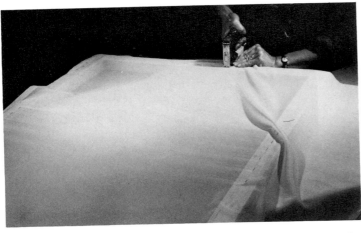

On the third side, pull tight, and shoot three or four more staples.

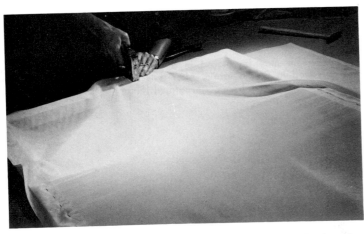

On the last side, pull tight, and put in five or six staples. Then work from side to side, adding staples from the inside out, pulling the silk tight with your fingers until the stapling is completed.

Use a double row of staples to insure strength. Hammer staples flat. They should not protrude at all.

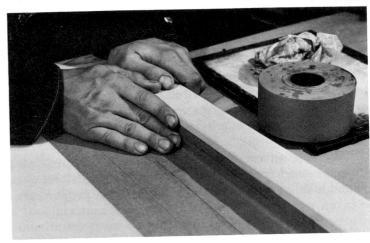

Seal all the joints with gummed paper tape. Do a neat, thorough job.

Tape the corners. Cover all the wood.

Below: Shellac a ½″ margin past the tape into the open screen. Two coats are a minimum.

termining the image opening, allow at least three inches of tape at top and bottom to allow for placing ink and squeegee during printing. Side taping should allow the squeegee a 1″ overlap on each side.

Shellac Application

After the tape is dry, apply two thin coats of clear shellac to all the taping. The shellac can also be extended ½″ onto the silk on the inside and outside of the screen to seal the tape edges. Take care to use a small flat brush about ½″ wide, and do not splatter shellac onto the image area.

Use a straightedge to guide the brush. Do not despair if an even edge is difficult to attain even with a guide. The edge of the image can be masked with thin visualizing paper at printing time.

When the shellac is thoroughly dry, the silk may be washed with mild soap and water to remove sizing and any surface dirt.

Norio Azuma uses lacquer instead of shellac to coat the tape.

Seal the paper tape with shellac. Thin with alcohol to brushing consistency. Two coats are better than one. The screen is ready when dry.

Baseboard

An ideal baseboard can be constructed of ½″ fir plywood. It should be about 2″ larger than the frame in all dimensions. Another good baseboard can be made of ½″ or ¾″ Nova ply. It is smooth and will not require a masonite top.

A top of ⅛″ tempered masonite cut to the same size as the plywood can be nailed to the plywood, to give a smooth surface to the base. Plywood alone often has a strong grain even after sanding that can create uneven printing. Masonite alone, even in ¼″ thickness, can warp.

After the base is assembled, a thin, carefully applied coat or two of shellac will seal the surfaces, top and bottom. Sanding before the second coat would be ideal.

Attaching Screen to Baseboard
Pin Hinges

A very easy method of attaching the screen to the base is to attach the frame to the base directly with removable pin hinges.

Begin by positioning the frame on the base with an even amount of base protruding around the frame.

Mark the position of the frame and hinges with a soft pencil.

Attach the hinges to the base with a piece of cardboard between the hinge and the base, to allow for easy removal of the pins. This can be attached by drilling the hole in the leg larger than the screw used to attach the leg to the frame. The leg should also have an application of shellac.

Place the screen frame securely against the hinges. Position the hinges at right angles and mark their locations. Screw the hinges carefully into the frame.

Hinge Bar

A very versatile method for attaching the frame to the base is to use a hinge bar the same height as the frame. The bar is attached to the base with bolts and wing nuts. The nuts and bolts allow the bar to be raised and lowered as

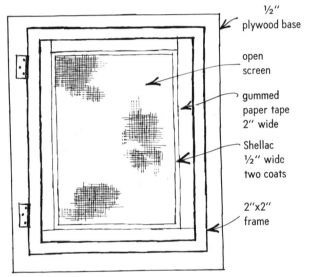

½″ plywood base

open screen

gummed paper tape 2″ wide

Shellac ½″ wide two coats

2″x2″ frame

SCREEN FRAME

Lift the screen. Place paper shapes on the board under the screen. The shapes will make the stencil and prevent the oil-based ink from passing through the screen when you start to print.

Paper doilies used as stencil on slik screen.

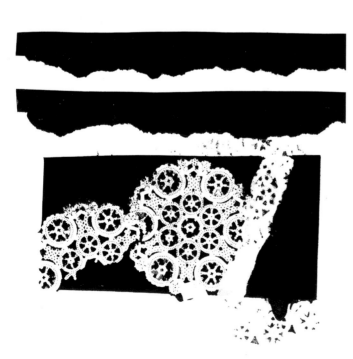

PAPER STENCIL

We have found the use of the paper stencil one of the best ways to become acquainted with what screen printing has to offer. It does not involve painting on the screen or washing out. It is very direct and very easy.

Although intricate forms can be cut easily with the x-acto knife, all the forms must be adhered to the screen with the ink deposited in the first pull of the squeegee. Therefore it would be wise to consider simplicity in designing the first stencils.

Materials

Visualizing layout pads (large size, 19″ by 24″)
X-acto knife with interchangeable blades
Single-edge razor blades
Sharpening stone
Masking or magic tape
LePage's glue

Stencil Paper

Visualizing layout pads manufactured for the commercial artist's layouts contain the best paper to use. It is semi-transparent, semi-absorbent and flexible and should not be confused with tracing paper. Tracing paper is too brittle in even a thin variety but it sometimes does adhere well enough. Other papers are usable and open to the artist's experimentation, but we have found visualizing layout paper most consistent in our own work and in students' work.

Stencil paper sold in art supply stores is too thick for our purposes and is designed for manual stencil brushes.

For certain mottled qualities, a very absorbent paper such as tissue may be tried. However it is useful only for a very short run because it disintegrates. It does give a soft printing quality that may be desirable. Some of our students have used wrapping tissue and bathroom tissue for stencil paper. These tissues produced interesting textures that held up after a nominal printing.

Stencil Knife

The kind of stencil knife desired depends upon the artist's "feel" for the tool. An X-acto knife with interchangeable blades is very useful. However, any sharp pointed knife is excellent.

Frequent sharpening of the stencil knife is important for detail and clean cutting. A fine-grained India stone is excellent for this purpose.

Cutting the Stencil

If a sketch of the work to be cut is made, register it in the register tabs and tape it to the baseboard. If no sketch is used, simply cut or tear the forms to be used.

Place the visualizing paper or other suitable paper over the drawing but not under the register tabs. Be sure the stencil paper covers the printing paper. Tape it to the baseboard.

Paper stencil silk screen in three colors. F. Culatta, Pratt Institute, Brooklyn.

If the drawing is easily seen through the visualizing paper, you may proceed to cut out the areas to be printed. Remember the areas you remove will be the areas that are printed. If the drawing is intricate or hard to see, you may want to trace it first, then cut it.

If there is a floating area in the stencil, place a few drops of LePage's glue on that spot through the screen after it is lowered just before printing. Allow the glue to dry before printing, to help insure attaching the small shape.

A floating area can also be fixed to the screen by cutting a small hole in the shape and placing magic tape behind it, with the gummed side face up; the tape will stick to the screen when finger pressure is applied just before printing.

Some images may require a freer edge than is achieved through cutting. Tearing the edge produces a rough quality that gives a very satisfactory effect. Some of our students have burned open areas in the paper stencil to create uneven edges.

Taping the Stencil to the Screen

Place strips of 3″ masking tape on the under edges of the stencil on all four sides, with the gum side up towards the screen. Allow about 1″ under the stencil and 2″ hanging freely beyond screen dimensions. Hold the stencil in position and very carefully remove the pieces of tape holding the stencil to the baseboard.

Lower the screen over the stencil so slowly that small pieces of the stencil will not ripple. Fasten the strips of masking tape attached to the back of the stencil to the sides of the screen.

If some parts of the stencil curl or ripple during the lowering of the screen, slip a thin steel ruler or metal letter opener under the screen and flatten the pieces.

After the stencil is taped to the screen, remove the tape from the working sketch and carefully slip it out. If this is difficult, leave it in position and print the first image onto the sketch, as a trial proof.

Printing the Stencil

Mix the ink to be used with roughly 50% transparent base, to allow smoother printing. If the ink is too transparent, add more color; if it is not transparent enough, add more transparency. The amount of transparency depends on the degree of transparency in the color being used. Mix enough ink to allow printing without interruption. A detailed discussion of ink preparation appears at the end of the section on the screen print.

Place an ample amount of ink across the top of the screen. Squeegee the ink firmly across the screen. The stencil should adhere easily with the first printing. Continue printing the edition. Do not let the screen dry out!

Cleaning the Screen, the Stencil, and the Squeegee

First place a thick bed of newspapers between screen and base. Remove all the excess ink from the screen and the squeegee with the cardboard squares. Save the ink in cans if it is reusable. The cleaner the screen is of excess ink, the easier it will be to clean.

Carefully remove the stencil. Place it on some clean newspaper. If the stencil is very simple, it can sometimes be cleaned with a small rag if great care is taken. However, the stencil is usually not reusable, and it is wise to print the whole edition at one time. The stencil cannot be left on the screen because the ink would dry and clog the screen.

Proceed to clean the screen and squeegee with clean rags and mineral spirits. Remove the newspapers as they soil, always working with clean newspapers and rags until the screen is thoroughly clean. A good test is to run a white rag over the screen; it is clean when color can no longer be seen on the rag. This cleaning method may be used for all screen cleaning.

When you have printed enough impressions, peel the paper from the bottom side of the screen and clean it with screen wash or mineral solvent. The paper stencil method is good for a small number of prints, as the screen may not be cleaned without ruining the image.

After the printing session is over, clean the screen with the appropriate solvent. For oil-based paint use screen wash or varsol, varnoline, etc. Place newspapers under the screen to absorb the solvent.

DIRECT GLUE STENCIL—NEGATIVE METHOD

An easy way to create a brushed-on stencil is the direct glue method, which is a negative method. The glue mixture can be applied to the screen in a variety of ways to produce free, painterly, textured effects, hard-edge forms, or line images. Nothing has to be washed out. When the glue is dry, the stencil is complete and ready for printing. The ink will print in the areas where glue has not been applied.

Materials

LePage's glue mixture #1, (50% Lepage's glue, 25% water, 25% color, thicken or thin as desired. The number one designation is used to differentiate it from the glue mixture #2 used for tusche and glue.)

Left portion painted with direct glue with some blotting to create tones. Alison Bury, Pratt Institute. Right portion; hand placed in glue mixture on slab and then on to screen, Joan Elliott, Pratt Institute.

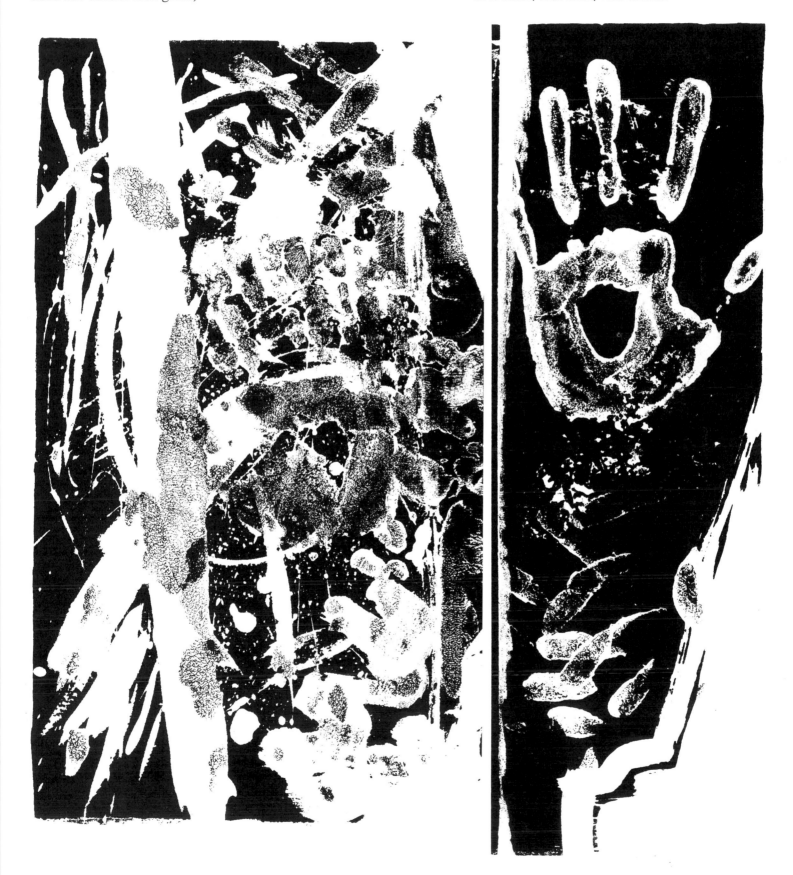

Robert Indiana
"Five" 1968
Screen print 23⅝" x 19⅝"
Courtesy of Pace Editions, Inc., N.Y.C.
Published by Editions Domberger, Bonlanden, Germany, 1968
Collection Richard Anuszkiewicz

For screens so large that it is inconvenient to stand the screen up to clean it, rest it on two tables and work with it in a horizontal position.

backing. The areas to be printed are carefully cut with a sharp knife, and stripped away from the backing. The film is then adhered to the underside of the screen with adhering fluid and the backing is peeled away, leaving a perfect stencil of lacquer film.

The lacquer film method is excellent when very precise detailed work must be done. Long editions can be printed without difficulty, and a screen with a lacquer-film stencil can be washed out and reprinted, a quality the paper stencil does not possess. However, the film is quite expensive, and the beginner may find the film a little more difficult to use than the paper stencil.

If the following instructions are observed with care, there should be success, even with a first screen.

Materials

Lacquer film (sold under various trade names such as NuFilm or Pro-Film. We have found the plastic-backed film the easiest to apply.)

Visualizing paper, glue, block out or lacquer (to cover areas of stencil not covered by film)

Adhering fluid (for adhering film to screen and removing film from screen)

Film solvent (for removing film from screen)

Stencil knife (X-acto or stencil swivel-blade knife, very sharp)

Masking tape

Rags (clean, absorbent, cotton)

Cutting the Film

Prepare a sketch, position it in the register tabs on the baseboard, and tape it down.

Cut a piece of film larger than the area to be cut and tape the film, lacquer side up, to the sketch.

Disengage the screen from the baseboard to make it easy to manipulate during the cutting.

Using the stencil knife, cut out the areas to be printed.

Make sure cuts, but do not cut through the plastic or paper backing. Overcut the corners of the shapes slightly to insure that the corners will be clean when the film is removed.

Removing the Film from Printing Areas

Remove the film carefully from all the areas to be printed, leaving the backing intact. Make some cuts in the backing to allow air to escape during the adhering of the film to the screen.

Pick up any loose bits of film on the film area to keep them from adhering to the screen.

Applying the Film

Be sure the screen is thoroughly clean to insure successful adhering. If a greasy cleaning agent like mineral spirits has recently been used, clean the screen with lacquer thinner or acetone. If the screen is new and may contain some sizing, wash it with a dilute detergent, rinse it well, and allow it to dry.

Adhere a piece of 3″ masking tape, sticky side up, to the backs of the four corners of the film, leaving 2″ free. Carefully remove the tape holding the film to the master sketch and lower the screen. Adhere the tape on the film corners to the screen, being careful to keep the film in position.

Remove the sketch from the baseboard and place a number of newspaper sheets as padding between the baseboard and screen. Lower the clean screen over the newspaper padding.

During the adhering process keep the cap on the can of adherent when not using it. It is wise not to inhale the fumes unnecessarily because they are powerful. It may be helpful to wear thin plastic gloves when applying the fluid and when using the solvent to clean film from the screen after printing.

Do not rush to adhere the film to the screen. Make pads from two clean cotton rags. Keep one dry and one wet with adhering fluid but not dripping.

Dampen a small area on the top of the screen with the wet rag. Quickly apply the dry rag to the spot and rub it. This drying action helps to adhere the film. As the film begins to adhere it will appear darker. Press hard when rubbing.

It is very important not to saturate the area with adhering fluid because too much fluid will dissolve the film or cause blurred edges.

A good place to start the adhering process is in the center of the image, working out to the edges on all sides simultaneously, to prevent wrinkling.

Work small areas at a time for the best control.

When the entire film has been adhered, allow the screen to dry for some minutes to be sure none of the areas are still moist. Then lift the screen into an upright position, remove the masking tape that held the film to the screen, and begin to remove the backing.

Removing Backing

Starting at the corners, peel the backing away from the screen very slowly. If the film has been properly applied it should come off easily.

If any film areas are not completely adhered and begin to come off with the backing, return the screen to the adhering position and repeat the adhering process, using small amounts of adhering fluid on the wet rag to be sure the film is not dissolved. After the film is thoroughly adhered and ready for printing, clean the underside of the screen with a cloth dampened with mineral spirits to be sure the screen is clear of adhesives used in manufacturing film.

If there are open areas of screen outside the film that are within the printing area, cover them with paper used for the direct paper stencil method or with lacquer blockout or glue. When all such areas are covered, the screen is ready to print.

Some artists save the pieces of film removed from the backing during the film stencil cutting and dissolve them in a jar with a small amount of adhering fluid. This mixture is useful as a blocking material and is easy to apply.

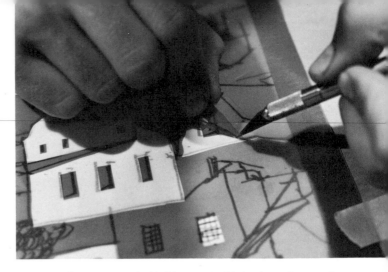

To cut a lacquer stencil (Nu-film or Pro-film) place the stencil on your drawing or sketch with the emulsion side up. Using a small frisket knife or sharp Exacto knife cut through the emulsion but not the backing paper. Peel away the lacquer film. Save the scraps in a jar.

When the stencil is cut put it in position under your screen. Take two rags, one in each hand, one soaked in adhering fluid and one dry. Rub the area over the stencil with the adhering-fluid rag, using heavy pressure. Quickly switch hands and, again with strong pressure, rub the area with the dry rag.

When the stencil has been adhered (by literally melting it into the silk) turn the screen over and peel off the backing paper from the lacquer stencil. Check carefully, and if any edges are not adhered, repeat the process in these areas. Too much adhering fluid will dissolve the stencil; be careful.

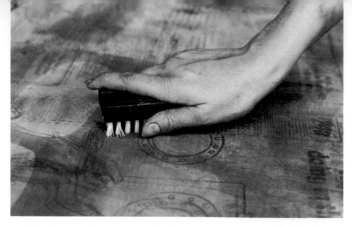

To clean a lacquer stencil from the screen, use film solvent or adhering fluid. Scrub with a brush if necessary. Hold to the light to check for clogged mesh.

Removing Film from Screen

The film may be removed from the screen after the required number of prints has been completed and all the ink has been thoroughly cleaned from the screen.

It is helpful to disengage the screen and lay it top side up on a bed of 6 or 8 sheets of newspaper.

Pour a generous amount of film solvent (for removing film) over the whole film area, allow it to sit for 4 or 5 minutes, and then rub the whole area with a large clean cloth.

After the solvent has been rubbed well over the entire area with the cloth, or a brush for difficult areas, lift the screen and remove the top layers of newspaper. Most of the film should come off with the newspapers.

Repeat the process of pouring the solvent over the screen and rubbing to clear any remaining areas of film.

If some small areas are difficult to remove, saturate two pieces of cloth with solvent, raise the screen upright, and rub the trouble areas vigorously with the two rags. Allow the screen to dry after the film is dissolved.

Adhering fluid can be used as a cleaning agent instead of film solvent, but it takes a little longer to do the job.

POSITIVE STENCIL

(Tusche, Wax, Rubber Cement, Maskoid)

The great advantage of the positive stencil is that the qualities of drawing and painting in line and mass and texture can be achieved with comparative ease. Its freedom of expression and direct positive image are often an attraction to painters who have never made prints. It is based on the principle that a waxy or greasy substance resists water.

Greasy substances such as liquid or stick tusche, liquid wax or wax crayon's rubber cement, maskoid, or even asphaltum varnish are used to design a positive image on the screen. A great variety of tools can be used: brushes, pens, sticks, rags, sponges, and so on.

A thick delineation is made with one of the substances or a combination of many of them. When the image is thoroughly dry, a thin coat of special glue mixture is thinly applied to the entire open screen area, acting as a blocking agent.

When the glue application is dry, the wax or tusche are washed out with mineral spirits, turpentine, or varsol, leaving a free, positive image ready for printing.

Materials

Glue mixture #1 for positive work
Glue mixture #2 for negative work
Lacquer blockout
Water-soluble blockout
Tusche, liquid and stick
Wax, liquid
Rubber cement
Maskoid
Asphaltum
Wax crayons, lithographic crayons (soft)

Rubbings with stick tusche and lithographic crayon of corrugated board and rough textured wood, writing with wax crayon and painting with tusche. Pratt Institute.

Brushes, speedball pens
Cardboard squares (for spreading glue, blockout, and lacquer blockout)

Glue Mixture #2

The glue mixture used for the tusche and glue, wax and glue, and rubber cement and maskoid and similar materials should be a little thinner than glue mixture #1, used for direct negative application, to make washing out the tusche or wax efficient.

The #2 glue mixture we have found very satisfactory is made by the following formula:

50% LePage's glue
40% water
8% vinegar (for longer keeping)
2% glycerine (for more resilience)

Tusche, Liquid and Stick

Many kinds of liquid tusche are marketed, under a variety of names. Some are prepared especially for screen printing. Most large supply houses list their own tusche products in their catalogs. A lithographic tusche manufactured for lithography and also used for screen printing is called Korn's Lithographic Tusche. Some tusche may be thinned with water, others with varnoline. All are soluble, when dry, with mineral spirits, varsol, and the like. In all cases it should be a thickish liquid; if too thinly applied, it will be hard to wash out. If it is too thin, pour a little onto a blotter or absorbent paper towel to let the liquid evaporate. Read the directions on the labels.

Tusche also comes in stick form that produces a drawn, crayon quality when used on the screen. Lithographic crayons may be used for the same purpose. A heavy deposit must be applied to the screen in all cases.

Wax, Liquid and Crayon

Liquid wax sold as a resist for ceramics is a good material for designing the positive image. It is soluble in water in liquid state and can be washed out with mineral spirits when dry. It can be colored with poster color for easier viewing.

Wax crayons can be used in very much the same manner as lithographic crayons and stick tusche. A heavy deposit of wax should be left when drawing on the screen.

After the wax is applied to the screen and allowed to dry, the glue blockout is applied as it is in the tusche and glue method. Directions for applying the glue are given at the end of this section.

Applying the Tusche

Be sure the screen is clean.

If a sketch is to be used, slip it under the screen in the register marks. Raise the screen slightly off the sketch by slipping some cardboard squares under each corner.

Stir or shake the tusche very well because thick particles often settle in the bottom of the bottle or jar. If the tusche is too thin, allow some liquid to evaporate overnight. If it is

Tusche and glue silk screen, one color. Alison Bury, Pratt Institute, Brooklyn.

In the "tusche and glue" process the tusche should be thick and heavy. It must fill the pores of the silk when it has dried.

It is not necessary to restrict your technique to brush strokes. Many implements can be used. This is a cardboard square dipped in tusche.

By rubbing the veined surface of a leaf through the silk with a soft litho crayon, the shape and textures of the leaf can be impressed into the silk.

Below: A coin has enough texture to mark the silk. The litho crayon should leave a heavy deposit of pigment.

too thick, thin with water or turpentine, depending on the type. In any case it is very important that the tusche be thick to achieve the best results.

Apply the tusche as heavily as possible with brush, pen, or other instrument. All the positive forms are created with the tusche.

Do not try to apply tonal effects with the tusche. Any tonal qualities can be developed through textures or with stick tusche or litho crayon.

The tusche must be applied with a solid black quality and fill all the screen mesh. For this reason you must work with a clean screen. Check the screen by holding it up to the light. Some areas may need a second application.

Applying Stick Tusche, Litho Crayon, and Wax Crayon

Stick tusche or lithographic crayon or wax crayon may be applied in some areas where texture or a variety of line is desirable.

In order to achieve a heavy deposit of crayon on the screen, it may be helpful to place a cardboard under the area being coated to keep the silk from being strained.

Texture Rubbing

Rubbings of textures may be made right onto the screen. An object or pattern with a rough surface is placed under the screen and the stick tusche or litho or wax crayon is rubbed over it. Be careful not to use any sharp objects that would damage the screen. Apply the stick tusche or crayon liberally. Apply glue as follows.

Applying Glue

Pour a moderate amount of glue mixture #2 on the screen margin, not on the image area. Be sure the screen is removed or raised at least ½" from the base to keep glue from seeping onto the base.

Squeegee the glue over the tusche area with thin, even, overlapping strokes of the cardboard squeegee, without letting the glue seep through.

Some artists prefer a second coat of glue after the first has dried. We rarely seem to need two coats if the glue is well applied. With one coat, little pin holes sometimes appear in the first two or three proofs, then disappear with printing.

Allow the glue coat to dry thoroughly.

Washing Out the Tusche

Reattach the screen to the baseboard and place a padding of newspapers between the baseboard and the screen.

Place the screen in down position and liberally pour a solvent such as mineral spirits, varnoline, or turpentine over the whole image.

Rub the tusche with a clean rag, remove the newspapers, and repeat the process.

Raise the screen and rub both sides of the screen simultaneously with solvent-soaked rags. Two cellulose sponges rubbed simultaneously on both sides of the screen will clean it well.

The tusche should wash out easily if it was applied thickly enough to the screen with a thin coat of glue over it.

If troublesome areas remain, use a soft nailbrush or two old toothbrushes face to face on each side of the screen to rub the difficult spots.

Cleaning Screen After Printing

After the edition is printed and the screen thoroughly cleaned of ink, wash the glue from the screen with warm water and clean rags.

Maskoid Stencil

The maskoid stencil method is similar to the tusche and glue but in many ways easier to use as it is removed easily and does not stain the screen.

Maskoid is a liquid synthetic latex sold under the names Art Maskoid or E-Z Liquid Frisket. When dry, it is insoluble in water and alcohol but can be easily removed from the screen by rubbing the dry maskoid with a piece of natural rubber or with a rubber cement pickup (eraser) made of dry rubber cement.

The maskoid is applied with a brush to the positive areas that will print. Free, fluid lines and masses are easy to define with the maskoid.

When the maskoid is dry, apply glue mixture #2 or any other water-soluble blockout medium over the entire screen with a cardboard square.

Spread the glue in a thin even coat as it is applied in the tusche and glue method.

When the glue is dry, remove the screen and place it on a flat clean surface of cardboard or paper.

Remove the maskoid with a piece of natural rubber. Rub the dry maskoid at a sharp angle. If the glue coat is thin, the maskoid should pick up (be removed) easily, and the screen can be printed.

Rubber Cement

Rubber cement sold in art supply stores as an adhesive may be used as a positive blockout with interesting effects. It should be fresh and liquid, not too dry, not too runny. Apply it in a medium coat with a brush, rag, sponge, cardboard, or similar tool. Allow it to dry thoroughly, and then apply glue mixture #2 in a thin coat. When the glue is dry remove the rubber cement with a rubber cement pickup (dry rubber cement rolled into a ball and used as an eraser). After all the rubber cement is removed you are ready to print.

MISCELLANEOUS METHODS

Impasto Printing

As the screen print produces an essentially flat surface, except when enamels are used, it may be interesting for some artists to exploit the use of impasto printing.

A folded piece of textured cloth will leave its imprint on the silk if rubbed heavily with soft litho crayon.

Here an old line cut of a business chart is rubbed with the litho crayon, and it can be transferred to the silk.

The solution of LePage's glue, water, glycerine, and vinegar is poured onto the side of the screen.

Below: When the glue has dried, wash out the tusche and litho crayon with mineral spirits, varnoline, benzine, or a similar solvent. Do not use lacquer thinner, alcohol, water, or any other than the proper solvent.

Harry Krug
"Bubble Gum Jungle"
Screen print 17½" x 23½"
Associated American Artists Gallery

Because the method involves paper and mat-board stencils and a heavy deposit of thickened ink, it is necessary to use a coarser silk of 10xx to 12xx in order to print more ink.

When many overprintings of enamel inks are used with ordinary stencil devices, a thick deposit of ink can be achieved because of the thickness of enamel inks. However, as the enamels take longer then poster inks to dry, the method can be laborious.

Norio Azuma utilizes a very effective method to achieve a thick, granulated deposit of ink. He opens the screen so that the underside is up and brushes some water on the underside of the screen over an entire area or just on an edge of a form. He then sprinkles some granules of sugar on the dampened area and allows the grains of sugar to settle in for about five minutes. He taps the screen underneath the area to shake off loose sugar particles. He drops the screen into printing position and squeegees his color through two to four times, in different directions, sometimes lifting the screen to check the deposit of ink, and squeegeeing again until he has the desired thickness. The granules of sugar adhere well to the screen and allow a thick deposit of ink in their area. Fifty to seventy five prints can be printed with one sugar preparation.

A simpler system utilizes heavy paper or cardboard for the ordinarily thin stencil. Thicken poster ink with household corn starch until it is the thickness of sour cream. Slowly and evenly squeegee the ink across the screen. The amount of pressure on the squeegee will determine the amount of ink deposited. Less pressure, more ink, more pressure, less ink. The thick stencil will allow a thick textured deposit of ink to print on the paper. If the cornstarch begins to clog the screen, clean the screen carefully and resume printing.

Norio Azuma utilizes a very effective method to achieve a thick granulated deposit of ink by placing a sugar and water mixture over an entire area or just an edge. Before the sugar is dissolved, the mixture is put on the screen over the section to be inked and left for about five minutes, then the color is squeegeed through.

Textured Objects

An additional method requires gluing down, with rubber cement or any other temporary glue, some textured objects such as burlap, rope, canvas, or cardboard to the base board. Place a thin printing paper, registered in position, over the glued objects. Then, using transparent inks, proceed to print. A heavier deposit of ink will occur in the recessions than in the raised areas, giving an interested effect. The uneven bed can produce register problems, so proceed carefully.

Mimeograph Stencil

Typewritten copy and drawings done on an ordinary of-fice mimeograph stencil can be used as a screen stencil. Prepare the stencil in the prescribed way as if it were to be used for a mimeograph machine. Tear the stencil sheet away from the supporting sheets and place it carbon side up on a piece of paper on the printing bed. Use visualizing paper, glue, or blockout filler to block out any areas between stencil and frame. Lower the screen and print. The stencil will ad-here with the first printing. Long runs are not possible, but the mimeograph stencil can produce interesting results.

Pochoir Process

The pochoir process can yield extraordinary effects if the artist designs especially for this technique. A stencil, usually brass, is cut by hand for each area of each color in the de-sign, and the color is applied to the paper by hand brushing through the open areas of the stencil. This process is used mainly in France for rather small editions of illustrated books. As hand-brushed effects can vary a great deal, the skill of the craftsman who applies the color is very im-portant to the finished result. If the artist personally applies the color, variations can occur at his discretion. Color can be added by the pochoir process to prints where a key block has delineated the main parts of the composition. Intaglio prints may have the color placed directly on the plate be-fore printing if rollers or small brayers are used in con-junction with the stencil. Thin oiled paper, tag stock, or tym-pan paper can be cut for stencils. Heavy acetate or vinyl, if

the needs of the image. The transparent base extends the ink and offers some economy. Be sure to mix it thoroughly with the ink.

A few drops of varnolene or thinner can be used sparingly to thin the ink if necessary. A 12xx silk works well with the poster inks.

Enamels

Enamels are more difficult to use because they dry by oxidation and require from 4 up to 24 hours to dry.

However, enamels possess qualities that can lead to interesting images. Because of the thickness of the ink, the printed surface appears raised, with an impasto effect. The printing quality is exceptionally sharp, and the inks retain the richness and brilliance of color when dry that they have in their wet state. The enamel inks are also extremely durable and flexible and have excellent adhesive qualities, making them very adaptable to printing on metal, ceramics, glass, and some plastics.

Care must be taken in clean-up of enamels because any ink left in the screen to dry is almost impossible to remove.

Vinyl Inks

The vinyl inks are specially formulated for printing on vinyl surfaces, whether soft or rigid, and dry by evaporation within 20 minutes, depending on atmospheric conditions. They are extremely durable and adhere exceptionally well, which makes them widely used for commercial purposes. However, in the last few years the Pop artists have created provocative screen print images on soft vinyl in both the dimensional and the flat; their example has led to the wide use of vinyl inks by fine artists.

The inks are manufactured opaque but can be made transparent by adding a special base made for this purpose and available through catalogs. They can be thinned more than most inks, but check your screen print supply house for correct thinners. Testing the printing qualities is especially advisable before beginning printing. One great plus is that vinyl inks do not dry in the screen, though they dry rapidly on the printed surface.

The inks and solvents for vinyl printing are very toxic and inflammable and should be used with adequate ventilation and fire precautions.

Howard Bradford
"Red Vase #2" 1971
Screen print 19" x 15"
Associated American Artists Gallery

Acrylic Inks

Acrylic inks are excellent for printing on rigid acetate, polystyrene, phenolics, plexiglas, lucite, and similar plastics families. Their adhesive qualities and durability are very good, enabling them to be used very successfully for the vacuum form process. However, acrylic inks cannot be used with lacquer film stencils or a lacquer blockout. Use glue, paper or a blockout without a lacquer base.

The inks can be used direct from the can or can be thinned with especially prepared thinners. Check your screen print supply house for compatible thinners.

The drying time under normal conditions is about 30 to

60 minutes. Caution must be taken to ventilate the room and to guard against fire hazards because acrylic inks and their solvents are inflammable.

Lacquer Inks

Industrial lacquers and decal lacquers are the two main types of lacquer inks. These inks have wide industrial application, but the artist may be interested in them because they print well on paper and cardboard and a special lacquer ink has been developed for metal foil. Do not use stencils with a lacquer base.

Their properties are interesting; they are available in gloss, semi-gloss, and high gloss inks, have a wide range of colors, and can be made transparent by adding base.

A group of ready-mixed transparent lacquers of intense color are excellent for printing on aluminum foil. These inks possess a luminous metallic sheen that adds to the reflectivity of the foil.

It is wise to do some testing before a run when using lacquers, particularly when printing on plastics. The inks dry by evaporation in 20 to 40 minutes for industrial lacquers and 1 to 2 hours for decal lacquers.

Use the lacquer inks and solvents with caution, as they are highly toxic and inflammable and require excellent ventilation and fire prevention care.

Artist Oil Colors

Artist oil colors dry by oxidation. They can be substituted for screen print inks when certain colors are desired. However, the high cost of good-quality artist oils is expensive for extensive use because so much ink is needed in silk-screen printing.

Inexpensive oil colors are not an economy because inexpensive colors contain little pigment and much oil.

A great advantage of the artist oil colors is that they are permanent and because the pigment is of high quality they can be used as tinting agents. They can be mixed with small or large quantities of transparent base to achieve a semi transparent or a transparent quality. The color and the transparent base must be mixed carefully and thoroughly. Add transparent base gradually to the oil color and mix it evenly with a large mixing spatula. The amount varies according to the intensity of the color. Norio Azuma uses only good quality artists oil color thinned with a little turpentine and with a little transparent base added. It must be pointed out, however, that the color sometimes takes days to dry, thereby delaying the printing operations considerably.

Fluorescent Inks

A new area of color statement is possible with daylight fluorescent inks. New images by Pop and Op artists have opened possibilities for the use of fluorescent inks, once used only for posters and billboards.

New formulations have produced fluorescent inks that are easy to use with a 12xx silk and dry in 20 to 25 minutes.

If the ink is used fairly heavily, it will print brighter and glow longer. The permanence of the fluorescent inks is ques-

adhering method previously described. Print the crossmarks as you print the image and finish the run. Position the second screen over the first print and add the crossmarks to the second screen to coincide exactly with the marks on the first color print. Prepare the image on the screen in relation to the first color image. Continue each color in this manner. Commercial color printing utilizes this crossmark system with great accuracy.

Reduction Printing Using One Screen

It is possible to print many colors using one screen in a method similar to the Picasso linoleum reduction prints. In this procedure, an accurate key line drawing in India ink is made on the screen. When dry, India ink will not wash out with varnolene or benzine or similar solvents. Each outline should conform to a specific color area, with a key given for each color. The first color is printed by printing the whole screen. If a white form is desired, it is blocked out before printing. After the first color is printed, the area it occupies on the screen is blocked out and the inking of the second color proceeds. This blocking out of the previous color printed continues until the last color is printed. Opaque ink should be used because of the continuous overprinting, which produces an interesting impasto quality in the finished print.

The Split Font

It is possible to achieve tonal effects of two or three colors on a screen without separate screens. Defined areas can be taped or blocked out on the screen and inks of different colors placed above the two areas and squeegeed across. Another, freer method is to place two or three different-color inks across the top of the screen and to squeegee them across the screen. The printing itself will create a gradual blending of colors. After 10 or 12 prints the blending will diminish, and more ink will have to be added.

Flocking

The technique of flocking is being explored by many innovating screen print artists. It is a method of applying fibers of wool, nylon, or viscose material to a screened adhesive. The flock has a velvety appearance when printed. For scores of years flocking has been used commercially, as in the wallpaper industry, advertising, and toy manufacturing.

A variety of adhesives are manufactured commercially for all surfaces. Most adhesives can be used with a 12xx or coarser silk and require that flocking be done immediately after the application of the adhesive. Overnight drying is also necessary. For mixing, mineral spirits and ordinary screen thinner work well; but check the specifications of your adhesive.

The adhesive is applied through any stencil form onto the surface to be printed. Be sure you buy an adhesive that works with your particular surface. Adhesives are made for printing on wood, paper, cloth, glass, and other surfaces.

After the adhesive is printed, the flocking material can be applied with a sieve, or flocking gun. Shake off the excess flock and allow the print to dry overnight.

A wide range of reflective material such as glass beads,

tinsel, spangles, mother of pearl flakes, and diamond dust can be applied in a similar manner.

The least expensive and simplest method is to use an ordinary flour sieve or to construct a sieve from a frame and wire screening.

Flocking guns costing from $4.00 for use with vacuum cleaner hose to $60 for separate units are available in well-stocked silk-screen supply houses.

Elaborate electrostatic flocking units have been developed for the industry, but they run into hundreds of dollars, making them impractical for the artist.

Cleaning the Screen

After printing is finished it is imperative to clean the screen immediately or the remaining ink will dry and make cleaning very difficult. The screen can be removed from its hinges or left in position for cleaning. Place layers of newspapers under the screen. Remove all remaining color from the screen with the sharp edges of the cardboard squares and save the ink in its container. Clean the screen with rags soaked in varnoline. Change the layers of newspapers under the screen frequently and change rags often until all the ink is gone from the frame and the taped areas of the screen. Hold the screen at an angle or upright in order to scrub its back and front simultaneously. We have found cellulose sponges useful in the clean-up when rags are in short supply. When clean white rags no longer show signs of color, the screen is clean. Hold the screen up to the light to check for difficult-to-remove ink. Clean the squeegee and your mixing slab well. Take care how you store rags soaked in solvents, as they are a fire hazard. A metal can with a lid especially made for holding discarded paint rags is a good safety measure.

The screen is either put away till the next printing or prepared for the second color; if several screens are used, a separate second-color screen may be set on the pin hinges, register guides checked, and new printing started. Because poster colors dry quickly, the first printing will be dry and the print ready to receive the second color.

Solving Common Printing Problems

Uneven Printing

Uneven printing may be caused by uneven pressure or a need to build up the printing bed with a moderate thickness of newsprint or newspaper. It may also be caused by poor mixing of ink with base; mix ink thoroughly. The ink mixture may also be too thick and not spread consistently. Add transparent base or thin it with a very small amount of varnolene. Check to see that the squeegee is smooth and sharp. Keep the quantity of ink consistent while printing. Replenish the ink as necessary for even distribution.

Clogging of Screen During Printing

If the screen clogs during printing, build up a bed of newspaper under screen to improve contact. Try increasing the pressure on the squeegee by scrubbing it back and forth to force ink through the screen and hopefully to loosen

Washing out the tusche from a "tusche and glue" stencil. Work both sides of the screen with two rags and mineral spirits.

Honore Daumier
"Robert Macaire, Excellent Placement"
Lithograph 10" x 7⅞" (from *Le Charivari*)
Collection of the authors

Norwegian, were inspired by the creativity of the French and produced work of note.

Picasso, the master graphic artist, was captivated by the possibilities of lithography and created innovating works particularly in the 1940s when he worked with the printers Mourlot.

There has been a rich resurgence of the medium, not only in France after World War II but also in England with notable works by Henry Moore, Graham Sutherland, Lynn Chadwick, Eduardo Paolozzi, David Hockney, and Allen Jones. In Italy works by the hand of Marino Marini, Afro, and Campigli have been significant.

In the United States, the renewal of the lithograph after World War II was implemented by large national and international exhibitions of prints, most notable, the International Biennial of Lithographs at the Cincinnati Museum when Gustav von Groswitz was its curator of prints and drawings. National exhibitions at the Print Club of Philadelphia, the Brooklyn Museum, and the Library of Congress did much to place in the forefront such artists of the lithograph as Romas Viesulas, Michael Ponce de Leon, George Miyasaki, Rudy Pozzatti, Will Barnet, and Federico Castellon.

Independent workshops in the fifties and sixties were extremely influential in involving the artist in lithography. The Tamarind Lithography Workshop in Los Angeles was able, through private funding, to commission both artists already involved with prints and painters and sculptors who had never done a print to try their hands. An impressive body of work has come out of this project, and selections were recently displayed at the Museum of Modern Art in 1969 in New York City. Louise Nevelson, John Hultberg, Antonio Frasconi, Peter Takal, Jacob Landau, and Adja Yunkers are a few of the many artists who worked at Tamarind.

Over the last 20 years the well-equipped workshop of Robert Blackburn in New York City has been an excellent place for artists to work independently with the lithograph. Pratt Graphics Center, in New York City, has also been a lively workshop in which both American and foreign artists take classes in lithography or simply use the fine facilities.

Universal Limited Art Editions, located in West Islip, Long Island, and directed by Tatyana Grossman, has published editions of lithographs by painters and sculptors of the New York School such as Robert Rauschenberg, Larry Rivers, Helen Frankenthaler, Grace Hartigan, Jasper Johns, and James Rosenquist.

With the revival of the workshop tradition, numerous shops such as the Bank Street Atelier and the Mourlot's workshop are successfully operating in New York City. The appearance of skilled artist-printers of lithographs promises a rich potential for future expression and exploration.

Opposite page:
Federico Castellon
"It was a gay and magnificent revel" 1968
Color lithograph 8¼" x 11⅞"
Collection of the authors
Aquarius Press, Baltimore

A light-duty lift at Indiana University will handle stones weighing several hundred pounds.

A stone rack in the graphic workshop of the Cooper Union. Art School in New York City. Storage cabinets are located above.

Stones have dimensions lettered on edge in the rack at the Bank Street Atelier in New York City.

Below: Pipe rollers are built into the Bank Street Atelier rack to help move the large stones.

THE PRINCIPLE OF LITHOGRAPHY

The princple of lithography differs from the other graphic processes in that lithography depends upon a chemical reaction instead of the physical separation of the inked and uninked areas. In relief printing the raised parts of the block receive the ink while the cut or recessed areas are not inked. The opposite is true for the intaglio techniques, where the incised lines retain the ink while the upper surface is cleaned and prints as a white. With silk screen the stencil process separates the inked from the uninked areas by a blocked screen that prevents the passage of color.

The antipathy of grease to water and water to grease is the basis for lithography. This method requires that the inking of the block, in this case a piece of Bavarian limestone or finely grained zinc, be accomplished only when a thin film of water is sponged over the printing surface. The water prevents the greasy ink from adhering to the undrawn surface while adhering to the equally greasy image or texture. The image is "etched" before printing with a mixture of dilute nitric acid and gum arabic, although the etching is not at all like the biting that takes place in the intaglio process. The purpose of the lithographic etch is to fix the greasy image firmly into the stone and to desensitize the white areas from receiving ink. The acid is so dilute that it does not eat the stone away as implied by the word "etch."

STONES AND PLATES

The traditional material for making lithographs has been limestone taken from Solenhofen and Kellheim in the Monheim district, north of Munich. Marble has been used occasionally, and stones have been quarried in England and France. Stones vary greatly in hardness, color and imperfections. Perfect stones should be treated carefully as they are very expensive. The stones' great weight makes them difficult to ship and dangerous to handle in the shop. Large stones are usually moved on a wheeled cart or table, and a large multicolor lithograph on stone requires lots of manpower to complete. Yellow or whitish stones are soft and will not take a fine grain while the blueish grey stones are harder and will take finer graining. Some stones will be mottled or contain combinations of colors. Be careful of cracks or fissures which will eventually split through, ruining the stone. Veining or slight spotting is common and does not necessarily impair the usefulness of the stone. Stones must be strong and thick enough to withstand the considerable pressure of the scraper bar. A thin stone may crack in the press while printing. Two inches is a minimum thickness for stones larger than 12" by 16", and very large stones should be even thicker. Storage racks must be very sturdy.

The expense and trouble involved in printing from stones has led many artists to use zinc plates. They are cheaper, more readily available, lighter, and store easily. The grain, which is applied by whirling steel balls over the surface of a spinning plate, is not as sensitive as that of stone, but it is suitable for a great variety of work done today. The zinc must be treated before beginning the drawing and is not so easy to scratch or scrape as a stone, but the many con-

Paul Wunderlich
"Behold Thou Art Fair, My Beloved, Yea, Pleasant:
Also Our Bed Is Green" 1970
from Song of Solomon, published by Aquarius Press
Color Lithograph 23¾" x 17¾"
Collection of the authors

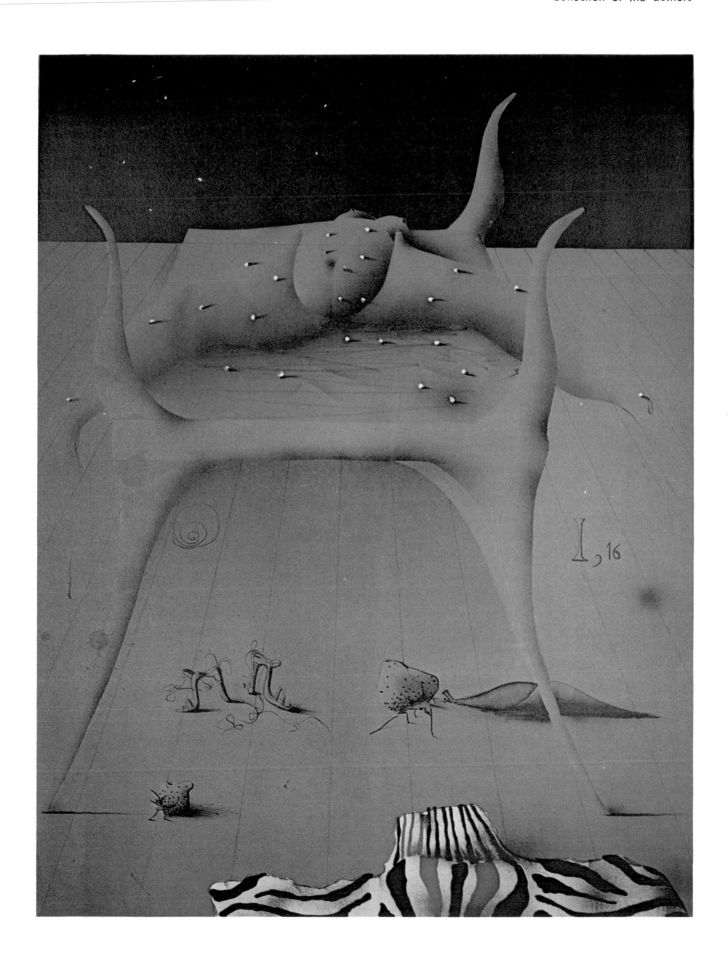

Joan Miro
No. 8A "Homenatge a Joan Prats" 1971
Color lithograph 21½" x 29½"
Barney Weinger Gallery

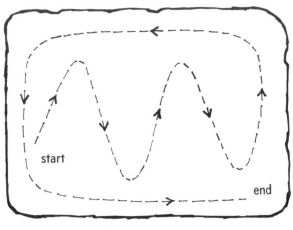

pattern for graining a large stone

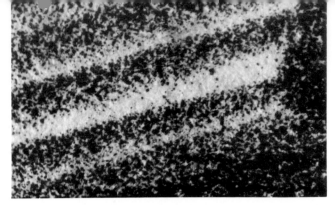

The grain of the stone is clearly evident in this enlargement of a lithograph by Daumier.

The graining table in the workshop of Edmund and Jacques Desjobert, Paris. The water and sludge drain out through a hole in the bottom into a pail, which is emptied every day or two. Elaborate equipment is not necessary for beautiful work.

Carborundum is sprinkled thoroughly over a stone by Rudy Pozzatti in the University of Indiana graphic workshop.

Below: Two stones are ground in Desjobert's workshop in Paris. Note position of the hands.

veniences of the light metal plates have won over a number of artist-lithographers. Zinc plates may also be regrained several times but this chore must be done by a special machine, usually found only in a commercial plate-maker's shop or in the largest schools or workshops. It is quite cheap to regrain a plate commercially, and it doesn't pay to buy a graining machine unless you have a large volume of work.

Graining the Stone

The surface of a stone must be smooth and flat if it is to serve as a support for a drawing that must be inked and printed. The simplest way to flatten the stone is to grind it smooth with a grinding disk, called a levigator, or with another stone. A strong table or sink is necessary if many stones are to be ground. The materials are simple and cheap, and a good, serviceable graining table can be made by a carpenter or handy man. You can turn an existing sink into a grinding sink, if it is large enough, by the insertion of a wooden rack inside the walls of the sink. If you build a sink, make it strong and solid because stones are heavy and the grinding action will eventually loosen a weak construction job. The legs can be made of 4" by 4" stock, the sides of 2" by 10" material, the bottom of the sink can be ¾" plywood, exterior grade. Bolt the legs to the basin for permanence. The basin may be painted and the joints lined with cloth tape and repainted, or it may be lined with heavy vinyl, folded from a large sheet and stapled above the water line. A first-rate job will line the sink with zinc, aluminum, or stainless steel. The drain should be so constructed that the heavy sludge that inevitably accumulates will not be washed into the soil line of the plumbing. The sediment will eventually clog the trap. In many graining tables a short piece of pipe protrudes an inch or so above the bottom of the sink, permitting the sludge to collect in the bottom, where it can be shoveled out at intervals. The drain pipe can be connected by a rubber hose to a pail or to the plumbing drain pipe.

Grinding is accomplished by a levigator (a round disk of cast iron about 2" thick) or by a smaller litho stone. Rough grinding done with sea sand or coarse (#150 or #180) carborundum should be continued until the old image is ground off the stone. Wet the stone, sprinkle a small amount of grit over the stone to be ground and, using a figure-eight pattern,

A small stone is used to grain the larger stone. The carborundum has mixed with particles of stone, lightening its color.

The levigator is used for rough grinding, because it spins rapidly on an off-center handle.

A power-driven levigator at a University of Indiana workshop is guided by Rudy Pozzatti.

Below: The stone is rinsed with water to remove all particles of stone and carborundum. It is then left to dry before it can be drawn upon.

move the smaller stone over the larger one in such a way that the entire surface is worked. The grinding should be continued until the stones become sticky and hard to move Wash off the sludge, add more carborundum, and continue until the stone is clear. The finer grits are used for succeeding grindings. The final grinding should be done after a particularly thorough cleaning of both stones, using #220 or F, 2F, or 3F carborundum. The smoother finish is suitable for fine-line pen or brush work, while the rougher finish is good for crayon and coarser brush strokes. Transfers of photo material, type, and similar material should be made on finely grained stones.

The edges of the stone should be rounded or beveled with a flat file and then polished with a coarse carborundum block, pumice stone, or Schumacher brick. If this is not done the sharp edges tend to catch ink and print when you are pulling the edition, and they tend to chip during handling.

When the grinding is finished, all the sludge and grit must be washed off the top, sides, and bottom of the stone, and it should be allowed to dry. The stone is now sensitive to both grease and water, and if it is not to be used at once, should be wrapped in clean, non-oily paper (not newspaper or printed matter) until you are ready to place the image on it.

DESIGNING ON THE STONE

Traditional ways of working the stone include greasy crayons and lithographic tusche as the drawing media. These materials are still used, but many other ways of working have been developed in recent years. Photographic techniques, transfers, rubbings, and the use of a number of unorthodox solvents and substances have expanded the possibilities of lithography enormously. While it is conventional to use prepared litho crayons or tusche as drawing agents, the only essential characteristic of your drawing material is its greasiness. Such items as animal fat, vaseline, soap, tallow, oil, or sweat may be used to produce textures and shapes on the stone or plate. Solvents such as gasoline, turpentine, alcohol, mineral spirits, lacquer thinner, and countless other chemicals have been employed to dilute, dissolve, or emulsify the grease to form unusual shapes, patterns, or textures. Individual preference as to imagery will direct the artist towards particular methods that will suit his artistic personality.

Drawing the Image with Crayon and Tusche

Lithographic crayon is a mixture of greasy material like soap with wax, shellac, and a coloring agent like lampblack. It is precisely formulated and numbered according to hardness, ranging from 0, which is very soft, to 5, which is the hardest. Crayons are sold in stick form and pencil form, and the medium grades are the most useful. They can be rubbed with the finger or with a cloth or stump to achieve grey tints or to intensify black areas. Most artist-lithographers find it desirable to have several grades of crayons on hand in the studio. They work equally well on zinc plates as on

Working directly on the stone with a litho crayon produces a grainy stroke. Protect the stone from the grease on your hand with a piece of stiff paper.

Starting at the top, clockwise, are some of the items used in placing the image on the litho stone; litho pencil, a straight pen, a ruling pen, a can of oil-based liquid ink, a snake-slip stone, a razor blade, and, at the lower right, some needles and a pointed Exacto-knife for scraping. At the lower center are a jar of liquid tusche and a block of solid tusche with some brushes. At top left are a selection of litho crayons of varying hardness.

The wash textures in this color litho by Castellon are defined be delicate crayon work.

stone, after the zinc has been sensitized. You may sketch your drawing on the stone with non-greasy pastel or sanguine chalk. A carbon sheet may be made by rubbing a piece of tracing paper with pastel or colored chalk, smoothing it with the side of your hand, and tracing through your original drawing with the carbon sheet facing the stone.

To create white lines in a black area or to erase portions of a form after it is on the stone, place a piece of cellophane or acetate over the offending part, then rub the end of a brush or any sharpened piece of wood over the acetate. The smooth surface will lift off the greasy crayon where you apply the pressure.

To achieve wash effects, the most commonly used material is lithographic tusche, which is a greasy substance dissolved in turpentine or emulsified with water-soluble

With a brush dipped in liquid tusche you can produce tones from deep black to delicate washes.

fibers of the paper enough to make it limp. If it gets too wet it may dissolve the crayon textures, so be careful. When the paper is pliable enough put it in position on the stone, which will be more receptive to the crayon if it is warmed in advance. Put several damp blotters or paper on top, put the tympan over all, and run it through the press several times with strong pressure.

TRANSFER LITHOGRAPHS

The method used to obtain textures is essentially the one that is used to make transfers of drawings, except that any drawing you make is liable to be more sensitive and delicate than a rubbing and to require more careful preparation. You may draw with greasy crayons on a variety of papers, depending upon your needs, but thin, tough papers are best. Remember that any greasy mark will transfer, even though you may not expect it. You may use tusche, but not the water-soluble kind, because it may blur or smudge. Use the turpentine-soluble tusche. It is possible to buy commercially prepared transfer paper such as Everdamp, which is excellent. Most transfer papers have been sized with albumen, starch, or gum solutions on one surface, which makes a very delicate crayon drawing transfer very well to the stone. However, the uncoated papers have the advantage of permitting immediate retouching of the transferred image, after it is placed on the stone. The coated papers desensitize those areas where the gum coat touches the stone, requiring a more complicated retouching procedure. When using any paper, however, the transfer will work better if the paper is limp and slightly damp, and the stone grained with a smooth surface. Some artists prefer warm stones to cool stones, but transfers will work on both, making it a matter of personal preference. Several passes through the press should transfer the image from the paper to the stone or

A leaf may be inked with liquid tusche and placed on a clean piece of board or paper. A clean large roller will receive the ink from the leaf. Many other textured items may be inked. *Below:* The impression from the roller is transferred to the sensitive stone. This roller is plastic, with a 2½" diameter and an 8-inch circumference.

plate. Naturally, the image will be reversed on the stone, only to print in its original position on the final impression from the stone; therefore, you may letter or write on your drawing as you wish and it will print correctly, an advantage over the direct method of drawing on the stone itself.

In all the preceding methods it is important to leave enough margin around the image to allow room for the scraper bar of the press. This bar requires a minimum of 1½″, although 2″ is better, particularly at the ends where the scraper starts and ends its pressure.

Etching the Stone

There are several types of etch used in lithography. The basic first etch is made from gum arabic (which can be obtained in lump or powdered form) mixed with water until it is the consistency of heavy cream or maple syrup, to make a quantity of about four ounces. If this solution is dirty, strain it through cheesecloth. Add to it enough nitric acid, technical grade, to make a medium strength etch. About 20 to 25 drops should be enough. As each drawing is different, it is not possible to make an inflexible formula. Delicate drawing requires less acid than strong, dark images.

Before applying the etch, dust a small amount of talcum powder (french chalk is the base for some powders) over the drawn image on the stone. Remove the excess with a pad of cheesecloth. Try a bit of the etch in the margin to check its strength; if it foams as soon as it touches the

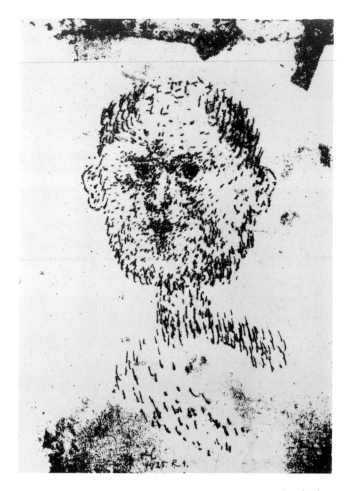

Paul Klee
Head of a man
Lithograph 8¾″ x 6″
Collection Richard Anuszkiewicz

KISTLER ETCH TABLE

(Proportion of acid to 1 ounce gum arabic)

QUALITY OF DRAWING	YELLOW STONE			LIGHT GREY STONE			DARK GREY STONE		
	Drops nitric acid	Drops phosphoric acid	Grains tannic acid	Drops nitric acid	Drops phosphoric acid	Grains tannic acid	Drops nitric acid	Drops phosphoric acid	Grains tannic acid
Very Delicate	0	0	6	0	0	6	3	2	8
Delicate	4	3	5	5	3	5	8	4	6
Light	6	4	6	10	4	6	13	5	6
Medium	12	5	6	15	5	6	18	5	6
Heavy	15	5	6	18	5	6	20	5	6

STANDARD ETCH TABLE

	Ounces Gum Arabic	Drops Nitric Acid
Weak	1	6-12
Moderate	1	13-18
Strong	1	19-26
Very Strong	1	27-33

Paper for Lithography

Good, all rag, smooth, hard-finished paper is best for printing lithographs. Avoid using wood-pulp paper, except for working proofs. There are many fine European sheets available, such as Arches wove, Rives BFK, Rives lightweight and heavyweight, Basingwerk heavy, Fabriano text and cover, Classico hard finish, and Umbria. Domestic American papers that are usable include Strathmore, water color, kid finish or hot pressed, Beckett cover (part rag content), Mohawk text (for proofs), and many other machine-made rag-content papers. Japanese papers are generally soft and have little sizing; therefore, they tend to "pick" or "fluff", leaving tiny particles of fiber in the ink. However, some of these papers are so handsome that they are used despite their shortcomings, including Kochi, Okawara, Shogun, Goyu, Masa, and Moriki (which is made in many beautiful colors). Almost no paper is handmade any more, except the Japanese stock, but the essentials are rag content or long-fibered plant material, no latent acid left to rot the fibers, and a smooth enough finish to pick up all the textures from the stone or zinc plate. Don't be afraid to try new papers; they give variety and texture to your images.

Dampening the Paper

Your paper should be prepared in advance for this moment. The best proofs are taken from damp paper, although adequate proofs can be taken on dry smooth stock, such as Basingwerk or index paper. To dampen a few sheets you may sponge some water over one side of each sheet, stack them, and place them under a blotter, with a weighted board on top to help the moisture soak evenly through the stack of moistened sheets. The fibers should be soft and pliant but not soaking wet, as excess moisture may interfere with the transmission of image from stone to paper. If you are in a hurry it is possible to immerse a few sheets in a tray of water for a few minutes, then put the sheets between blotters and roll out all the excess moisture you can. This is the same method used when printing etchings, but the paper should be more thoroughly blotted for lithography.

To dampen a large number of sheets for printing an edition or for class work in a workshop, a damp box should be constructed. One is easily made from 1" by 6" pine stock and ¼" plywood or pressed board for a bottom. Line the box with vinyl or sheet plastic, leaving enough plastic to fold over and wrap completely around the stack of paper. Put the paper in the box, dampen every other sheet with a wet sponge, and cover the stack with the plastic. Place a plywood sheet on the bundle, with a weight on top. After 10 to 12 hours the moisture should permeate each sheet evenly. A little experimenting will tell you how much water is enough for each type of paper you use. Do not leave paper in the damp box too long, or mildew will form.

The Press

The usual press has several basic parts: a frame holding a traveling bed that moves back and forth transporting the

DAMP BOX FOR PAPER

weight

¾" Plywood top covered with vinyl

cut top smaller than box

1" x 6" wood sides plywood bottom covered with vinyl

Damping a plate with a sponge at the Atelier Desjobert.

Rolling up a stone with a leather roller to bring up the black. Atelier Desjobert.

The greased tympan sheet is placed on a packing board which cushions the scraper bar pressure. The dampened rag paper is under all, on top of the freshly inked stone. Atelier Desjobert.

stone or plate, a yoke that holds the scraper box and scraper bar, and some sort of mechanism to bring the stone into tight contact with the scraper bar. There are several variations, all of which are efficient and practical, and the selection of one press over another is a matter of availability or individual preference. An etching press with an unwarped bed can be used to print zinc plate lithographs, but good quality of impression is more difficult to obtain from it than from a lithograph press.

The bed of a litho press is usually covered with linoleum or a smooth sheet of zinc or soft steel, or occasionally masonite or pressed wood. It should be kept clean and free of lumps or chips of any kind. The pressure exerted on a stone is very strong and they do crack and break, especially if there are irregularities in the bed or in the stone itself.

The stone is pulled under the scraper bar with the lubricated tympan sheet aiding the sliding movement. This is a typical French press from the Atelier Desjobert.

Printing the Lithograph

To pull the first proofs from a stone, you should have your inking slab in convenient proximity to the press, and your supply of dampened paper should be at hand. After you have rolled up the stone or plate to what seems to be the proper position, place a sheet of paper on the stone, without dragging or smudging the surface. Put a blotter or newsprint sheet on it, and then place the greased tympan sheet on top. The tympan can be an old zinc sheet or a piece of fiberboard. It must be greased with vaseline or heavy grease to let the scraper bar move across it.

Push the entire bed under the scraper until the scraper bar is directly over the leading margin of the stone. Lower the bar that raises the bed and stone into contact with the leather-covered scraper bar. Turn the handle that works the gears, travelling the bed under the scraper. Stop the press when the scraper reaches the other margin of the stone. Do not run the bed too far or the scraper will drop off the edge of the stone.

Raise the lever that releases the pressure. Lift off the tympan sheet and the blotter and, finally, carefully pull the dampened litho paper off the stone. This is your first proof. It is usually too light, because the inked image has to be

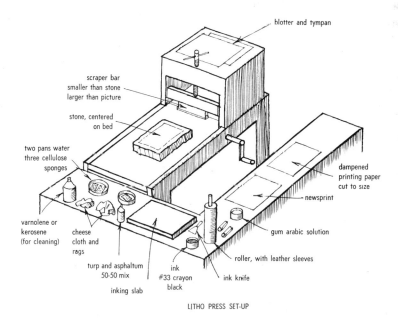

LITHO PRESS SET-UP

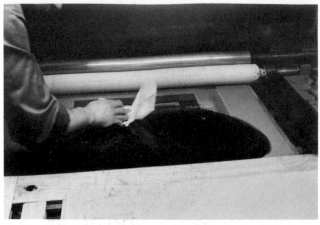

A plate is washed with mineral spirits to remove the old ink before printing on one of the power presses at the Bank Street Atelier in New York City.

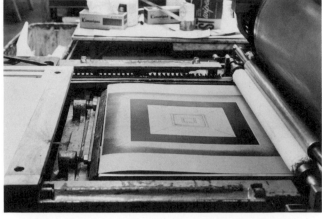

The plate has been reinked prior to printing. Bank Street Atelier.

One of the French power-driven flatbed litho presses at Bank Street Atelier. Note the inking distribution rollers necessary to provide thorough even inking in one pass of the stone.

built up slowly. Damp the stone and roll it again, pulling proofs until the image on paper is at the proper strength. At this point you must evaluate the print and decide if it fulfills your expectations, a rare occurrence. If it does, the edition can be printed. It is more likely that corrections or additions will have to be made.

If you can not make changes at once, you must "close" the stone again with a coat of gum arabic and wrap it before putting it into the rack. Whenever the stone is going to be left for any length of time, even overnight, it should be gummed. If left for many months, the ink must be refreshed periodically to prevent it from drying out. To prolong the life of the ink put a sheet of brown kraft paper onto the freshly gummed stone. Rub all the air bubbles out. This cover will keep the ink protected for a year or more, but even this is not permanent protection.

Corrections and Additions

When you are ready to make corrections and additions, the stone should be opened by removing the old ink and the gum. The gum dissolves in water, and the ink in turpentine. Do not dissolve the ink unless there is a thin coating of gum over the stone to protect the open areas. Sensitize the clean stone by brushing on a saturated solution of powdered alum. This is called a counteretch. Leave it on for three or four minutes, wash it off, and dry the stone. You can now add crayon, tusche, or textures to your images.

If you want to remove small lines or shapes, scrape them with a sharp knife or a razor blade. If you want to remove areas and then redraw in the same spot, you can regrain the stone in that place with a snake slip, a pumice block, or some carborundum and a small sharpening stone. Wash off the grit and sludge with plenty of water and redraw the new image. Do not grind the stone too deeply, or it will not print properly later on. After making all your additions, you must etch the new work in the same manner as the first drawing on the stone.

Corrections on stone are easy, but corrections on the zinc plate are not. Zinc will not stand much scraping or regrinding, but with care, some work can be done. Gum the plate and dry it. Remove all unwanted work with potassium hydroxide brushed over the areas to be erased. Leave this on for about 5 minutes, then wash off with running water. The

After a correction has been made on an "open" stone it is regummed before printing can resume. Atelier Desjobert.

The edges of the drawing may be straightened by using a snake slip, an abrasive stone, against a straight-edged ruler.

area must be resensitized with alum and water and washed off after 3 or 4 minutes.

To sensitize aluminum plates, use 1 part of oxalic acid to 20 parts of water. To erase areas from aluminum plates, use carbon tetrachloride (a dangerous chemical because the fumes are very poisonous) or gasoline (also dangerous in any workshop).

Color Registry in Lithography

Normally each color in a color litho needs its own stone and must be printed in correct register with all the others in order to complete the image. There are several methods to register lithographs, all basically very simple.

The use of pins or needles set into two wooden handles is one of the simplest ways to help register the proofs. In the margins of your first stone or plate draw two small crosses, well away from the image area. Ink the stone full strength and pull a proof on smooth paper, including your register crosses. Place this proof face down on your new stone and run it through the press. The inked proof will transfer the image to the new stone. Wash the stone with a gasoline-soaked rag. Be careful, this is an inflammable and hazardous procedure! The ink will be removed, but it will leave a faint stain on the stone that can be used as a guide for the second color. Now you can finish the second color image in correct juxtaposition to the first. If there is to be more than one color you can transfer each image onto the succeeding stones, in sequence, to place the images in position as they are finished.

To pull the proofs in register, take a proof of the first stone on your paper. Puncture holes in the centers of the register crosses, turn the sheet over, place the needles through the holes, hold the paper with needles in place (which may require two people with a large stone) and place the paper over the next stone (which, of course, must be prepared and inked with the correct color). Keep the paper away from the surface of the image until you can place the needles into the register crosses on the second stone. Now let the taut paper slide down the needles until it touches the stone, in register and ready for the printing of the second. In printing the edition, you will print all the prints

Jasper Johns
"Fragment—According to What-Bent Stencil"—1971
Color lithograph 27½" x 20"
© copyright 1971 Gemini G.E.L.

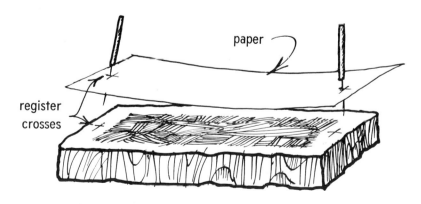

paper

register crosses

PIN HOLE
REGISTER
FOR LITHO
STONES

Rubbing-up Printing Area on Multimetal Plates

Rubbing-up ink is supplied as liquid or in a spray can. While the plate is wet with counteretch, rub in this ink with a rag until the copper takes the ink completely.

Now the gum etch may be brushed or wiped on. Lithographic suppliers make a mohair-covered plastic pad for this purpose that works admirably. The gum etch can be made from gum arabic with one part phosphoric acid to 30 parts of gum solution. Wipe to a thin film and let dry. The rub-up ink should be removed with varnoline and asphaltum solution and the gum etch removed from the plate with clean water; the plate is now ready for printing. A scraper-type litho press may be used and so may an intaglio press. The thin plates print very well on etching presses, using a blotter between the felts and the back of the printing paper. Large editions are more easily printed on multimetal plates than on single-metal litho plates because scumming is removed with little trouble and the physical separation of the image from the non-image area makes a consistent edition possible.

Paper-Plate Lithography

An inexpensive and simple substitute for a litho stone or a zinc plate is the paper plate manufactured by Anthony Ensink of Chicago. These plates are easy to draw upon, using grease or wax crayons and tusche; because they are paper they may be carried easily, used as outdoor sketching paper and, with little effort, can be printed on a variety of presses.

The quality of tone obtained does not equal the tonal variety yielded by stone or zinc, but the simplicity of the process may be attractive. The plate must be moistened between each inking with a proprietary solution called Litho-Sketch plate solution, which is applied with a cotton pad or sponge. The ink must be a greasy litho ink and should be rolled over the surface with a thin film and image built up by three or four printings, as in stone or zinc lithography. Write to Anthony Ensink for further information. See list of suppliers.

White Lines on a Black Background

Draw on a sensitized stone or plate with a gum solution to which has been added some watercolor (any color but black); it is added only that you may see what you are doing when you draw. Draw with brush, pen, or stick dipped in this gum solution, or soak fabrics or texturing materials in the solution. It will print as white after the process is completed. After the gum has dried, paint over the area with a heavy solution of tusche or litho ink dissolved in turps. The gummed areas will reject the greasy ink and can be washed out with water. The stone must be etched with a fairly strong etch and the litho process followed as previously described.

DRY LITHOGRAPHY

A new planographic printing process has been under experimentation by Harry Hoehn at the C. W. Post Graphic Workshop in Brookville, Long Island. This method uses a chemical coating that repels ink in much the same manner as the dampened litho stone repels ink, although no water is necessary in the new process.

The materials needed are:

236 Dispersion (manufactured by Dow Chemical)

Solvent for Dispersion (Dow VM & P Naptha or gasoline in an emergency)

Two brayers or rollers in good condition (One for dispersion, one for ink)

Support or base plate (a grained litho plate, all-rag matboard, oak tag, or hard-surfaced cardboard or illustration board)

Litho ink

Printing paper (Hosho, Troya, Mulberry, or other smooth-surface papers)

Glass or plastic slabs for rolling ink

Solvent for ink (varnoline, mineral spirits)

There are many ways to use this new process. We will describe several approaches. An interested artist will naturally pursue those methods that satisfy his creative needs.

The brayer can be used to spread the dispersion liquid evenly over the plate, in a flat film. The dispersion repels the ink so that a plate covered in this manner will accept no ink at all. It is not until the coating is scratched, abraded, or removed in some other manner, exposing the base plate underneath, that the image can be made printable. If the artist likes the normal white surface of paper or the litho stone, this method may be the most suitable. After the dispersion is applied, a silicone rubber compound is rolled evenly over the plate. It must be allowed to dry, which takes about 5 hours. The drying can be accelerated by a hot plate, on low heat, or a low oven (250°F.). Do not overheat. The coating should be completely dry before printing. The design or drawing can be scratched through the coating with needles, razor blades, knives, sandpaper, or any sharp implement. The dried coating can be removed with Dow VM and P Naptha, which can be brushed on and then blotted up. You will have a positive image, with your drawing printing as a black and the coated plate resisting the ink and therefore printing as white.

The Transfer Method

The dispersion may be rolled onto fabric, metal grating, leaves, or other textured material and then be transferred to the plate, where it must dry and be printed as usual. All sorts of textures may be devised; it should be possible to roll a film of dispersion on to a photoengraver's halftone plate and then transfer that image to another paper before placing it on the plate. It will print as a white or negative impression, but it will not be reversed.

Harry Hoehn has floated the emulsion on water, stirred or agitated the surface, and then submerged the support plate into the water, transferring the image to the plate. Those plates with strong patterns of emulsion seem to be most successful, and they make good background plates.

The Lift Process

It is possible to make a lift-ground drawing using the dispersion as the covering ground. This procedure enables the artist to draw directly with crayon or tusche and have his drawing act as the positive printing image.

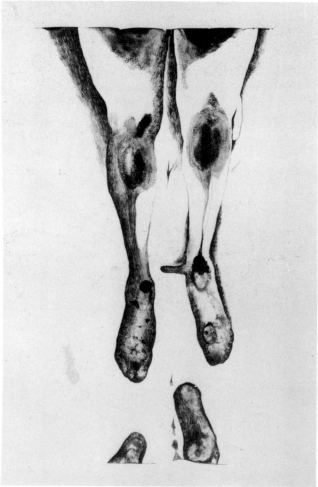

Clean the support plate with acetone and let it dry. Draw with #1 litho crayon or paint with tusche onto the plate. Now roll the dispersion evenly over the entire plate. When it has thoroughly dried, the dispersion may be lifted from the plate where it covered your drawing by rubbing it gently with a benzine-soaked rag. The dispersion cannot stick to the greasy drawing, which will therefore be revealed. If you must touch up with dispersion emulsion, allow the full drying time before attempting to print. If you have not deposited enough crayon or tusche, your "lift" may not be complete; work with a heavy deposit of crayon for best results.

Because the dispersion repels most substances it does not accept preliminary drawings easily. A chalk transfer will work well, however, and can be rubbed off when the scratching is completed. A felt marking pen will make a faint image usable as a guide for complex images.

One of the great advantages of this new medium is that it allows the artist to remove unwanted portions of a design by painting them out with a coating of the dispersion liquid.

Printing

When the plate is thoroughly dry, it is ready to print. Roll up a quantity of litho ink on a slab with a good-quality brayer and start to ink the plate. At first the ink will stick at random but a continued inking will produce an even coating of the image, while the dispersion will resist the ink and keep the background clean. The plate must be placed on a smooth even surface during the inking. Place the paper directly on the plate. It may be rubbed or burnished directly with a rice spoon, a door handle, or other implement, but an etching or litho press makes for a much more efficient printing procedure. If an etching press is used, only one thin blanket or a couple of blotters are necessary as packing. Use a clean newsprint between the back of the paper and the blanket to keep the blanket clean. Clean the plate after printing with benzine, but do not rub the plate or the dispersion may be removed. Blot the plate dry.

Colors may be used, of course, and one of the good qualities of this method is the ease with which you may make color plates for complex color prints.

For further information on this process write to:

Harry Hoehn
C. W. Post Graphic Workshop
Fine Art Center
C. W. Post College
Brookville, Long Island, N.Y.

Marisol Escobar
"1 Trial Proof May 1971"
Lithograph 48" x 31¾"
Whitney Museum

PHOTOGRAPHIC TECHNIQUES

INTRODUCTION

The images that photography can capture have caused many artists to develop techniques designed to exploit the photographic process. These techniques are suitable for many areas of printmaking, such as lithography on metal plates, etching on zinc or copper, photo-silk screen and relief etching on metal plates. There are many approaches to photography in printmaking, and they vary from straightforward reproduction of photographs, such as Andy Warhol's screen prints *Jackie* and *Marilyn*, through Robert Rauschenberg's more complex lithographs to Joe Tilson's and Eduardo Paolozzi's prints combining screen printing and lithography.

It is possible to use images on photoengraving plates made by a commercial engraver by relief rolling the image with a good quality brayer and then transferring that image to an etching or a litho plate. The photoengraving can also be printed directly into your print. Negative effects will be produced by intaglio inking and wiping followed by printing the plate through an etching press. Plastic mats, electrotypes, and commercially prepared litho plates can be incorporated into the print, either directly or by the transfer method. Collage plates can accomodate a variety of photographically produced images (See Lindner's *The Parrot Lady*).

However, if an artist wants to make his own photographic plates he can use a number of different methods to place the image onto the plate or stencil. We will describe several processes and note the advantages and disadvantages of each.

THE TRANSPARENT POSITIVE

(Acetate, Paper, Glass, and the Like)

In many cases it will be advisable to have your image put on transparent film (usually Mylar or Estar based for dimensional stability). Other transparent sheets can be used, however, with good results. For instance, you can draw with any opaque ink or pencil on a thin, good-quality tracing paper to make a transparent positive through which light can pass

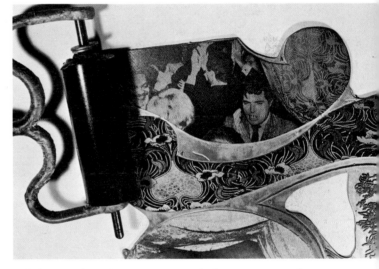

A half-tone plate, from a commercial photo engravers shop, is inked with a 6-inch plastic composition roller. A thin even film of ink is necessary.

Below: The impression from the half-tone engraving is transferred to the stone from an 8-inch plastic roller.

A zinc plate lithograph may be printed in an etching press with excellent results. A student of Jack Sonenberg at Pratt Institute in Brooklyn is about to place the dampened paper on the plate.

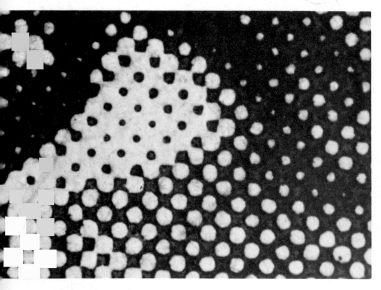

The half-tone dot breaks up the picture into thousands of black or white dots of varying size, depending on the depth of tonality in the original copy.

to expose the sensitized plate or stencil. You can also use cellophane or acetate as a base and paint or draw on it with non-crawl paint, ink, or crayon. There is a prepared acetate sheet that will accept water-based paint without bubbling or shrinking. You can even paint or draw on glass to make a transparent positive.

In general, two types of positives are used in photographic work. A line shot is one in which all the image is translated into black or white lines or masses. The film used is not sensitive to greys and renders them as either black or white, depending upon their density. Solid areas are flat. Greys must be achieved by texture or a network of fine lines.

The second photographic process, called half-tone, renders grey values by breaking up the areas into black and white dots of varying sizes. A finely ruled screen is placed between the art work and the film, separating the picture into thousands of tiny squares, each one registering as a single dot, of a size commensurate with its grey value. The screens range in fineness from a low of 40 or 45 to a normal high of 133 lines to the inch. Some screens go up to 300 lines, but they are too fine for normal commercial printing. Screens are quite expensive and must be handled with care, as one scratch can ruin the ruled surface. The coarser screens are easier to print. A delicate wash drawing or a subtle grey photographic tone will reproduce in correct values, by virtue of the tiny dots of black. These half-tone dots can be seen in an enlarging glass.

Positive Transparencies with the Copy Camera

Although a copy camera setup is not inexpensive (a good 14″ by 17″ camera costs about $2000), it is the most efficient instrument for producing consistently good transparencies to be used in photographic printmaking. These films can be used in many ways and in many processes, such as screen printing, lithography, intaglio etching, and relief etching. A trained technician is desirable to help the artist achieve the best results from his material.

The step-by-step procedure of making transparencies will be described, using commonly available materials, such as Kodalith Ortho #3 film, no. 4556, which can be used for both line and half-tone shots (Gevaert 082 Film can also be used). Exposures range from 20 seconds to 1 minute, depending on the intensity of the lights and the density of the material to be photographed. The half-tone shot needs a longer exposure than the line shot. This film is sensitive to yellow light and needs a red safelight in the darkroom. The photographs show the procedures. When the first film has been developed, washed, and dried, you will have a negative transparency, with the originally black lines now showing as white on a black background.

To make a positive transparency, place the negative back on the camera in the horizontal position, on top of another piece of Kodalith Ortho #3, 4556. Place a piece of clear glass on top of both, if necessary, to assure good contact. Expose for 30 seconds in yellow light. Develop, stop, fix, and wash as described above. This exposure will make the positive transparency, with the lines that were black in the original now black in the transparency. This exposure can be made in a

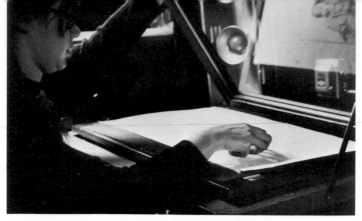

The copy to be photographed is placed in the copy board vacuum frame. (Line drawing by Al Blaustein.)

The copy board is sealed and the vacuum pump operated to insure that the drawing has good contact with the glass.

The copy is placed in a vertical position by Donna Moran, technician at Pratt Institute in Brooklyn.

Exposure and focus are computed and the camera is adjusted. The lens opening is set.

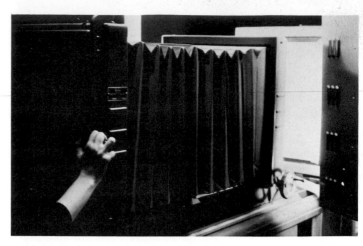

Both ends of the bellows may be adjusted. Focus can be checked on the ground glass at the back of camera.

Two vertical rows of lights are positioned to properly illuminate the copy.

Below: The film holder (back) of the camera is lowered. When film is inserted, only a red safelight may be used. The light at the top of this photo is a yellow light and is used for a "bump" exposure on half-tones to extend the grey scale. For this procedure the back is opened flat. This step completes the exposure.

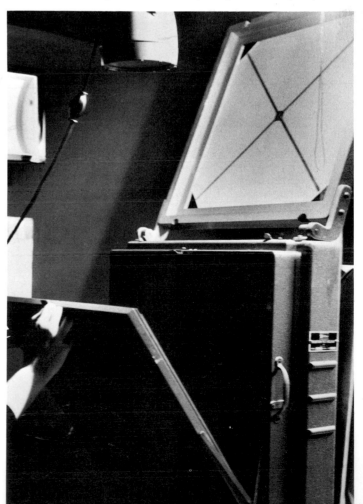

Still in red safelight, the film is inserted into the developer. Kodalith liquid developer, 1 part A solution, 1 part B solution, 6 cups of water at 70°, for 2½ minutes average time.

From developer to stop bath (4 ounces of acetic acid to a gallon of water). Then into 3M Rapid Fix or Kodak Liquid Fix Concentrate with hardener for three times the length of time it takes to clear. Then wash in water at 70° for 10 minutes.

Below: Hang film to dry after it has been squeegeed to remove excess water. This process has produced a negative transparency.

vacuum frame, if available, or on a table top with any available high-intensity light. You will now have, on transparent film, a photographic image that can be used in a variety of media.

Positive Transparencies with an Enlarger

Small photographic negatives can be enlarged onto Kodalith Ortho #3 film, up to the greatest size the enlarger can handle. A certain amount of detail is always lost in excessive blow-ups, and a sharp edge is difficult to achieve. The enlarger should have a condenser system to concentrate the light rather than diffuse it, and the lens should be a high-resolution lens that can produce good definition. 35 mm. or 2¼"-square negatives will lose sharpness when enlarged 10 times or more. The Kodalith film will translate certain types of negatives that do not rely upon tonal gradations without a halftone screen, with occasionally unusual effects. Of course, if you use a normal negative your enlarged transparency on Kodalith will be a positive and will yield a positive intaglio plate or, conversely, a negative-relief etching plate. Film negatives exposed onto an etching plate will yield a negative intaglio or a positive relief etching plate.

PHOTO-ETCHING

In general there are two approaches to photo-etching a zinc or copper plate to prepare it for intaglio or relief printing. The first method involves sensitizing the plate yourself with a solution that will react to light. The second method involves buying a presensitized plate from a commercial photoengravers supply house. Both methods are suitable, depending on your location and the quantity of plates which you consume. The commercially prepared plates have a uniform coating that gives high-quality results. They must be stored carefully, in a cool place, and should be used within a few months. The additional cost per plate is moderate (about $1 extra per plate). The self-prepared plates can be made as you choose, and the chemicals have a shelf life of about a year. Unless you prepare the plate properly you may not get results as good as from a commercially sensitized plate. We will describe both processes.

Self-Sensitized Zinc or Copper Plates

The materials needed to sensitize zinc or copper plates include Kodak KPR chemicals, which cost approximately $25:

> 1 qt. KPR Photo Resist
> 1 gal. KPR Photo Resist Developer
> 1 qt. KPR Photo Resist Dye

Also needed are:

> Zinc, copper, or brass plates
> Stainless steel trays
> Acetone
> Webril-wipe or lint-free cloth

The plate should be thoroughly cleaned with acetone and rinsed well with water. Avoid touching the surface. A clean

Pravoslav Sovak
"With a Tank, August 21, 1968"
Photo Intaglio 16¾" x 12¾"
Pratt Graphics Center
Photo Eric Pollitzer

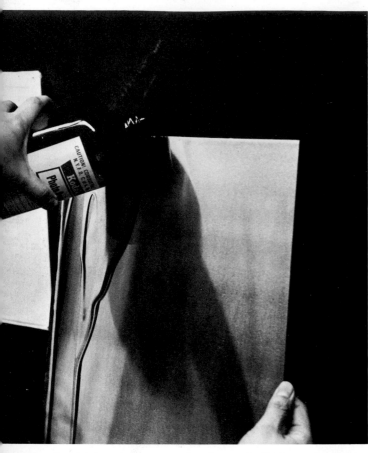

In a darkened room pour the photo-resist fluid over the plate so that it is covered with a thin, even coat.

Below: The plate should be standing in a tray to catch the excess solution for reuse. Let the plate dry.

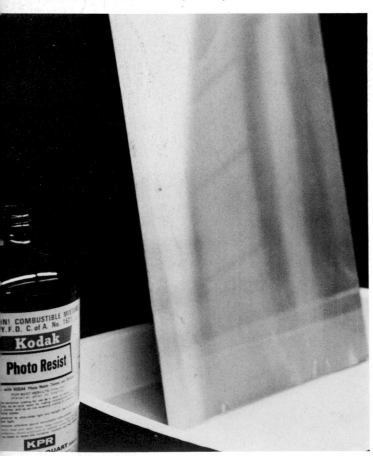

surface is essential, and all grease or dust must be removed. Dry by heat, over hotplate or in oven.

In the darkroom, under a yellow safe light, place the clean plate in a clean tray in a vertical position and pour the Photo Resist over it. The liquid should cover the plate evenly and drain into the tray. The plate can be removed from the tray and leaned against a wall while the remainder of the resist can be funneled back into the bottle. The plate will dry in about 10 to 15 minutes.

Still under the safe light, in the darkroom, place the plate face up on the exposure table, with the film transparency on top. (See section on preparation of transparencies). Cover it with clean glass, either in sheet form or in a vacuum table. The emulsion side of the film should touch the emulsion side of the plate for sharpest results. With a carbon arc lamp, exposure will range from 2 to 4 minutes. With a group of four #1 photoflood lamps in reflectors, exposure could be as long as 20 minutes, but normally it will take somewhat less time.

Remove the plate from the exposing table and slide it into the tray with KPR Photo Resist developer. Develop for 2 or 3 minutes without agitation, then wash the plate with cold water. Pour a coat of KPR Photo Resist dye over the plate while it is in a vertical position, and let it drain for 30 seconds, or submerge the plate in a tray. Place the plate under running water and wash it until the image is visible. The developer can be rebottled and stored in the darkroom.

Now the plate can be etched. Use a weak etching solution (12:1), of nitric acid for zinc or copper and of Dutch Mordant for copper or brass. Ferric chloride is good for very fine biting of copper but must act with the plate face-down in the acid. See section on biting.

To remove the resist prior to printing, wash the plate with lacquer thinner. Bevel the edges and pull the first proofs. Half-tone plates require delicate wiping, and coarse screens work better than fine screens.

Presensitized Zinc or Copper Plates

You may want to use presensitized plates from a local photoengraver's supply house. We use H. Pitman and Sons in Secaucus, New Jersey. These materials may also be obtained from Ball Metal and Chemical Co. in Brooklyn, New York. We use Micro-Metal presensitized plates and the developing solution is, naturally enough, Presensitized Micro-Metal Hi-Speed Developer. Also needed is Presensitized Micro-Metal Print Cleaner Solution. Webril Wipes are convenient to apply the solution. A hotplate is necessary as is some mineral spirits or varnoline.

In the darkroom (yellow safe light) place the presensitized plate on the exposure table face up. Put the film transparency on top of the plate, emulsion side down. Cover with glass or close the vacuum table. If you use an arc lamp, the exposure should be about 3 minutes. Photoflood exposure will take much longer. The light will harden the emulsion where it strikes it. The rest of the emulsion will be softened and washed away by the developer, leaving these areas open to the attack of the acid.

When the exposure is finished place the plate into the developer, either in a tray or in a vertical stainless steel tank.

Place the plate, face up, on the exposure table. Put your photo positive with the desired image on top of the plate. In this case a vacuum frame holds all the elements together, but a piece of plate glass could be sufficient, if handled carefully.

Expose the plate. Normally several minutes are required with photoflood lamps. Carbon arc lamps require only a fraction of the time but are expensive.

Develop the photosensitive emulsion on the plate by immersing it in the developer. Stainless steel trays are best. Some plastics are softened by the photo-resist developer.

Now stand the plate in another tray and pour photo-resist dye over it so that an even coat drains over the surface. This will stain the developed resist so that the image will be visible.

Wash the plate under running water. The exposed sections will have hardened upon exposure to light and will be insoluble in water.

Below: Bite the plate. It may be aquatinted or retouched first, if desired. (Herb Youner at Pratt Graphic Art Center.)

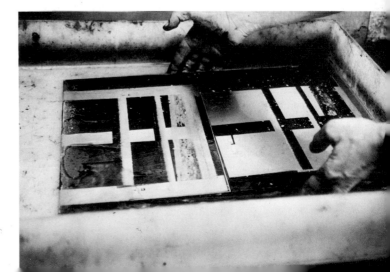

doesn't affect any part of the ground which received adequate exposure. The dissolved residue and developer are sprayed off with a gentle aerated spray and the image dyed with KPR dye for better visibility.

"The plate can be etched in the manner normal to any etching procedure. I have obtained best results with 42° Be ferric chloride heated to 100°F., suspending and agitating the plate upside down with the aid of tape handles on the back for small plates and C clamps at the edge for large plates. I use about 5 stopping-out steps and a total final etching time of around 24 minutes.

"The prime advantage of the photosensitive ground procedure is its enormous, almost hair-raising flexibility. Not only can a drawing be transferred at any or all stages of its development, but in any combinations with other drawings, or even high-contrast photographic positive transparencies, all this either simultaneously or at different etching stages—and I have only begun to explore the possibilities.

"This has been a fairly casual explanation about a very exacting set of procedures, and anyone interested can find all the necessary details in the two Kodak pamphlets P-79 and P-125 ($1.00 each, Department 454, Eastman Kodak Co., Rochester, N.Y. 14650)."

PHOTO LITHOGRAPHY

There are two basic methods of achieving the photographic image in lithography. One procedure requires the purchase of presensitized plates from a commercial supplier. We will describe this process after we present the other method, which requires the artist to prepare the surface himself by placing the photosensitive emulsion on the plate.

Sensitizing the Plates

It is relatively easy to sensitize your own zinc plates for photo lithography. The plates may be purchased from suppliers who stock the .012" or heavier thickness that the artist-lithographer requires. Most commercial offset plates are thinner and may curl or buckle in the printing process, unless they are firmly adhered to a smooth support. The materials needed for preparing the plates are the ST chemicals and ST plates. If you use plates of another brand, they must be absolutely clean and free of dust or grease.

Materials

ST Super D Powder   ST Wipes
ST Base Solution   2 Cellulose Sponges
Super D Developer   Super D.A.G.E.

Opposite:
Peter Milton
from "The Jolly Corner" 1971
Etching and photo-etching 14¾" x 10"
Aquarius Press, Baltimore

The work was begun with a sheet of d'arches cover on which had been printed in black by traditional hand zinc lithography a random selection of circular shapes. The sheet, folded, cut, punctured and re-assembled into a construction, was mounted on the face of a copy board, carefully illuminated to deepen the shadows and tonal scale. A Robertson Overhead Graphic Arts Process Camera with 150 line elliptical dot contact screen (gray, Kodak) was used for photographing the halftone negative. Ortho type #3 film (Kodak) was used throughout.

From the original negative, two contact positives were made. The film negative and two positives were securely taped together to produce yet another contact for a visual montage with moires. A press plate was made from this negative. An outline drawn on acetate by hand with opaque ink was used for the flat color plate. Press plates were then made from the final film negative and the acetate drawing using 3M pre-sensitized S Plates. The images were burned in with an arc lamp and developed. Five hand drawn zinc plates (tusche) were prepared for the color runs, and all six plates were printed on d'arches cover on a ATF #26 off-set press.

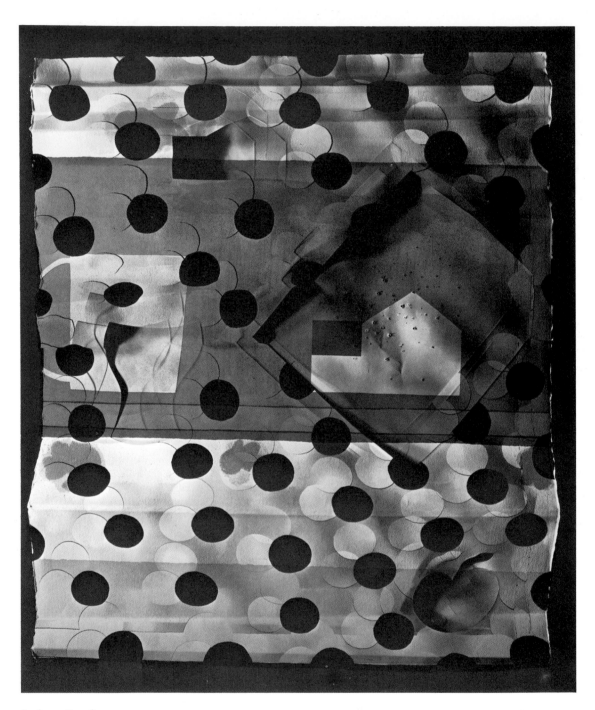

Andrew Stasik
"Still Life Landscape #5" 1969
Photo lithograph 24" x 20"
Courtesy of the artist

The process worked out by the artists and technicians at Pratt Graphics Center in New York requires that the steps be undertaken in subdued light, avoiding flourescent lights. Make the sensitizing solution by adding the ST Super D Powder to the Base Solution and shaking well until it is dissolved. This solution will keep for about two or three weeks. Pour the solution onto the plate and, with an ST wipe, coat the plate evenly, first in one direction, then in another, in overlapping strokes, until the plate is covered. Using a second wipe as a pad, polish the coating until it is smooth and dry. Keep the plate in subdued light until exposure. It should be used promptly.

Exposing the Plate

Put the plate on the exposure table or into the vacuum frame. If working on a table, use a rubber mat under the plate, then place the previously prepared film positive (see section on film transparencies) on top of the sensitized plate, emulsion to emulsion. Put a clean glass sheet on top of the transparency to insure good contact. Exposure can be made with a single photoflood lamp, 250 watts, in a reflector positioned about 18″ from the plate for 5 to 8 minutes. When using a vacuum frame and an arc lamp at a distance of 3 feet, you can cut exposure time to 2 to 3 minutes.

Developing the Plate

Still working in subdued light, prepare the Super D developer by shaking it vigorously. Pour some on the plate and spread it evenly over the surface with a damp sponge for about 2 minutes until the image has become an intense black. Rinse off the excess developer with water and clean the plate with a cotton swab. Now pour Super D.A.G.E., a gum etch, on the plate and spread evenly over the surface with a second sponge. Add a second application of D.A.G.E. and wipe it down with a cheesecloth pad, as is usual when gumming a plate. The plate is now ready for printing. If scumming appears, add one teaspoon of fountain solution to a pan of water, to use when plate is charged with ink.

Deletions and Corrections

Corrections are made on ST plates by using ST image remover. Using a Q-tip, rub it into the lacquer surface, then gum those areas. To make photographic additions to the plate, the entire process has to be repeated, from the sensitizing base solution through exposure, developing, gumming, and so on. A kit is available that allows you to resensitize areas with deletions. See list of suppliers.

The Presensitized Litho Plate

Plates coated with a light-sensitive emulsion may be purchased from a commercial lithographers' supply house, ready for exposure. They are relatively inexpensive and work very well. See list of suppliers. Additional necessary materials include subtractive plate developer and subtractive plate gum from Minnesota Mining & Mfg. Co. (Hereafter called 3M).

Exposing the Presensitized Plate

Place the plate on the exposure table or in the vacuum frame with the transparent film positive on top of it, emul-

Andy Stasik times a carbon-arc lamp exposure of one of his plates at the Pratt Institute workshop in Brooklyn. The sensitized plate has been positioned in the vacuum frame under a photographic positive of the image.

Robert Rauschenberg
"Sky Hook" 1969
Lithograph 42½" x 31½"
© Copyright 1969 Gemini G.E.L.

sion to emulsion. Cover it with a clean glass sheet if working on a table, or close the vacuum frame. With a carbon arc as the source of light, exposure time will vary from 20 seconds to 2 minutes. As carbon arc lamps vary in strength and the distance from the copy is critical (3 feet is average), you must run tests to determine the proper exposure time. Photo lamps take much longer to work and can require 5 minutes to expose a plate.

Developing the Presensitized Plate

Pour a puddle of Subtractive Plate Developer (from 3M) into the center of the plate and spread it evenly with a lint-free pad (Webril Wipes are good). Leave it on for 30 seconds and wipe off with the same pad. Rinse thoroughly with water. A spray attachment on the hose is convenient, and you may have to rub with your hand. The image should be visible at this point. After the plate has been rinsed pour on the S-gum (Subtractive Plate Gum) and spread it evenly with a pad or a sponge until a good even coat is achieved. This is the gum and etch process. Let it dry and the plate is ready for the initial roll-up and printing.

PHOTO SCREEN PRINTS

Direct Emulsion Methods

Several procedures can be used for preparing photographic screens for printing. The self-prepared screen, for which the artist places the emulsion directly on the screen, is easy and cheap to produce. However, even though it is possible to remove an emulsion from all synthetic fabrics, such as nylon, polyester, stainless steel, it is not easy to remove an emulsion from silk. Another disadvantage of the direct method of making screens is in its timing; the dichromate sensitizer frequently used to make the emulsion must be used the same day it is mixed, and the screens remain sensitive only a few hours. Because of this disadvantage, new emulsions have been developed that last longer than dichromate and enable the sensitized screens to be stored for weeks before exposure. In any case, the fabrics should be thoroughly cleaned and degreased before any photographic emulsions are placed on them.

Direct Method—Azocol Sensitizer

One process uses a nondichromate sensitizer, Azocol, manufactured by Colonial of East Rutherford, New Jersey.

Materials

Stretched nylon screen (wet nylon before stretching)
Azokleen Concentrate and Nylon scrub brush
Azocol R Direct Eulsion and Sensitizer
Azocol Blue Dye (optional)
Plastic Squeegee

Cleaning the Screen

Remove all grease, lint, dust, and the like by washing the screen. Ajax or other abrasive cleansers will work but may harm the screen or clog the mesh if not rinsed away. Screen washes such as Azokleen (1 part Azokleen Concentrate to 3 parts water) are more efficient. Scrub both sides of the wet screen with the brush and flush with hot water until all trace of the cleaner is removed. Let the screen dry in a dust-free area.

Coating the Screen

The sensitizer comes in powdered form; add water to the bottle and shake it until the sensitizer is dissolved. Pour this sensitizer into the basic emulsion and stir until thoroughly blended. Do not shake or whip it, as that may cause air bubbles that will encourage pinholes in the emulsion. If you want to tint the emulsion to see the image more clearly, add some of the blue dye at this time. The prepared emulsion can be used now or stored in a cool dark place for many weeks.

The plate has been developed and is now being washed with water to remove the excess developer. It may be necessary to rub it with a sponge or cotton to clean the plate.

The
LUNCH EDITION
Bela Lugosi Journal
THE OFFICIAL PUBLICATION OF THE AMERICAN BELA LUGOSI FAN CLUB
Vol. 1 — No. 1 48 *Joe Tucson 2/70* SUMMER - FALL, 1969

Special

MEMORIAL ISSUE

MISS POLICE
WORLD

**MISS POLICE
WORLD**

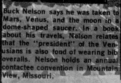

SOCIAL GREETING a bela monkey was recorded on motion picture film. When an acquaintance appears, lip-smacking (top, note protruding tongue) rapidly turns into an exaggerated grin is meant to demonstrate a lack of hostility.

Buck Nelson says he was taken to Mars, Venus, and the moon in a dome-shaped saucer. In a book about his travels, Nelson relates that the "president" of the Venusians is also fond of wearing bib overalls. Nelson holds an annual contactee convention in Mountain View, Missouri.

sions properly. Screens must be completely clean, degreased, and prepared to receive the emulsion. The emulsion should be sensitized by the addition of the dichromate on the same day it is to be used, as it should be discarded at the end of the working day. Screens should be exposed within several hours after sensitizing. The ammonium dichromate, usually supplied in crystal form, should be mixed with water in a ratio of 4 ounces of crystals to one quart of warm water. Add one part of this mixture to 5 parts of emulsion (Naz-dar's Indicote or Advance's Polycop are good) and stir until mixed. Mixing may be done in normal light, but the subsequent steps should be done in subdued light (yellow light is good).

Coating the Screen

Squeegee the emulsion over the outside of the screen (printing side), then turn it over and immediately place another coat or two of emulsion on the inside of the screen, using a plastic, stainless steel, or aluminum scraper coater. The screen should dry in the horizontal position.

When using a coarse screen (up to 16xx silk or 196 nylon) let the first coat dry, then squeegee another coat onto the outside of the screen. This second coat will give a more even screen coating to insure better contact between screen and printing stock. Let the screen dry, in the dark.

Exposure

Good contact is essential between the film positive and the screen. Exposure time under a carbon-arc lamp might average 2 minutes at 4 feet, and a vacuum frame would be the best device to insure the firm contact necessary for good exposure. A vacuum frame is best, of course, but a sheet of glass on top of the film will help if the vacuum is not available. A good level work surface is also essential, and a rubber mat will be a great convenience in this respect. Four photofloods with reflectors will usually suffice. Exposure time will vary from 3 to 8 minutes. Bulbs should be 18" to 36" from the film. Too much heat will ruin the dichromate. Try various exposures to test the strength of your lights.

Developing or Washing Out

Protect the screens from daylight or fluorescent light until they are washed out. First wet both sides of the screen with warm water (110°F.), mainly from the inside of the screen. Turn screen after it is three-quarters open and wash the outside of the screen. Work quickly and finish the wash with a cool-water rinse. Too much water may damage the softened emulsion. You may have to clean off the residue and scum with Scum-X (from Advance) or another manufacturer's product. Inspect the screen for pinholes, and block them and the edges of the screen with Water-Sol block-out before printing.

Opposite:
Joe Tilson
"Bela Lugosi Journal" 1969
Photo Screen Print 38¼" x 25"
Marlborough Graphics

Screens are exposed from underneath in this light box at Cooper Union Art School in New York City.

Carbon arc lamps in front of vacuum frame at Cooper Union.

Washing out a photographic emulsion with warm water spray. Cooper Union.

Below: A pinpoint warm water spray washes out the remaining bits of the photographic emulsion. The Art Center of Northern New Jersey.

weight mat board is not heavy enough, corrugated board or some of the new styrofoam boards are excellent because they are rigid and weigh very little; however, they are more expensive.

Measuring the Mat

The size of the mat should not be excessive. Three- to five-inch margins are fairly good as a general rule, with the 3″ size for small prints and up to 5″ for large prints. We usually make the top and side margins the same width and the bottom an inch larger. The cut-out area of the mat should be about ¼″ larger than the print size on top and sides and about ½″ larger on the bottom to allow the number, title, and signature to be easily seen.

Start by setting up a clean large measuring and cutting table. The ideal studio space should have a table just for cutting mats and wrapping packages, but that is a luxury of space few artists seem to be able to keep free. Use a large piece of chip board to top the table and to serve as a cutting board. Sharp mat knives and razor blades will soon dull if a hard, rough surface is used for cutting mats. Use a medium pencil with a good long point and do not press hard while marking, or marks may show even after erasing. Use a steel straightedge with a piece of masking tape attached to the underside to keep the straightedge from slipping. Trim both boards to size. Measure and mark off the opening to be cut.

Cutting the Mat

There are many methods for cutting a good, clean, professional mat. The important thing is to find the method that best suits you. Many students come close to hysteria at the thought of cutting a mat. Once the procedure is thought out and simplified, most people should be able to cut a reasonably good mat.

A number of varieties of good mat knives with changeable blades are sold in art supply stores. They are comfortable to hold, but we find the thickness of the blade and the constant need for sharpening a handicap. We prefer single-edge industrial razor blades, 100 to the box, fitted into a sturdy razor-blade holder obtainable in a hardware store. The razor blade is so thin and sharp and cheap that there is no excuse for a dull tool.

We often use two or three blades for one mat. Use the steel ruler as a cutting guide. Some people prefer a steel T-square. Hold down firmly on the ruler or T-square with one hand and cut straight through the board with one stroke to insure an even cut. However, if you don't have the strength for this, two or three careful cuts without moving out of the line will work. Be careful at corners and don't overcut. Some people prefer to mark and cut the mats from the back to avoid erasing and to have better control of corners. It is customary to cut the board at a slight bevel from the edge of the mat and with a little practice this should be possible. Some artists use the slanted side of the steel T-square as a guide, others use mat-cutting devices available in art supply stores.

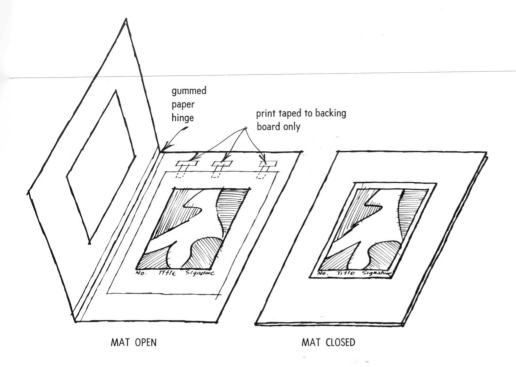

gummed
paper
hinge

print taped to backing
board only

No. Title Signature

No. Title Signature

MAT OPEN   MAT CLOSED

Hinging Mat and Print to Backboard

After the mat is cut, hinge it to the backboard, using gummed linen tape for a permanent mat or gummed paper tape for an impermanent one. Always hinge the longest sides of the mat and backing.

The print is always attached with a hinging device to the backboard, never to the mat. First, position the print carefully with the mat in a closed position, taking care to have even spacing between the print and the edge of the mat. The print should have adequate clean margins so that there will be a sufficient margin area to allow for taping. After the print is positioned, open the mat and attach two strips of gummed linen tape about 2" in length to the top back of the print, protruding 1" beyond the print. Place two more strips of gummed linen tape about 3" in length across the two protruding strips, fastening them securely to the backing. The print now hangs freely from the top only, allowing for the shrinkage and expansion caused by changing dry and humid weather. Strips for hinging may be made from the same paper used for the print. Cut strips from paper scraps and use library paste to adhere the strips to the backing. If a print is large and on heavy paper, three or four hinges might be required, with a spot of Elmer's glue to insure sticking.

Floating the Print

Another method of mounting used widely today, especially for oversized prints, is to float a print on a linen backing for framing. Some artists print their images flush to the edges of their papers, particularly in lithograph and silk-screen prints. The effect can be quite handsome when the deckle of the paper is utilized. Prepared linen boards of actual linen cloth, in a variety of textures and some tones are sold in many art supply stores. Trim the board to the correct size, and place small amounts of Elmer's glue in the two upper back corners and glue it to the backing. The bottom will hang free. The print can then be acetated for shipping to exhibitions or framed for permanence, although the print surface may be damaged by condensation on the inside of the glass.

Acetate or Vinyl Protective Covering

When you send work out to some of the smaller, less well-equipped galleries, it is well to back the prints with a sturdy backing board and to acetate them to protect them from excessive handling in print bins. A good cover is .003 gauge acetate or a clear vinyl wrapped around the print and taped to the backing. The corners can be folded with excess bulk cut away. Acetate can also be trimmed a fraction smaller than the backing and a white tape used to neatly seal the edges.

FRAMING THE PRINT

Framing a print properly is a huge specialized area. There is nothing quite as handsome as professional, first-rate framing. There are many excellent framers, particularly in large cities, and there are framing accommodations in print galleries where the people know prints and can mount and frame them properly. Avoid framers who know nothing of the proper handling of prints because they can do damage. We have seen prints trimmed unmercifully by inept framers to fit a standard mat, and we have also seen one sad job of a print that was dry-mounted to a backing, making the print impossible to remove. Find a reputable framer who specializes in prints, who has a wide selection of framing to choose from, and who will make a dustproof, tightly assembled frame.

One area of print framing that is new and must be dealt with on an individual basis is the framing of dimensional prints. If the structure is paper that has been built up through molding, cutting, or constructing, special frame boxes, usually plexiglas and sometimes glass, must be devised either by the artist himself or with a sympathetic framer. If plexiglas, metal, acetate, mylar, or any other hard nonabsorbent surface is used for the base of the actual print, it can be shown without glazing but will need some kind of mount for hanging or displaying. Vacuum-form printing makes possible a finished product of plastic material that may still be fragile because of the dimensional depth of the projecting image and, if not adequately protected, can crack or crush and be totally ruined.

Opposite:
Clare Romano
"Cape View I" 1968
Collagraph 23" x 17¾"

Glazing

A standard rule for glazing is that work done on paper must be framed under glass to prevent dirt and humidity saturation by the absorbent paper. Any glass unfortunately dulls the image somewhat but is necessary to preserve the work. Avoid glare-proof glass because it distorts the tonal quality of the print. Plexiglas is a good substitute and produces less glare than glass, but unfortunately it is expensive and must be very carefully handled because it scratches easily. Colors fade less under plexiglas than they do under glass.

Metal Section Frames

We have found an easy and less expensive substitute for commercial framing in the metal section frames available in many art supply stores and some bookstores. There are two or three varieties based on similar principles and quite simple to assemble. They are often manufactured in natural aluminum and anodized aluminum that looks golden. The glass must be purchased from a glazier and slipped into the frame.

John Ross
"Sisak" 1966
Collagraph 18" x 30"
Joseph Hirshhorn Collection

THE DEALER AND THE EDITION

As there are many more dealers and distributors who handle prints or purchase individual prints and editions outright than there were 10 years ago, it is much easier now for an artist to find an outlet for selling his work. However, certain pitfalls are worth mentioning. Usually the beginning artist leaves a group of his prints on consignment with the dealer for sale at a specified commission. The percentage that the dealer takes can vary from one third to one half. If the dealer wants your work badly enough, he will sometimes arrange an outright purchase of a number of works at a discounted price. Such a sale can be desirable for the artist in most cases. Distributors of prints will often buy whole editions from an artist at a greatly reduced price, which can vary from 10% or 15% to 30% of the price of the print. The attraction of a large sum of money must be weighed against the time it takes to produce the print.

When an artist leaves work on consignment, he should prepare duplicate sheets with a simply stated agreement specifying amount of commission, his request for monthly payment for work sold, and his request to be able to withdraw his work from the dealer on demand. A listing of prints should then follow, with edition numbers and selling prices. The dealer should be presented with two copies to sign, one for the dealer, one for the artist. Some years ago the Print Council of America, 527 Madison Avenue, New York City, prepared such a form as a guide for artists. It was very useful to us when we began working with numerous dealers.

Investigate all small out-of-town dealers. You can ask for the names of artists handled by the dealer and contact them to inquire about the dealer's working arrangements and general reputation. Remember, it is difficult to retrieve work once it is shipped to distant cities and much easier to do a little investigating before you are involved. Too many artists have suffered badly at the hands of unscrupulous dealers or just from dealers who sold their galleries intact with consignment work to new owners who may or may not be ethical.

RECORD-KEEPING

Unfortunately the very system of edition-making requires some kind of record-keeping. The artist, like the grocery store owner, is dealing with an inventory, and the inventory is his prints. Use the simplest method possible for a very dull job. We generally hate this aspect of printmaking but unfortunately it is necessary. Our system is to keep two large looseleaf notebooks of different colors, one book for noting editions, where sold, where consigned, and the date, and one book to hold agreements and print listings from each gallery, all placed alphabetically (by print titles) in the books. When a print is sold it is checked off in the edition book and in the gallery listing book. This system is fairly accurate. A separate listing of exhibitions where you exhibit each year is also helpful so that a record of the print shown, date and place of show can be made.

SIZE OF EDITION

The handling, signing, numbering, and cataloging of the prints is difficult because the print is produced in a multiple edition. Each print is unique, yet part of a designed quantity of prints called an edition. A similar situation exists in the making of a limited edition of castings by the sculptor; however, such castings are not always numbered.

The printing of the edition itself may be handled in a variety of ways, depending on the probable demand for a print, the ease of printing, and whether the edition is printed by the artist or by a printer for artists. The artist decides on the number to be printed unless a dealer in prints commissions an edition and designates the number for the edition. The usual number for an artist-printed edition used to be 25 or 50. However, so many changes have occurred in the last few years with the appearance of numerous new print galleries and publishers and distributors, coupled with a general increase in demand for prints, that the number of prints in an edition has drastically increased. Editions of 200 to 300 prints are produced quite regularly, and some artists have been known to sign up to 2000 prints, printed by professional artist printers and produced as special editions.

The size of the edition used to be kept small in order to insure the value of each print and hopefully to raise the price of each one as the edition sold out. However, with the wide distribution and demand for the print today it is impossible to speculate on supply and demand in relation to size of edition.

Some artists decide on the size of the edition but do not print the whole number immediately. They may print 10 or 15 to start with, numbering the first group 1 through 15, for an edition of say 50, record the number printed in a book, and then fill out the rest of the edition when they have more printing time or can engage assistants or give out the remainder of the edition to a printer for artists. We often prefer this method for our complicated color collagraphs so that we can be free for new work. A very accurate, detailed printing chart must be kept so that the edition can be filled out exactly as it began. This system has worked very well for us because our diagrams are very good and we supplement them with color saved in wax paper packages and recipes for color mixtures. This method is discussed at length in the chapter on the collagraph.

Other artists prefer to print their whole edition immediately to free themselves from reprinting. Time and experience will determine the method best suited to your work. Of course the deferred-printing system cannot work for lithography or for silk screen. For lithography the stones would be difficult to store, and silk-screen printing is a relatively fast printing technique that allows for fairly easy edition work. Interrupted printing applies best to relief and intaglio printing.

A number of artists feel that the limited-edition numbering system protects only the dealer and the collector at the expense of the artist and refuse to use the system. Instead, they sign the prints and mark them as artist's proofs or only sign them.

When an edition is complete, the blocks, plates, screens, stones, or whatever contains the image should be destroyed or defaced. This precaution against further reproduction is usually requested when editions are commissioned. It is done in many cases by scratching, cutting, or drawing a line through the printing surface. However some unscrupulous dealers have attained possession of plates and then proceeded to print them and sell them unsigned and defaced. Many important 19th- and 20th-century French artists' prints may be found along the Quais in Paris or in small dealer's shops in this condition.

Occasionally an artist prints his edition, retains the blocks or plates, and decides at a later time to pull new prints. The artist may alter his color relationships or perhaps even make structural changes. Any editions pulled from altered blocks or plates should be designated as second editions.

NUMBERING, TITLING, AND SIGNING

The numbering, titling, and signing of the edition has traditionally been done with a medium pencil on the bottom of the print. The number of the print and the size of the edition are written on its lower left side with the designation 1/50 for the first print of an edition of fifty, 2/50 for the second, and so on until 50/50 is numbered. The title is usually written in the bottom center and the artist's signature in the lower right. Whether the edition is printed all at once or over a period of time, the prints should be printed as much the same as possible. The numbering then designates the sequence in time and not prime value for low numbers and less value for higher numbers. Probably the question most asked by laymen is whether print number 1 is more valuable than print number 50. Many artists avoid the whole problem by simply writing edition 50 in the lower left corner of each print. However, the traditional method of individual numbering does afford the artist an accurate bookkeeping device if he sends out many prints to exhibitions.

ARTIST'S PROOFS

Traditionally, 10% of an edition should be designated *artist's proofs*. These prints are of the same quality as the numbered edition and are designated as artist's proofs because they are the prints retained by the artist if an entire edition is sold outright or printed and sold one by one. If an edition is sold outright at a discounted price, the artist's proofs will sell at the artist's usual selling price or more, at the discretion of the artist if the edition is sold.

Artist's proofs are also numbered with Roman numerals like I/X and XX/XX or with a system of letters, A, B, C, and so on.

Years ago it was customary for collectors to covet artist's proofs, most often because in the French tradition of printmaking the artist worked closely with a printer and inspected the proofs submitted by the printer and marked his choice "bon a tirer" and signed the print as guide for the edition. As these collectors felt this print was the first to meet the artist's approval, it was therefore more desirable. Because artists now print editions themselves and give equal care to the first and the last prints in an edition, this fixation on the artist's proof as the most accurate state has diminished.

WORKING PROOFS

During the early stages of the development of the print the artist may experiment with a number of color combinations, different wipings, or rolling, and the like. Though these prints may not be the final choice for the edition, they often contain many interesting variations and should be marked working proofs and numbered in the sequence pulled. These prints will no doubt have value as an edition is depleted and, more importantly, are of considerable value in studying the development of a print. If you have ever had the opportunity to see the numerous stages of many of Rembrandt's etchings that can be studied, you will understand how interesting the working proofs of an artist can be for the total comprehension of a work of art.

THE RESTRIKE

A restrike is a print that has been pulled from a block or plate at a much later date than the original printing. Many restrikes exist of Rembrandt etchings, pulled in the 18th and 19th centuries. Numerous restrike prints exist of work by Goya and Kollwitz. Such impressions may be inferior to the prints printed in the artist's lifetime. Sometimes the plates are reworked, usually being steel-faced in order to obtain long runs. When the prints are sold as restrikes at modest prices they are often interesting to study and to own. When the restrikes are sold as artist-pulled proofs for large sums, it is most unfortunate for the unsuspecting buyer. The best advice in this area would be to always buy from a reputable dealer and be wary of "fantastic" buys in master prints. Finding such a buy is highly unlikely.

RAPHAEL · VRBINAS +

Ugo Da Carpi
"The Descent from the Cross," after Raphael
Chiaroscuro Woodcut
The Metropolitan Museum of Art
Rogers Fund, 1922

Käthe Kollwitz
"Weavers Cycle: March of the Weavers"
Etching 8" x 11½"
Collection of the authors

COLLECTING PRINTS

The burgeoning interest in the fine print has caused many artists to explore printmaking techniques. It has spurred galleries to exhibit and commission new prints for a new generation of print collectors. It has prompted museums to mount survey and retrospective exhibitions of contemporary and historic prints. And, to exploit this renaissance, print dealers, agents and wholesalers have sprung up like mushrooms all over the country. The print has many lovers, and new processes and techniques follow each other with increasing rapidity. It is a complex scene which greets the collector who has become intrigued by the print.

What Is An Original Print?

Definitions which once seemed to be complete, final, and absolute only a decade ago now seem ambiguous and unclear. An original print was described in a brochure issued by the Print Council in 1961 as a work of graphic art, the general requirements of which are:

1. The artist alone has made the image in or upon the plate, stone, wood block, or other material, for the purpose of creating a work of graphic art.

2. The impression is made directly from the original material by the artist or pursuant to his directions.

3. The finished print is approved by the artist.

This is still a helpful definition but it does not cover many of the situations which are arising now. The modern methods of printing, particularly in offset lithography and screen printing, have offered artists ways to create images and textures that have not been attainable in prior years.

Photographic methods that were considered reproductive are now being used by artists, with the help of skilled technicians from the commercial printing plants that abound in our mass-communicators society. Museums are accepting as original prints those impressions which would have been rejected ten or twenty years ago. The press-printed lithograph or silkscreen can be turned out in editions of thousands, and some galleries are offering color lithos in signed editions of from 3000 to 10,000 impressions. *Art in America* has printed 60,000 impressions of photographically prepared plates which are claimed to be original prints. The addition of the artist's signature is said to make the impression 100 times more valuable!

It is difficult to tell a photo-lithographic reproduction from an original lithograph, especially when the reproduction is printed on fine rag paper and has a pencilled number and a forged signature in the corner. Even well-known artists succumb to the temptation of ready cash and let craftsmen interpret watercolors, drawings and other art work into the print media. Sometimes these prints are carefully supervised by the artist but often they are not. When another artist or craftsman redraws the image on to a stone or plate the resulting print often changes in character and may distort the original drawing or design. An ethical practice would dictate that the artist-designer and the craftsman both be identified as having created the print. Some artists have been known to sign blank paper in advance of the printing of the edition. Eventually these practices will cause the discriminating collector to re-examine the prints offered for sale, with an eye to quality of impression, the strength of the image, and the size of the edition. All of these factors, plus the reputation of the artist, enter into the pricing of the print.

The print market, which in the 60's seemed to be insatiable, was affected by the general economic recession of 1970–71 and sales dropped considerably. Many galleries retrenched, some went out of business and prices of some contemporary artists either leveled off or went down. The market for old master prints held up quite well, however, and these prints are still demanding very high prices, with masterpiece prints by Rembrandt and Goya exceeding prices in six figures. The print market will undoubtedly be responsive to new changes in business and economic conditions.

Should The Collector Specialize?

The cost of amassing a good general collection of prints, with first-rate examples of great masters, is so high that only the rich can attempt it. Most people will be attracted to a certain period, or to a style, or even to an individual artist whose work they admire. A collector can restrict his interest to a single country, to a certain type of image which has special meaning to him, or in any manner which satisfies his desire to collect. Some people acquire prints as an investment against the seemingly perpetual inflation which erodes the value of currency. Certainly it is more rewarding from an esthetic point of view to study the etchings and engravings of the masters than those rather formal portraits of the presidents on paper money. The art work seems to have better durability than the cash!

In order to understand the area in which you collect it is vital to acquire some knowledge in the field. This means that the collector should first collect a few books or catalogs which describe the prints which interest him. There are catalogue raisonne's which list the entire production of an artist over his life-span. These are helpful to a serious collector who needs to know details of states and editions. Many print dealers issue catalogs which describe the prints being offered

Clare Romano
"New Jersey Landscape I" 1968
Collagraph 23½" x 24"

for sale. When prices are listed these catalogs form a record of print values over the years which can be fascinating (or frustrating) to collectors. The Print Collector's Newsletter 205 East 78th Street, New York, New York 10021, is published as a bimonthly brochure in looseleaf format which gives latest prices and information on new editions of original prints. It also lists upcoming auction sales of prints as a service to its subscribers.

The way to learn about prints is to study them, find an area that interests you and then pursue that area, looking at as many prints as you can. You will then know what books and catalogs will help you in your search. If a workshop class in printmaking is available it will be helpful for the collector to enroll in order to better understand the diverse techniques which are used by artists. Many colleges and art schools offer evening courses in printmaking on a non-matriculated basis, some taught by respected and productive artists.

Where To Find Prints

Dealers have appeared all over the country. Some have elaborate gallery facilities, others operate from a closet in the hall. Some know a great deal, others know very little. A reputable, established dealer is the best source for continued acquisition of prints, of course, but sometimes a good print will appear in a gift shop, or in a decorator's boutique, or in a furniture store. When this happens, you must rely on your own knowledge and judgment as to current values. Despite recent history, print values cannot constantly go up. Therefore you should be as informed as possible in order to protect yourself from ambitious dealers or overpriced editions. Many larger companies send traveling salesmen on the road with thousands of prints, covered with acetate or vinyl, to mount one-day sales in such places as college or university galleries, libraries, or schools. Many of these exhibits contain excellent prints, but they usually include some restrikes (impressions from a plate pulled without the approval of the artist, usually after his death). There is nothing wrong with restrikes so long as they are labeled as such and it is clearly understood what they are. The general public could not afford a Durer, Goya, Rembrandt, Callot or Kollwitz if the plates were not reprinted many times. Variations in price between early and late printings of the same plate can be enormous because the plates wear rapidly, especially delicate areas such as aquatint or drypoint. Early printings have the richest blacks and the strongest tonality.

John Ross
"Boulevard" 1964
Collagraph 16¼" x 26¾"

Some prints being offered for sale are cut from old magazines, such as "Verve," which were printed in very large editions (often in the thousands). These prints may be technically "originals" but should be priced accordingly.

It may be possible to buy work directly from a living artist, when you are in his neighborhood. Some artists will be distracted by this, however, and their work may be obtained only from their dealers. The most direct contact is usually the best, with the least amount of "handling" and "wholesaling" producing the best guarantee of authenticity and often the lowest prices.

A few print societies publish prints of contemporary artists, usually at favorable prices. These prints are normally restricted to members but often membership in these groups is a simple matter of joining and paying an annual fee. The Society of American Graphic Artists (S.A.G.A.) at 1083 Fifth Avenue, New York, New York 10028, offers prints by its distinguished artist members to its associate members at very low prices. The International Graphic Arts Society (I.G.A.S.) at 410 East 62nd Street, New York, New York, 10021, also offers editions of especially commissioned prints to its membership at prices much less than normal. The Print Club of Philadelphia, 1614 Latimer Street, Philadelphia, Pennsylvania, has been active in the field for many years and publishes small editions of prints, with a preferential price to its members. Many other non-profit societies and groups offer prints to a select group, usually at a distinct price advantage over the normal commercial channels.

Many museums offer prints to the public which are not available through commercial galleries or dealers. The sponsoring institution can not guarantee the immortality of any of its selections but, as the panel which chooses the print to be published is likely to be composed of experts the chances are that their choice will have some validity, at least.

Auctions and special sales are usually publicized in local newspapers. These may contain many worthwhile impressions but the buyer is completely on his own, as items purchased can rarely be returned. A collector may locate other collectors who will either sell or trade prints in order to build a collection in a certain field. Many publishers are releasing portfolios and deluxe volumes of illustrated books which contain fine prints, usually at a reasonable price because of the number of prints involved. The collecting of fine books which contain original prints is an area which combines literature and the visual arts in a particularly satisfying way.

How To Show and Store Prints

Most collectors display only a portion of their treasures on the walls. Like the tip of an iceberg, these may just indicate the bulk of the work stored in cabinets or closets. Color prints, especially, should be displayed only in subdued light, preferably away from reflected sunlight, and should not be left on display for extended periods of time. All colors will eventually change if exposed to bright light. The careful collector will be content to view his most brilliant color pieces at intervals.

Prints should touch only 100% rag mounts and should be hung from the back portion of the mount with non-staining

Prints can be stored vertically or horizontally in Romano-Ross workshop. Shelves are spaced three to six inches apart.

Permanent storage of prints can be obtained by using solander cases, with dust proof lids and spring catches.

hinges. Cardboard mats are not necessary, except for very large prints (over 30″) because they bulk up the collection and take up too much room. Heavy paper will suffice for most prints of small and medium size. These may be stored flat in solander cases, which are dustproof and have positive spring latches to close the lid. Portfolios are good when they have flaps to keep out dust and if they are closed tightly to prevent warping. They are not as good as solander cases for long term storage.

When prints are to be displayed on walls, they should be covered with glass to protect them from dust and dirt. The edges of the glass should be protected by a frame and the back sealed. The surface of the print should not touch the glass because condensation on the inside of the frame might cause water staining. This can be achieved with a suitable mat or strips to separate the print from the glass.

Patented brackets and other devices are good for temporary display of prints and should not be used as permanent fixtures. Dimensional prints need special boxes, often made of plastic, which scratches from the continual cleaning necessary to keep the dust away. Sheet plastic has a curious magnetic quality which attracts dust. Very large prints are difficult to store and need large cabinets or strong crates to keep them. Some may be rolled and kept in cardboard tubes. As a collection grows it may need its own room, which should have a large work table, good general illumination, and a movable small lamp for close examination of prints. A magnifying glass of 8 or 10 power is a help when studying some prints.

THE
PRINT
WORKSHOP

INTRODUCTION

The activities of the printmaking workshop are quite specialized and require careful organization and purchase of equipment to ensure an efficient, productive setup. It is possible to use one room for more than one process, but it is rarely possible to equip a shop for all the techniques (etching, lithography, relief printing, and screen printing) unless the room is larger than 1800 or 2000 square feet. A one-man studio can be slightly smaller but not much, because the presses and storage racks take up large amounts of space. It is better to have separate rooms for etching and lithography, although relief printing and screen printing can be accomplished on sturdy tables in almost any room large enough to hold them. When a number of printmakers work together it is wise to limit the number of techniques to two or three, particularly in a school or teaching situation. Screen printing takes a tremendous amount of table space, and each printer needs his own drying rack to accommodate the rapid flow of prints. Etching workshops need the smallest amount of space, while the relief print needs the least amount of expensive equipment, if prints are to be printed by hand rubbing and a press is not used.

THE ROOM

Although the size of a printmaking workshop can vary greatly, it should not be less than 800 to 1000 square feet if paper is stored in the room. The handling of paper requires a clean table, and this area must be kept away from the ink, acids, and other chemicals used in the workshop. Each additional artist requires about 40 to 50 square feet of workspace. The number of people working in a shop should not exceed 16 to 20, with 10 a much more workable number.

The light values in a print workshop should be fairly high. The general level of illumination should not fall below an exposure value of 10. A good photographic exposure meter will check this reading when held about one foot from a sheet of white paper in the work area of the room. Storage

Intaglio inking area at Bank Street Atelier. Convenient storage of inks and chemicals and good lighting (both natural and artificial) commend this workshop.

a good item to keep in the shop. Corrugated board in 36″ by 48″ flat pieces is useful for backing and for general packaging. It should be purchased from a commercial supplier in quantity and needs a large area for storage.

Ink, plate oil, chemicals, and paints should be stored in shallow wall cabinets for ease of access. Deep cabinets are hard to stock, and it is difficult to see what is in the rear. Acids should be kept in cabinets with doors and locks to prevent unauthorized usage. In New York City, nitric acid is considered a weapon, and its sale to unauthorized persons is discouraged. If the shop services 20 or more printmakers, mineral spirits should be purchased in 55-gallon drums and then siphoned into gallon safety containers. Lacquer thinner, alcohol, adhering fluid, shellac, and other solvents should be kept in covered metal containers.

Racks can be constructed from 2′ by 4′ verticals with ¾″ plywood shelves for litho stones (shelves should have horizontal 2″ by 4″ stringers underneath for support). Zinc plates for litho and etching should be stored flat on plywood shelves. A school might want to lock up certain items, such as paper and plates, because of their high cost. Silk-screen inks, which are used in quart cans for certain colors and in gallon cans for extender and transparent base, require a large amount of storage space. Screens may be stored in overhead racks with vertical dividers every 8″ or so.

Finished prints should be kept in metal blueprint-file cabinets. In schools, each student could be assigned a drawer for his completed prints. In the private workshop, boxes or solander cases may be used to store completed editions before they are shipped to galleries and exhibitions.

VENTILATION AND ELECTRICITY

Acid fumes should be vented to the outside by an electric fan with the ductwork and vents made of stainless steel or of galvanized steel painted with asphaltum paint. Fumes from solvents used in screen printing are very toxic and should be vented efficiently. Spray paints used in aquatints are particularly harmful and should be used outdoors or in very well ventilated areas. Cellar rooms with small windows are a poor choice for print-making workshops.

Electric hotplates may require 220-volt lines if two or more are needed. One hotplate will function on a 110-volt line if it is on a separate circuit. Outlets should be liberally placed throughout the workshop because electric hand tools are very useful in a busy shop. Grinders, routers, polishers,

The acid room at Pratt Institute in Brooklyn. Different strengths of acid should be clearly labeled.

saws, and sanders are being used in more and more work-shops. Motorized presses need electric power. Table lamps are helpful when high-intensity light is needed, and they need power, too. A radio is frequently welcome, especially while printing editions.

PHOTOGRAPHIC EQUIPMENT

A well-equipped professional or college printmaker's studio will have facilities for making positive transparencies and for exposing them on to screens, plates, or stones. The most expensive piece of equipment is a large process camera, which will cost about $2,000 in the 14" by 17" size. This camera will need its own darkroom with sink and running water. A carbon arc lamp with a vacuum table for exposing the plate will cost about $600 for a 22" by 28" unit. Although photoflood lamps make a workable substitute, a high volume of work may make the cost of a vacuum table a good investment as it cuts the exposure time by a considerable amount. The popularity of photo images and techniques is increasing rapidly, and many schools and shops are purchasing this equipment.

SAFETY MEASURES

Every workshop must have at least one (preferably more) fire extinguisher of the chemical foam type. They should be checked regularly to insure their workability. A first aid kit is also essential, including antiseptics, bandaids, bandages, and burn lotion.

Robert Blackburn's Printmaking Workshop in New York City has five geared etching presses, and two lithograph presses.

Many large diameter rollers are used in Blackburn's shop for relief and intaglio prints. They are stored in notched racks.

PRINTMAKING FOR CHILDREN

INTRODUCTION

We have included this section on printmaking for children for a number of reasons. We know from our own experience how our sons enjoyed many hours working alongside us in our printmaking studio from the time they could hold tools. We know the value and joy of their early endeavors with printmaking. Now that they are older, their knowledge of printmaking has produced two helpful printers for edition printing. Numerous friends who teach elementary and junior high school art classes often come to us to ask how they can adapt some of our techniques and materials for use in their children's classes. Essentially, the methods we list on the following pages are relief print methods and should relate to children from the ages of six to thirteen. High school children from the ages of fourteen to eighteen should be able to utilize the adult approach in the main body of this book as long as they show a strong interest and are supervised. Many high school art departments are extremely well equipped and often have both etching and lithograph presses and offer highly sophisticated programs. In our New School and Art Center classes, which are run on a workshop basis, whether for credit or not, we have occasionally had gifted young people of fifteen or sixteen who showed remarkable feeling for printmaking and were a welcome and inspiring addition to an adult class.

The merits of introducing printmaking to the very young are many. The experience of expressing themselves in another medium and developing their tactile sense is especially important. The combined quality of the constructed or cut-away surface gives them a sense of the bas relief and is a fine way to lead them on to explore three-dimensional construction and sculpture. The magic of the print process through the inking of a surface and the production of an image that is not drawn or painted is an exciting experience for them.

An excellent way to introduce the concept of the print to very young children from six to eight is to have them make monoprints. Although the monoprint is not a true print medium because it cannot be duplicated, it does show quickly how an impression can be made from an inked surface. We have found that another excellent way to introduce the print to this age group is to have them experience a new place, by taking a walk or an excursion to gather objects that can be inked and printed. Our son Tim's early experiences at the seashore each summer and his insatiable appetite for scavenging shells, pebbles, and the flotsam and jetsam of the sea led him to assembling the objects, gluing them on a cardboard, printing them, and then making a color woodcut of his own interpretation of the shells and the sea.

The tools given to young children must of course be carefully selected. Sharp tools must be eliminated unless groups are very small and carefully supervised. Simple, easily obtainable materials are best. Water-based inks are always available and easy to clean up. Oil-based inks are excellent because they do not dry too quickly, allowing more time to ink surfaces; but they are harder to clean up and present added problems when clothing gets into the ink. For cutting linoleum and wood, it would be best to eliminate knives except for older children who are closely supervised. Gouges for cutting are very satisfactory as long as the child is taught to keep the non-cutting hand behind the cutting one. The bench hook for holding the block discussed in the section on the relief print is a useful aid in cutting and helps to avoid cutting accidents. In each of the following methods we do list all the simple tools required. However, as all the methods are relief methods it would be helpful to read the material in the section on the relief print.

MONOPRINT (All Ages)

Materials

A smooth, nonabsorbent surface such as glass, lucite, Masonite, enamel pan, linoleum, or vinyl can be used for drawing the monoprint.

Water-based or oil-based ink or paint

Flat sticks or brushes for painting

Palette knife, rollers, rags

Newsprint paper, kitchen wooden spoon for rubbing print

Water or mineral spirits for clean up

The monoprint can be quick and spontaneous, depending on textural qualities, or it can be thoughtful and painterly, and it usually produces interesting results. The monoprint is exactly what the word indicates. It is one print, taken from a design developed or drawn by a variety of means on a hard, nonabsorbent surface with either water-based or oil-based inks or paint. A sheet of paper is then placed over the image, and the paper is rubbed by the hand, a soft rag, or a spoon, and an impression or *monoprint* is printed on the paper.

Numerous colors can be applied, by brush or by roller. A palette knife can blend colors, and mineral spirits can be poured or dabbed onto the surface to achieve blending or running effects in the colors. If a brush is used, a free, painterly drawing with numerous colors can be made. Fingers, rags, sticks, and rollers can also be employed to draw into the colors.

Monoprint
Image painted on glass with stiff brush and printing
ink thinned with mineral spirits. Grass texture made
with stick drawn through ink.
James, age, 11

Still another method, similar to stencil printing, is to lay thin cut-out paper shapes on an inked surface of one or many colors and to take an impression of the partially masked surface. The paper shapes will print as open white forms with color around them.

OBJECT PRINT (All Ages)

Materials

Shells, flat pebbles, leaves, feathers, coins, embossings, and so on.

Wood in a variety of shapes and textures, cut to shapes or from old packing cases, driftwood, and the like.

Stamped metal grating, flattened tin cans, bottle tops, raised letters, old plastic blocks, and other materials.

Water-based or oil-based inks, soft rollers, a spoon for rubbing.

Newsprint paper or rice paper (Rice paper has a soft absorbent quality that makes it receptive for printing hard objects. Troya is a soft domestic paper that works well. Tableau, a paper made in Boston for filters and sold in rolls, is relatively inexpensive and very good. Check supply sources at back of book.).

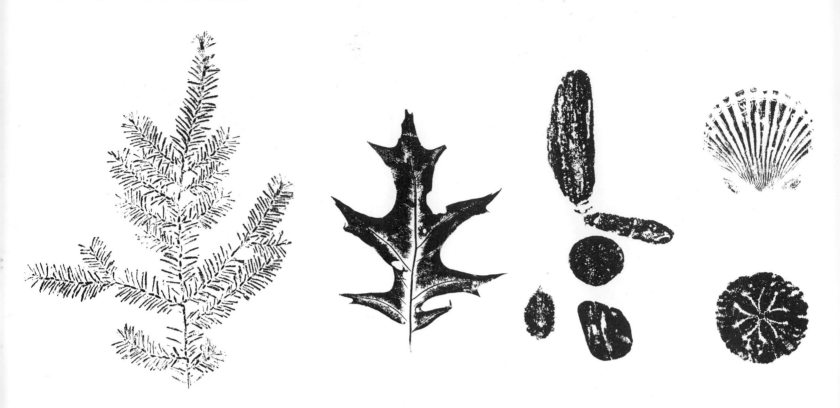

Object Print
Pebbles, Shells, Oak Leaf, Hemlock branch.
Mary and Ruth, ages eight and nine

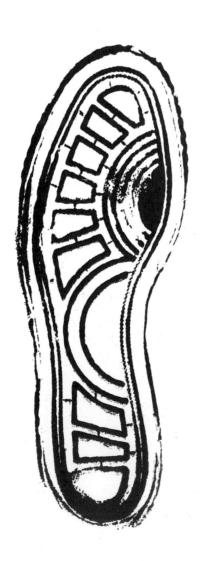

A smooth inking palette can be any nonabsorbent, easily cleaned material: glass, lucite, masonite, enamel pan, and so on.

Rags, water, or mineral spirits for cleaning up, depending on whether water or oil-based inks are used; palette knives to clean palettes.

If an object has a flat enough surface, to receive the roller, it can be inked and printed. Avoid sharp or especially rough surfaces because they will be hard to ink and will tear the paper.

Ink objects with a variety of colors, place a sheet of paper over the inked objects, and rub it with fingers or spoon. Print either on single sheets or in a variety of arrangements on a large piece of paper. Impressions made on small papers can be cut out and pasted down on a large sheet of paper for a small mural.

OFFSET ROLLER PRINT

Materials

    2 soft rollers, 2" or 3" in diameter
    Some interesting textured object
    Water-based or oil-based ink
    Newsprint paper
    Inking palette, palette knives, rags, water or mineral spirits

A variation of object printing is to ink an intricate object with a roller until a good quantity of ink is built up on the surface. Take a second clean roller and run it across the ob-

Offset Roller Print
Bottom of a child's sneaker rolled with a heavy build up
of ink. Clean, soft roller rolled over inked sneaker, picking
up pattern on clean roller, and rolled on to paper.
Robert, age nine

ject. The clean roller will pick up an impression from the inked intricate surface. Now roll out the impression on the clean roller onto a piece of newsprint paper. The image will offset the object's image onto the paper.

STENCIL PRINT
(All Ages, Simplified for Young Children)

Materials

Thin, stiff bristol board, scissors
One or two soft rollers
Water-based or oil-based inks, inking palette
Newsprint paper
Rags, solvent or water for clean-up

Following the principle of stencil printing, cut the image to be printed out of the stencil paper. Tape the stencil on to a table. Slip a sheet of newsprint paper under the stencil. Roll an inked roller across the open surface to produce the print. If stencil areas are isolated, more than one color, each with its roller, can be used. Older children might make a two-color stencil with two stencils by taping the stencils, carefully cut to register, onto a cardboard with four cardboard stops glued to the cardboard to serve as paper guides.

Stencil Print
Cars drawn on stiff paper cut out with small scissors.
Ellen, Age 6

CARDBOARD AND PAPER PRINT (All Ages)

Materials

Shirt cardboard (thin cardboard used in laundries to package shirts), corrugated board, two-ply chip board, stiff paper

Elmer's glue, brushes, inking palette, rollers, oil-based or water-based ink

Cardboard and Paper Print
Heads cut out of shirt cardboard and paper,
glued with Elmer's glue, and left
as a silouhetted relief.
Louisa, age 13

Rags, mineral spirits or water, texture tools such as a dressmaker's wheel, a rasp, and so on.

For older children, 9-13, X-acto knives with a variety of blades

Cut images out of thin cardboard and paper with scissors. Glue shapes down on two-ply chip board or corrugated board with Elmer's glue. Coat the surface of the plate with a dilute mixture of Elmer's glue: ⅓ water and ⅔ Elmer's glue. Be sure that all the cardboard forms are well glued and the surface is dry before printing. It is necessary to coat the cardboard surface with the dilute mixture to seal the surface; if this is not done the cardboard will disintegrate and peel up during inking.

In a well-supervised small group, older children can be allowed to cut into two- or three-ply chip board or corrugated board with an X-acto knife. A drawing or guide lines can be made right on the board with a soft pencil. The cardboard can then be cut and peeled away from around the form, leaving the image in high relief. Textures can be hammered and rubbed into the surface with anything that can make a mark, such as a dressmaker's marking wheel, a pizza cutter, a rasp, or bottle caps hammered into the cardboard to make impressions that will print. Coat the whole surface of the plate with dilute Elmer's glue to seal the surface. Ink it and print it.

COLLAGE PRINT (All Ages)

Materials

Cloth of various textures, lace, actual pieces of clothing such as a boy's shirt, part of a pair of dungarees, paper in various textures, flat sticks such as popsicle sticks, scraps of thin, flat wood, string, sand, sawdust, cat litter, metal mesh grating, wire mesh, crushed tinfoil, oil cloth, sandpaper, beans, noodles, scotch tape, masking tape, and other materials.

Stiff cardboard or thin Masonite on which to glue the materials

Scissors, Elmer's glue, acrylic gesso, polymer medium, inking palette, newsprint paper, Troya, filter paper, soft rollers in a variety of sizes, a rubbing spoon.

Water or mineral spirits for clean-up, oil-based or water-based inks

The collage print is a most versatile print medium. It affords a great textural experience for children because the materials can be selected by them and used with a thought to building a design through textures. The only limitation is whether or not an object or materials can be glued down and inked. If it can be inked, it can be printed.

The plate can be developed by making a sketch in pencil on the cardboard or Masonite backing board. Glue down the materials in relation to the sketch with Elmer's glue or acrylic gesso. Be sure the materials are adhered well to the backing. A thin coat of dilute Elmer's glue should be applied to the entire surface. The plate can also be made by just a free assemblage of interesting textures and forms, without any sketch. Be sure the plate is thoroughly dry before inking. An overnight wait may be advisable. Small soft rollers should be used for inking and the ink applied generously because

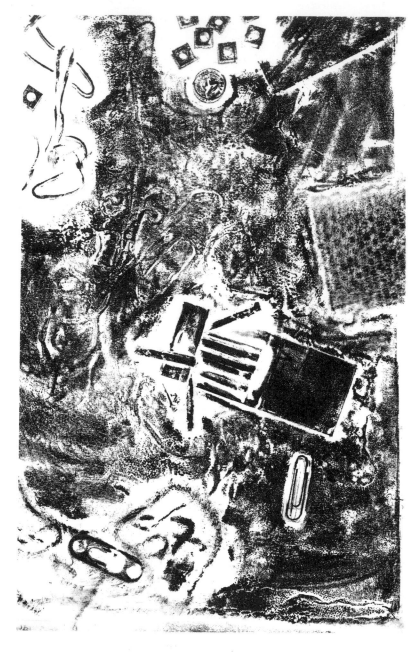

the textured nature of most of the material requires more ink than a hard surface.

Interesting prints can be made by gluing down pieces of clothing such as a man's shirt or part of a pair of dungarees on a stiff backing with Elmer's glue or gesso. A whole garment can even be immersed in polymer medium, glued to a backing, allowed to dry, and printed.

Masking tape and cellophane tape can be used to build interesting linear plates. Beans, noodles, or string can be used for background textures and to build a whole image. Sand and sandpaper and sawdust can also be used for textures. The textured images produce some surprises when printed. Smooth surfaces such as oilcloth and smooth paper print very black, while textured surfaces such as sand and sandpaper and corduroy fabric print with light textures.

Different colors on small rollers can be used to ink the same plate to produce a colorful print. During printing, rub the back of the paper well with your hand, a rubbing spoon, or a rag rolled into a ball, depending on the material to be printed. Use soft rice paper such as Troya, Mulberry, or filter paper because it is more pliable than newsprint. However, if only newsprint is available, it will produce adequate results.

Woodcut
Woodcut cut with simple
Japanese tools in soft pine.
Martha, age, 11

WOODCUT, LINOLEUM, HEAVY VINYL, AND BALSA-WOOD PRINTS (All Ages)

Materials

Linoleum, heavy vinyl, knotty pine, balsa wood. Buy heavy-duty linoleum, and vinyl unbacked in a floor covering store. It is less expensive than the mounted kind found in art supply stores. The pine can be obtained in a lumber yard in 8″ shelf widths cut to size. Scraps are often obtainable free of charge. Balsa wood used in model building can be found in art supply stores.

Inexpensive Japanese woodcut tools sold in small wooden boxes in many art supply stores or Japanese novelty shops are very good. They usually include a gouge or two, a knife, a chisel, and a sharpening stone. Do not buy the plastic bagged kind sold in dime stores. They break easily.

Though we do not suggest the Speedball tools for adults, the sets made with removable nibs are adequate for children.

Wire brushes, stamping objects, rasps, oil-based or water-based ink, soft rollers, inking palette, bench hook, newsprint paper, water or mineral spirits for clean-up, rags.

Simple designs and drawings can be cut in linoleum or wood if the child is shown how to carefully handle the tools, always keeping the supporting hand behind the cutting hand. Use a bench hook to hold the block. Check the woodcut equipment section for instructions on how to make one. It is a simple device and easy to use.

When using wood, select soft, easily cut pieces. Some lumber yards are very sympathetic to the idea that their scraps can be used for woodcuts and often give large quantities to schools. Blacken the wood surface with some dilute India ink or printing ink so that the cutting can be easily seen. White chalk can be used to indicate a design. The children can begin by selecting a piece of wood that has an interesting grain or knots. The grain can be made more visible by rubbing a steel brush into it to wear down the soft areas and allow the grainy ridges to stand out. Sometimes the wood itself will suggest a landscape or features of a figure will seem apparent in the distribution of knots.

Use simple gouges at first for cutting. Try stamping and pounding textures into the wood and printing them. This is very easy with balsa wood and pine shelving.

The linoleum and vinyl are easier to cut than the wood and can be cut with simple gouges for quick results.

3M VINYL
LUCITE and ACETATE PRINTS

A new material produced by the Minnesota Mining and Manufacturing Company is quite a fine print material. It is thin enough to be cut with scissors and can be cut with gouges. It is called 3M vinyl.

Heavy acetate and vinyl can be cut with scissors and scratched into with old dental tools or any sharp instrument. Very good prints can be made from the round vinyl tops used on coffee cans. Cut away the ridge and you will have a good material to scratch, gouge or cut with scissors. The interesting quality of the 3M material and the vinyl and acetate is that pieces of these materials can be cut in many parts, inked separately, then reassembled and printed at one time.

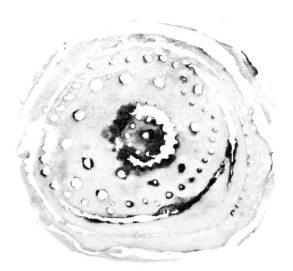

PLASTICINE PRINT (Young Children)

Materials

Plasticine, oil-based ink, soft roller, inking palette, rubbing spoon, newsprint paper, solvents, interesting objects to press into plasticine such as bottle caps, coins, textured objects, and so on.

Simple prints can be made by flattening some plasticine with a roller or pressing it with a piece of wood, to about ⅛″ thickness. Press any interesting objects into it to make an impression, or draw into it with a sharp tool such as the back of a brush. Roll ink over the surface, using oil-based ink because the oily plasticine may repel the water-based ink. Place the paper over the inked surface of the plasticine and rub the back of the paper with your hand or softly with a spoon so that the plasticine images are not crushed.

Plasticine Print
Shapes flattened out, punctured and scored with a stick.
Charles, age, 6

GLUE PRINT (All Ages)

Materials

Elmer's glue, acrylic gesso, cardboard, oil-based and water-based ink, soft and bristle brushes, cardboard cut in 2″ squares for drawing linear images, inking palette, soft rollers, solvent or water for clean-up, newsprint paper, rags

Very interesting prints can be made with glue or acrylic gesso. Elmer's glue can be squeezed right out of its plastic container and used as a drawing tool or be dripped or painted on a cardboard backing, allowed to dry, then given a thin coating of dilute Elmer's glue, inked, and printed.

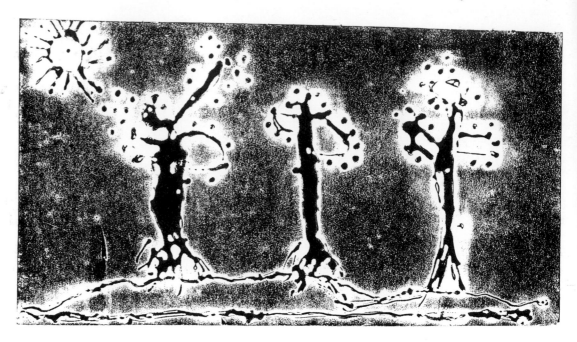

Glue Print
Elmer's Glue squeeze bottle used to draw and drip image.
Ellen, age, 6

More controlled images can be made by using soft and stiff brushes to paint on cardboard backing, building it up by drying and repainting so that some higher surfaces can develop. Acrylic gesso, when not too liquid, can produce some fairly good relief areas. The cardboard squares can be used to apply gesso in linear forms or, if folded, can be used to apply texture areas.

Allow the design to dry thoroughly, then coat it with a diluted Elmer's glue to seal the surface of any open cardboard areas. Ink the plate with soft rollers, place newsprint or rice paper over the surface, and rub with your hand or a spoon.

STAMP PRINT (All Ages)

Materials

Ruby erasers (any firm rubber erasers usually manufactured in a variety of colors for pencil erasing)

Two- and 3-ply cardboard, large firm potatoes, X-acto knives, paring knife, oil-based and water-based inks, inking palette, soft rollers, solvents, rags, newsprint paper.

Inventive little stamps can be made by cutting into the firm colored erasers used for pencil erasing. X-acto knives can be used to cut little designs in the flat surface of the erasers. Heavy layered cardboard can also be cut and peeled away to produce a simple high relief design. Attach a little handle made of masking tape to the stamp and ink the image either by tapping it in some ink rolled out on an inking palette or surface-roll the ink onto the relief surface of the stamp. Stamp the design in multiple colors, repeats, and overlaps on newsprint paper with some newspaper padding under it to insure a sharp image.

Another old, quick, simple method for very young children is to make stamps from potatoes. A simple design can be cut into halved firm potatoes with a not-too-sharp paring knife. Water-based ink can be rolled onto the relief surface of the design, or the potato stamp can be tapped into ink rolled out on an inking palette. The printing can proceed as just discussed.

Stamp Print
Leaves, and stars cut out of soft red erasers and cardboard.
Thomas, age, 12

SOURCES AND CHARTS

SOURCES OF SUPPLIES FOR PRINTMAKING

General Supplies (tools, paper, ink, and so on)

1. Craftool Company
   1 Industrial Road
   Woodridge, New Jersey 07075

2. Sam Flax
   25 East 28 Street
   New York, New York 10016
   (Also in Chicago, Los Angeles, San Francisco, and Sacramento)

3. Arthur Brown
   2 West 46 Street
   New York, New York

4. Fine Arts Materials Co.
   531 LaGuardia Place
   New York, New York

5. Rembrandt Graphic Arts Co.
   Stockton, New Jersey 08559

6. F. Weber Co. (order from local dealers)
   Wayne and Windrim Avenue
   Philadelphia, Pennsylvania 19144

7. Graphic Chemical & Ink Co.
   P. O. Box 27
   728 North Yale Avenue
   Villa Park, Illinois 60181

Cherry or Poplar Type-High Blocks:

8. Reliance Blocking
   9419 Railroad Avenue
   North Bergen, New Jersey

9. American Wood Type Co.
   42–25 9th Street
   Long Island City, New York

Birch Plywood from Finland:

10. Stewart Industries
    6520 North Hoyne Avenue
    Chicago, Illinois 60645

End-Grain Maple or Boxwood Blocks:

11. J. Johnson
    51 Manhasset Avenue
    Manhasset, Long Island
    New York

Tools (gouges, knives, chisels, stones, and so on)

12. E. C. Lyons
    16 West 22 Street
    New York, New York 10011

13. E. C. Mueller
    3646 White Plains Road
    Bronx, New York 10467

14. Frank Mittermeier, Inc.
    3577 E. Tremont Avenue
    Bronx, New York 10465

15. Sculpture Associates
    114 East 25th St.
    New York, New York

16. Wilfred C. Kimber, Ltd.
    24 King's Bench Street
    Blackfriars
    London, S.E.1, England
    (also Hunter, Penrose, Littlejohn Ltd. See No. 33.)

Felt Blankets

17. Continental Felt Co.
    22 West 15th Street
    New York, New York

18. Pacific States Felt & Mfg. Co.
    843 Howard Street
    San Francisco, California 94103

Pigments (for ink and paint):

19. Fezandie & Sperrle Inc.
    103 Lafayette Street
    New York, New York 10013

20. Interchemical Printing Corp.
    16th and Willow
    Oakland, California

21. E. I. DuPont De Nemours Co.
    Pigments Department
    Wilmington, Delaware

Acids and Chemicals:

22. Amend Drug and Chemical Co.
    83 Cordier Street
    Irvington, New Jersey

23. Philip Hunt Co.
707 Army Street
San Francisco, California 94124

24. for Gentry Clove Oil:
Beacon Chemical Co.
244 Lafayette Street
New York, N. Y. 10012

Photoengraving Supplies, Including Copper and Zinc Plates:

25. Harold Pitman Co.
515 Secaucus Road
Secaucus, New Jersey 07094

26. For small quantities:
National Steel & Copper Plate Co.
653 10th Avenue
New York, N. Y.

Litho Plates (new and regrained)

27. City Litho Plate Co.
429 Vandervoort Avenue
Brooklyn, New York

Rollers and Brayers:

28. Apex Roller Co.
1541 No. 16 Street
St. Louis, Missouri

29. Ideal Roller Co.
21 39th Avenue
Long Island City, New York

30. Jomac, Inc.
181 Broad Street
Carlstadt, New Jersey

31. Speedball Soft Rubber Brayers
Hunt Manufacturing Co.
Statesville, North Carolina
(Many local dealers)

(Leather) Rollers for Litho:

32. Roberts & Porter Inc.
4140 West Victorial Ave.
Chicago, Illinois 60646

(also Siebold Ink Corp. See No. 37.)

(also Craftool Co. See No. 1.)

33. Hunter-Penrose-Littlejohn Ltd.
109 Farringdon Road
London, E.C.1, England

34. Ault & Wiborg
Stander Road
Smithfields
London, S.W.18, England

Cylinder Rubber (for rollers)

35. Miller Products Co.
29 Warren Street
New York, New York

Printing Ink (letterpress):

36. IPI (Interchem Corp.) (Everyday Ink)
636 11 Avenue
New York City, New York

37. Siebold Ink Co.
150 Varick Street
New York City, New York

38. Sun Chemical Corp.
General Printing Ink
750 3rd Avenue
New York, New York 10017

Ink (intaglio):

39. Cronite Company
88th Street & Kennedy Blvd.
North Bergen, New Jersey

(also Graphic Chemical & Ink Co. See No. 7.)

40. F. Charbonnel
13 Quai Montebello
Paris, Veme, France

41. Lorilleux-Lefranc & Co.
16 Rue Suger
Paris, VIeme, France

42. Usher-Walker Ltd.
Chancery House
Chancery Lane
London, W.C.2, England

Ink (litho):

43. Sinclair & Valentine Inks
Secaucus Road Extension
Secaucus, New Jersey 07094

44. California Ink Co.
501 15th Street
San Francisco, California 94103

45. Borden Chemical Corp. (Inks)
1100 Vail Avenue
Montebello, California 90640

46. Handschy Chemical Co.
2525 North Elston Avenue
Chicago, Illinois 60647

(also Siebold Ink Co. See No. 37.)

(also IPI. See No. 36.)

47. Superior Printing Inc. Co.
295 Lafayette Street
New York, New York

Crinoline or Tarletan:

in large quantities only (100 yds. or more)
48. Gross-Kobrick
370 West 35th Street
New York, New York

49. A & S Textile Co., Inc.
236 West 27th Street
New York, N. Y.

Silk-Screen Ink, Paint, and Supplies:

50. Advance Process Supply Co.
400 N. Noble Street
Chicago, Illinois 60622
Offices in:

51. 570 McDonald Ave.
Brooklyn, New York 11218
and

52. 3101 San Jacinto
Houston, Texas 77004
and

53. 6900 River Road
Pennsauken, New Jersey 08110
and

54. 1965 East 57th Street
    Cleveland, Ohio 44103

55. Colonial
    East Rutherford
    New Jersey 07073

56. The Naz-dar Company
    1087 N. North Branch Street
    Chicago, Illinois 60622

57. Naz-dar Co. of New York Inc.
    33 Lafayette Avenue
    Brooklyn, New York 11217

58. Naz-dar Co. of California
    756 Gladys Avenue
    Los Angeles, California 90021

59. Naz-dar Canada, Ltd.
    925 Roselawn Avenue
    Toronto, 19, Ontario

60. Serascreen Corp.
    147 West 15th Street
    New York, New York

Paper:

large stock of imported and domestic papers:

61. Andrews/Nelson/Whitehead
    7 Laight Street (on Canal St.)
    New York, New York 10013

for white index and cover stock:

62. Crestwood Paper Corp.
    263 9th Avenue
    New York, New York

tableau paper in sheets and rolls:

63. Technical Paper Corp.
    729 Boylston Street
    Boston, Massachusetts 02116

cover stock, blotters

64. Saxon Paper Co.
    240 West 18th Street
    New York, New York

Corrugated board in quantity:

65. Standard Corrugated & Case Corp.
    686 Grand Avenue
    Ridgefield, N. J. 07657

West coast dealer for A/N/W

66. Zellerbach Paper Co.
    234 South Spruce Street
    South San Francisco, California 94118

Mat, chipboard in quantity:

67. Miller Cardboard Co.
    80–82 Wooster Street
    New York, New York

68. Fine Arts Material Co. See No. 4

Hand made Japanese papers:

69. Yasutomo & Co.
    Dept. AA-4 24 California Street
    San Francisco, California 94111

Japanese papers and tools:

70. Aiko
    714 North Wabash
    Chicago, Illinois

for blotters, commercial cover stock:

71. Lindenmeyer, Schlosser Corp.
    5301 11th Street
    New York, New York

for Kizuki-bosho paper, used by Uchima:

72. Shimizu-Seirindo
    8–1, Honmachi Nihonbashi,
    Chuo-ku, Tokyo, Japan

Photographic Techniques

For Kodak KPR Chemicals & Ortho Film:

73. Treck Photographic Inc.
    1 West 39th Street
    New York City, New York 10018

For Print-E-Mulsion & SC 12 Superfast:

74. Rockland Colloid Corp.
    599 River Road
    Piermont, New York 10968

For Subtractive Plate Developer & Gum

75. Minnesota Mining & Mfg. Co.
    St. Paul, Minnesota 55101
    Available through local suppliers

for Presensitized Micro-Metal chemicals:

76. Ball Metal and Chemical Co.
    210 Van Brunt Street
    Brooklyn, New York 11231

For Lacquer Toppings (grounds):

77. Teaneck Chemical Co.
    197 Washington Avenue
    Carlstadt, New Jersey

For ST Super D Chemicals:
Harold Pitman Co. See No. 25

Plastic Sheets

78. Commercial Plastic & Supply Corp.
    630 Broadway
    New York, New York
    or local supplier

Carborundum for Litho Stones

79. King and Malcolm
    57–10 Grand Avenue
    Maspeth, Long Island, New York

Benelux Press Beds

80. Laminated Sheet Products
    Industrial Park Corporation
    Norwood, Massachusetts

Litho Drawing Supplies (crayons, tusche)

81. William Korn
    260 West Street
    New York, New York

Paper Plate Lithography

82. Anthony Ensink
    400 West Madison Street
    Chicago, Illinois 60606

Hard Ground (mixed with lacquer thinner)

Heims Etching Ground

83. John L. Heim
    1205 Virginia Avenue
    Glendale 2, Calif.
    (Available from Cronite Co.)

Steel Facing of Copper Plates

84. Anderson & Lamb
    Fulton Street
    Brooklyn, New York

Check commercial catalogs for additional types.

PAPERS FOR PRINTMAKING

Name	Size (in.)	Composition	Intaglio	Litho	Relief	Silk Screen	Notes
American Etching	38 x 50	100% rag, machine-made.	x	x		x	Large size for intaglio plates. White, soft finish, prints well.
Arches Cover	22 x 30 29 x 41	90% rag, mould-made.	x	x	x	x	Available in white and buff; smooth, even, beautiful texture. Handsome finish.
Arches Text	25 x 40	90% rag, mould-made.	x	x	x	x	Light, even, white, laid and wove finish.
Basingwerk Heavy	26 x 40	45% Esparto pulp, machine-made.	x	x	x	x	Very smooth, even surface. Good for proofs. Inexpensive, useful paper.
Beckett Cover	26 x 40	25% rag, machine-made.	x	x	x	x	Inexpensive, smooth, brilliant white permanent paper, very useful.
Classico Watercolor	22 x 30	100% rag, mould-made.	x				Beautiful, heavy, handsome, white, textured, expensive, for intaglio prints.
Copperplate	22 x 30 30 x 42	33% rag, mould-made.	x	x		x	Soft, white. Fragile when damp and should be handled with care. Prints well.
Copperplate Deluxe	22 x 30 30 x 42	75% rag, mould-made.	x	x		x	Permanent, white, soft, needs little dampening to soften fibres, expensive.
Crisbrook Etching	22 x 31	100% rag, handmade.	x	x		x	Soft, white, unsized. Prints well. Fairly expensive.
Domestic Etching	26 x 40	50% rag, machine-made.	x	x	x	x	Cheap, white, useful paper.
English Etching	22 x 31	100% rag, mould-made.	x	x	x	x	White, nice texture, moderately priced, handsome sheet.
German Etching	22 x 30 30 x 42	75% rag, mould-made.	x	x	x	x	Beautiful finish, soft, white, even, moderately expensive.
Goyu	21 x 29	Part Kozo, handmade.			x	x	Thin, off-white, even texture. Prints delicate detail well.
Hosho	19 x 24	Part Kozo, handmade.			x	x	White, soft, small sheet, good for color woodcuts. Picks up fluff on press.
Hosho (student)	16 x 22	Part Kozo, handmade.			x	x	Cheap, uneven, small, good for student proofs.
Hosho Pure	—	Part Kozo, handmade.			x	x	Expensive, beautiful, strong off-white handsome sheet. Available only from Japan.
Index	26 x 40	100% sulphite pulp, machine-made.	x	x	x	x	Cheap proof paper. Strong, white, turns brittle with age.
Inomachi (Nacre)	20 x 26	100% Kozo, handmade.	x	x	x	x	Elegant threaded texture. Prints etchings well but must be carefully dampened. Expensive.
Italia	20 x 28 28 x 40	67% rag, mould-made.	x	x	x	x	White, soft, handsome finish. Moderately priced. Does not erase well.
Iyo Glazed	17 x 22	Part Kozo, handmade.			x	x	Uneven texture, white, small sheet, inexpensive.
J. Green Watercolor	27 x 40	100% rag, mould-made.	x	x		x	Nice texture, warm white, prints well, handsome sheet.
Kizuki-bosho	17 x 24 25 x 35	100% Kozo, handmade.			x	x	Sized on both sides, for Japanese method with water-based inks. Made by same family for seven generations.

Name	Size	Composition				Description
Kochi	20 x 26	Part Kozo, handmade.		x	x	Warm off-white, handsome finish, elegant look, moderately priced, uneven thickness.
Masa 225	21 x 31	Manila and sulphite, machine-made.		x	x	Cheap, flecked, natural color, good for black-and-white proofs. Not permanent.
Millbourn 140 lb.	22 x 30	100% rag, handmade.	x			Expensive, beautiful, lovely texture. Strong white. A handsome sheet.
Mohawk Text	26 x 40	100% sulphite, machine-made.	x	x	x	Cheap, proving paper only.
Moriki 1009	25 x 36	Kozo, handmade		x	x	White, soft, unsized, useful paper.
Moriki (colors)	25 x 36	Kozo, handmade		x	x	Many beautiful colors. Soft, unsized, moderately priced.
Mulberry	24 x 33	Part Kozo, handmade.		x	x	Thin, off-white, tears easily. Not expensive. Good for general woodcut printing.
Mulberry Student	24 x 33	Sulphite, handmade.		x	x	Cheap paper for proofs and student work.
Murillo	27 x 39	33% rag, mould-made.	x	x	x	Very heavy, strong, buff color, even texture, good for deep intaglio and very sensitive.
Okawara	36 x 72	Kozo, handmade.		x	x	Very large, natural tan color, fairly opaque, even texture, handsome finish.
Opaline Parchment	22 x 28	100% sulphite, machine-made.	x	x	x	Smooth, even finish. Good for wood engravings and delicate relief prints. Discolors.
Pericles Cover	26 x 40	Rag and sulphite, machine-made.	x	x	x	Fairly permanent, white, smooth, even, good for silk-screen editions.
Rives Heavy	19 x 26 / 26 x 40	100% rag, mould-made.	x	x	x	White, slight texture, not heavy enough for deep embossing, but very useful.
Rives BFK	22 x 30 / 29 x 41	100% rag, mould-made.	x	x	x	A standard paper with many uses. White, even smooth texture, almost opaque. A classic paper.
Sekishu	24 x 39	Kozo, handmade.	x	x	x	Two colors available, white and natural, thin, soft, inexpensive, tears easily.
Strathmore Artists	—	100% rag, machine-made.	x	x	x	Strong, white sheet with monotonous texture.
Suzuki	36 x 72	Part Kozo, handmade.		x	x	Very large, white, slight texture. Good for large woodcuts, medium weight.
Tableau	40" rolls	Machine-made.	x	x	x	Unlimited length, very tough, will not discolor, used as a filter paper. Available in cut sheets.
Torinoko	21 x 31	Part manila hemp.		x	x	Strong, white, opaque, expensive, nice texture.
Troya #40	24 x 36	Hemp, machine-made.	x		x	Cheap, smooth, even paper, good for proofs. Will discolor to pale brown, turns brittle with age.
Tuscan Cover	26 x 40	100% sulphite, machine-made.	x	x	x	Good for etching proofs, is cheap, smooth, turns brittle with age.

Note: Esparto is a grass fiber. Kozo is a plant fiber.

ETCHING PRESSES, Domestic Currently Available

Manufacturer	Bed Size	Gears	Weight	Micrometers Available	Price*	Motor Available	Comments
Charles Brand 84 East 10 St. New York, N.Y. 10003	12 x 24	No	90	No	295	No	Well-made, highly respected machines custom-made to your order.
	16 x 30	Yes	350	Yes	795	No	
	18 x 36	6:1	760	Yes	1460	Yes	
	22 x 24	6:1	880	Yes	1770	Yes	
	24 x 46	6:1	970	Yes	1890	Yes	
	26 x 48	6:1	1100	Yes	1995	Yes	
	30 x 50	6:1	1300	Yes	2310	Yes	
	36 x 60	6:1	1900	Yes	2930	Yes	
Sturges	18 x 48	9:1	290	Yes	480	Yes	Solid, sturdy, slow.
Graphic Chem. P.O. Box 27 Villa Park Illinois 60181	28 x 48	9:1	1300	Yes	1375	No	
Dickerson Combination (from Graphic Chemical Co.)	27 x 48	Yes	400	No	985	Included	Motorized rollers must be shielded.
Craftool Co. Woodridge New Jersey 07075	12 x 24	Yes	61	No	160	No	Complicated mechanism.
	14 x 20	Yes	242	No	450	No	
	18 x 30	Yes	395	No	575	No	
	24 x 40	Yes	—	No	1450	No	
	24 x 40	No	1240	No	1950	No	
Rembrandt Graphic Arts Co. Stockton, N.J. 08559	16 x 32	No	—	No	270	No	This company also sells used presses when available. Many models.
	24 x 42	3:1	1200	Yes	1530	Yes	
	28 x 48	7:1	1200	Yes	1650	Yes	
	30 x 50	7:1	1200	Yes	1950	Yes	
Sam Flax 25 East 28 St. New York, N.Y. 10016	10 x 18	No	50	No	115	Yes	Small presses only.
	13 x 25	Yes	77	No	175	Yes	
	17 x 33	Yes	260	No	650	Yes	
	19 x 29	Yes	550	No	900	Yes	
Meeker-McFee 309 Parkway Madison Wisconsin	25 x 48	120:1	400	Included	1600	Included	An unusual frame design. A solid press.
Glen Alps 6523 40th Ave. N.E. Seattle Wash. 98115	40 x 66	60:1	2850	No	2600	Included	Heavy, strong, large presses.
	28 x 66		2000	No	2000	No	

Company	Size						Notes
Griffin Co. 2241 Sixth St. Berkeley Calif. 94710	24 x 40	Yes	500	No	—	No	A new design.
	30 x 50	Yes	700	No	—	No	
F. Weber Co. Wayne & Windrim Aves. Philadelphia, Pa. 19144	10 x 18	No	50	No	150	No	Small presses only.
	13 x 25	Yes	77	No	225	No	
American-French Tool Co. Route 117 Coventry, Rhode Island 02816	24 x 48	4:1	1845	No	1685	No	Simple, well-built machines.
	30 x 52	4:1	2115	No	1985	No	
	36 x 60	4:1	2420	No	2285	No	
Craftsmen Machinery Co. 75 W. Dedham St. Boston, Mass. 02118	24 x 48	4:1	485	Included	1200	No	Easily taken apart for travelling.
William Crull 155 South Lakeshore Rd. Lakeside, Mich. 49116	24 x 36	12:1	1200	Included	1400	No	
	30 x 48	12:1	1450	Included	1750	No	
	36 x 60	12:1	1800	Included	2250	No	
Martech P.O. Box 36 Northport, New York, 11768	12 x 24	Yes		No	275	Yes	Motorizing $300 extra. Many good features.
	16 x 30	Yes		No	750	Yes	
	18 x 36	Yes		No	1400	Yes	
	20 x 40	Yes		No	1600	Yes	
	24 x 46	Yes		No	1850	Yes	
	28 x 50	Yes		No	2050	Yes	
	30 x 50	Yes		No	2300	Yes	
	36 x 60	Yes		No	2900	Yes	

*Prices are changing constantly, usually upwards, check with manufacturer for latest information.

Michael Ponce de Leon's hydraulic press, made by Charles Brand, can exert tremendous pressure in a vertical motion, enabling the artist to print very deeply embossed bas-relief plates.

Charles Brand 30'' by 50'' motorized etching press with micrometers and blotter storage shelf. Studio Romano-Ross.

Brand 24'' by 46'' geared etching press, no micrometers, springs holding roller off bed. Chain is normally covered with steel box.

Laszlo (Rembrandt) 24" by 42" geared etching press. Covered chain drive, #1376.

Rembrandt etching press, 28" by 48", with 36" dia-circular drive wheel. G-1 gearing, #1411.

Sturges etching press #CP4, planetary gear, 18" by 36" steel bedplate or 18" by 48" Benelux bedplate.

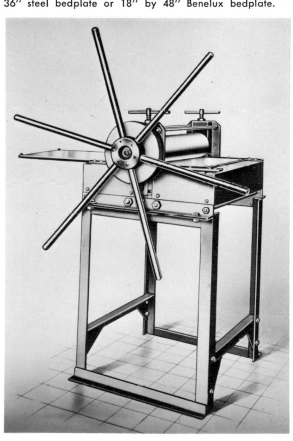

Sturges etching press #CP5, 28" by 48", steel bed, 8-1 planetary gear. Calibrated adjustment gauges are available.

Dickerson Combination press, 27'' by 48'',
prints etchings and lithos with changeable
top roller and scraper bar. Motorized
only. Lightweight. Available from Graphic
Chemical.

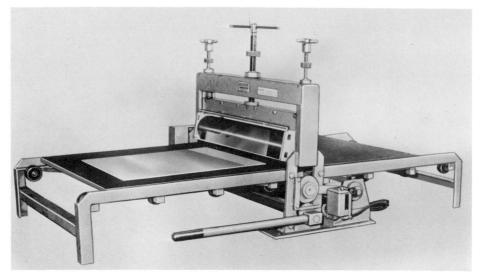

Glen Alps, motorized model ''B'' etching
press, 40'' by 66'' steel bed, large rollers.
Also available in a geared model hand
driven by a large wheel.

Meeker McFee, motorized etching presses,
24'' by 48'' printing surface, Benelux bed,
shielded top roller, lightweight. University
of Wisconsin.

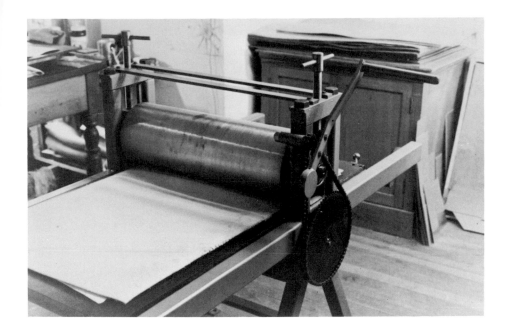

Griffen geared etching press (experimental model), 24" by 40" bed of fir plywood.

Craftool geared etching press, 24" by 40", steel bed, covered operating parts.

Old clothes wringer with wooden rollers. This press will print an etching if the depth of the line does not exceed 2/100 inch.

German press installed in Bank Street Atelier. Motorized.

American French Tool Co. 36" by 60" geared etching press has cable restraints to keep bed on press.

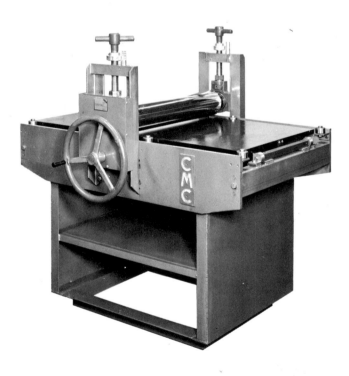

Craftsmen Machinery Co. (formerly Fox Graphics) make this 24" x 48" Benelux bed, geared etching press.

Fox Graphics press has 24" by 48" bed with a choice of gear ratios, 4 to 1 or 10 to 1. Benelux bed.

ETCHING PRESSES, Imported Currently Available

Manufacturer	Bed Size	Gears	Weight	Micrometers Available	Price*	Motor Available	Comments
Wilfred Kimber	8 x 14	No		No	Write	No	Available in nine models
24 Kings Bench	12 x 20	No		No	to	No	and many sizes. Solid,
Blackfriars,	16 x 24	Yes		No	manu-	No	strong presses of con-
London, S.E.1	16 x 30	Yes		No	facturer	No	ventional design. Large
England	19 x 36	Yes		No	for	No	sizes are expensive and
	19 x 36	Yes		No	latest	No	heavy.
	23 x 36	Yes		No	prices.	No	
	23 x 42	Yes		No		No	
	26 x 48	Yes		No		No	
	31 x 54	Yes		No		Yes	
	36 x 60	Yes		No		Yes	
	42 x 60	Yes		No		Yes	
Bottega D'Arte	15 x 28	No		No	690	No	
Grafica	16 x 28	Yes		No	800	No	
6 Via Degli Artisti	18 x 35	Yes		No	1100	No	
Florence, Italy	26 x 48	Yes		No	1425	No	
Sakura Color	11 x 20	No	50	No	—	No	These presses are avail-
Products Corp.	16 x 36	No	331	No	257	No	able with gears for a
1-1 Nakamichi	18 x 36	No	440	No	341	No	little more money.
Motoamachi	21 x 43	No	705	No	483	No	
Higashinari-Ku	27 x 51	No	926	No	1181	No	
Osaka, Japan	21 x 43	Yes	771	No	1291	Yes	
	27 x 51	Yes	992	No	1593	Yes	Floor models.
	40 x 85	Yes	4846	No	3968	Yes	

An 18'' x 36 steel bed with a geared drive features this imported Sakura press.

NEW LITHOGRAPHIC PRESSES (Currently Available)

Maker	Bed Size	Wgt. in lbs.	Approx. Price	Bed Material
Charles Brand 84 East 10 Street New York, N.Y. 10003	16 x 30 20 x 38 24 x 40 30 x 50 32 x 52 36 x 52	800 1380 1580 2000 2700 3200	1800 2350 2650 3040 3640 4220	Steel Steel Steel Steel Steel Steel
Craftool Company Woodridge, N.J. 07075	24 x 40 14 x 20	— 320	1550 515	⅝" Steel Plastic.
Dickerson Combination (From Graphic Chemical Co.)	27 x 48	400	1035	—
Graphic Chemical Co. P.O. Box 27 Villa Park, Ill. 60181	30 x 48 36 x 60	1175 1770	1345 1750	Steel Steel
Rembrandt Stockton, N.J. 08559	26 x 42 28 x 42 30 x 50	1300 1300 1300	1850 1895 1950	Maple, cork Linoleum.
Griffin Company 2241 - 6th Street Berkeley, Calif. 94710	26 x 48 32 x 60 39 x 72	500 700 900	1700 2100 2500	Laminated fir ⅛" neo- prene Galv. steel.
Kenneth Tyler Gemini G.E.L. 8365 Melrose Ave. Los Angeles, Calif., 90069	Large Presses			Custom made hydraulic, automatic motorized, expensive
American Graphic Arts, Inc. 628 West 45th St. New York, N.Y. 10036	Standard Sizes			New variations of old designs
Garo Antreasian Tamarind Institute University of New Mexico Albuquerque, New Mexico	Large Presses			Custom made hydraulic, automatic motorized, expensive

Custom-built oak frame litho press, built for University of Indiana. Formica bed.

Graphic Chemical Litho press, geared, model LP-3, 36" by 60" bed size, planetary gears 8-1, steel bed covered with heavy linoleum.

Rembrandt lithographic press, 28" by 42", maple bed, ½" cork with linoleum covering, geared.

Charles Brand litho press, 30" by 50" steel bed, button clutch, many safety devices.

Dickerson combination press, 27" by 48", here adjusted for lithography, motorized, Benelux bed, lightweight.

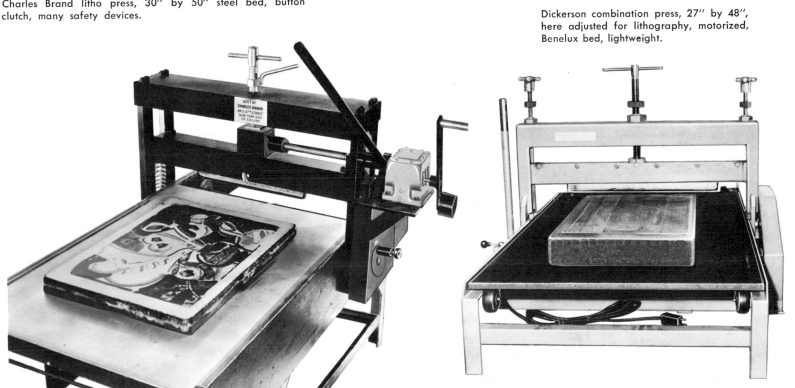

Only the books and articles that might be useful to a working artist-printmaker are included. The literature on prints and printmaking is vast, and works that are essentially scholarly in nature are listed separately. The tabulation of monographs on individual artists is listed alphabetically by artist and is intended as source material to reveal what some of the most inspired artists throughout the centuries have done with the creative print. In general, emphasis is placed on works that are currently available as reprints.

General

Eichenberg, Fritz (editor), *Artists Proof* (Magazine and Annuals), All issues, Pratt Graphic Art Center, New York. The most complete and best-produced survey of contemporary printmaking.

Getlein, Frank and Dorothy, *The Bite of the Print*, Clarkson N. Potter, Inc., New York 1963. A sympathetic and enthusiastic outline of satire and irony in prints.

Gilmour, Pat, *Modern Prints*, Studio Vista|Dutton Pictureback, London, 1970. A small format survey of contemporary prints.

Hayter, Stanley William, *About Prints*, Oxford University Press, London 1962. A innovator in contemporary printmaking discusses some aspects of the field.

Ivins, William, *How Prints Look*, Beacon Hill, paperback 1943. Analysis and enlargements of techniques by an expert.

Ivins, William, *Prints and Visual Communication*, DaCapo reprint, New York 1969. Some fascinating insights into prints as information bearers.

Karshan, Donald, *American Printmaking*, Smithsonian Institution Press 1969. A readable, historical survey.

Karshan, Donald, *Language of the Print*, Chanticleer Press, New York, Random House, 1968. Selections from a remarkable, recently acquired collection of master prints.

Mayor, A. Hyatt, *Prints and People*, Metropolitan Museum of Art, New York 1971. A brilliant and witty survey of prints, written with great style by the Curator Emeritus of the Metropolitan.

Roger-Marx, Claude, *Graphic Art of the Nineteenth Century*, McGraw-Hill, New York 1962. Informative, brilliant discussion of an intensely interesting period in printmaking. Small format.

Sachs, Paul J., *Modern Prints and Drawings*, Knopf, New York 1954. Small format, readable, well-chosen illustrations.

Sotriffer, Kristan, *Printmaking, History and Technique*, McGraw-Hill, New York 1968. A good, general introduction to the history of printmaking. Some worthwhile illustrations.

Zigrosser, Carl, *The Book of Fine Prints*, Crown Publishers, New York 1956. A classic short history of printmaking. Clear, readable text, small reproductions.

Zigrosser, Carl, *Multum in Parvo*, G. Braziller, New York 1965. An appreciation of miniature prints.

General Techniques

Brunner, Felix, *A Handbook of Graphic Reproduction Processes*, Visual Communication Books, Hastings House, New York. Highly useful. Good layout and design.

Heller, Jules, *Printmaking Today*, University of Southern California 1965, Revised 1971. Elementary survey of print techniques.

Peterdi, Gabor, *Printmaking*, Macmillan 1971. Recently updated, this is one of the most useful books on the intaglio processes by a creative and innovative artist.

Relief Print Techniques

Green, Peter, *Introducing Surface Printing*, Watson-Guptill, New York 1967. Lots of pictorial material and good ideas about the relief print.

Green, Peter, *New Creative Printmaking*, Watson-Guptill, New York 1964. Excellent for its uninhibited approach to new forms in printmaking.

Karshan, Donald, *Picasso Linocuts 1958–1963*, Tudor, New York. A lucid explanation of a remarkable new approach to the color linocut.

Kent, Cyril and Cooper, Mary, *Simple Printmaking*, Watson-Guptill, New York, 1966. Intended for children but is useful for all beginning students.

Mueller, Hans A., *Woodcuts and Wood-engravings and How I Make Them*, Pynson Printers, New York 1939. A popular illustrator of the 30's and a fine craftsman talks about his approach.

Rothenstein, Michael, *Frontiers of Printmaking*, Reinhold, New York 1966. Introduction to some contemporary solutions to print problems.

Rothenstein, Michael, *Linocuts and Woodcuts*, Watson-Guptill, New York 1963. A highly respected teacher presents some new approaches.

Rothenstein, Michael, *Relief Printing*, Watson-Guptill, New York 1970. A really fresh and creative view of relief printmaking.

Intaglio Techniques

Bosse, A., *Traicte' des Manieres de Graver en taille-douce*, Revised by Cochin in Paris 1745, 1758. Illustrated technique of engraving and etching.

Brunsdon, John, *The Technique of Etching and Engraving*, Reinhold, New York 1965. Straightforward, direct exposition of processes and methods.

Buckland-Wright, John, *Etching and Engraving*, Studio Publications, London 1953. First-rate work book; still very valuable.

Gross, Anthony, *Etching, Engraving and Intaglio Printing*, Oxford, New York and London 1970. Mainly traditional methods.

Hayter, Stanley William, *New Ways of Gravure*, Oxford, New York and London 1966. The intaglio methods, explained by Hayter.

Lalanne, Maxime, *A Treatise on Etching*, Estes and Lauriat, Boston 1885. Still has much useful material for the artist.

Lumsden, E. S., *The Art of Etching*, Dover reprint, paperback, New York. First published 1922. Witty, knowledgeable, and helpful to the serious student.

Morrow, B. F., *The Art of Aquatint*, G. P. Putnam's Sons, New York 1935. Practical approach to traditional methods.

Pennell, Joseph, *Etchers and Etching*, Macmillan, New York 1931. Reflections by an admirer of Whistler.

Screen Print Techniques

Auvil, Kenneth, *Serigraphy*, Prentice-Hall paperback 1965. Good, clean, concise workbook. Well illustrated.

Biegeleisen, J. I., *The Complete Book of Silk Screen Printing Production*, Dover paperback, 1963. Although primarily for commercial applications, this has much material of use for the artist.

Biegeleisen, J. I. *Screen Printing*, Watson-Guptill 1971. A most complete and up-to-date survey of methods and materials used in screen printing.

Carr, Francis, *A Guide to Screen Process Printing*, Vista Books, London, 1961. Some excellent technical material, including photo processes.

Chieffo, Clifford, *Silk Screen as a Fine Art*, Reinhold, New York 1967. Large format; good, clear illustrations; not enough variety in reproductions.

Kosloff, Albert, *Elementary Silk Screen Printing*, Naz-Dar Company, Chicago 1954. Good, clear directions. Written for a materials supplier.

Shokler, Harry, *Artists Manual for Silk Screen Print Making*, Tudor, New York 1960. Simple, poor format, but covers elementary approaches.

Sternberg, Harry, *Silk Screen Color Printing*, McGraw-Hill, New York 1942. Basic, simple guide to elementary procedures.

Lithography Techniques

Antreasian, Garo and Adams, Clinton, *The Tamarind Book of Lithography: Art & Techniques*, Harry Abrams, New York 1971. The highly publicized Tamarind workbook in a lavish production. A massive work. The most useful book in print.

Arnold, Grant, *Creative Lithography and How to Do It*. Dover, New York, paperback, 1965.

Cliffe, Henry, *Lithography*, Watson-Guptill New York 1965. Good, workmanlike approach to the method.

Dehn, Adolf, and Barrett, W., *How to Draw and Print Lithographs*, American Artists Group, New York 1950. Direct, to-the-point, somewhat outdated.

Knigin, Michael and Zimiles, Murray, *The Techniques of Fine Art Lithography*, Van Nostrand Reinhold Co. 1970. An up-to-date, clear explanation of most litho procedures. Handsome format.

Senefelder, Alois, *A Complete Course of Lithography*, DeCapo reprint, New York 1969. A reprint of the classic text and still useful.

Weaver, Peter, *The Technique of Lithography*, Reinhold, New York 1964. Simple, easy to follow, worthwhile.

Weddige, Emil, *Lithography*, International Textbook Co., Scranton, Pa. 1966. Handsome reproductions, concise explanation of methods.

Weber, William, *A History of Lithography*, McGraw-Hill, New York 1964. Informed and well-produced survey.

Japanese Woodcuts

Binyon and Sexton, *Japanese Colour Prints*, Frederick Publications 1954. Much information in a tiny format, including publisher seals.

Gentoles, Margaret, *Masters of the Japanese Print*, Asia Society, Harry Abrams, New York 1964. Paperback catalog of a distinguished exhibition at Asia House, New York.

Hillier, J., *Utamaro*, Phaidon, London 1961. A giant of Japanese prints.

Michener, James, *The Floating World*, Random House, New York 1954. A popularized but worthwhile account of the Japanese print. Poor reproductions.

Robertson, Ronald, *Contemporary Printmaking in Japan*, Crown Publishers, New York 1965. An analysis of how the new wave of Japanese printmakers has expanded the traditional procedures.

Yoshida, Toshi and Rei Yuki, *Japanese Printmaking, a handbook of traditional and modern techniques*, Charles E. Tuttle Co., Rutland, Vermont, and Tokyo. A thorough and definitive study of Japanese water-based techniques.

Monographs on Artists
(Listed alphabetically by artist)

Leonard Baskin, The Graphic Work 1950–60, FAR Gallery, New York 1970.

Bonnard Lithographe, by Claude Roger-Marx, Andre Sauret, Monte Carlo 1952.

Georges Braque; His Graphic Work, by W. Hofmann, Harry Abrams, New York.

Bresdin, Rodolphe, by K. G. Boon, Amsterdam 1955. A fantacist of the highest rank whose lithographs are well worth study.

Graphic Works of Peter Brueghel the Elder, by A. Klein, Paperback Dover 1963.

Jacques Callot, by Edwin De. T. Bechtel, Braziller, New York 1955.

The Graphic Art of Mary Cassat, by Donald Karshan, Smithsonian Institution 1967.

Marc Chagall, His Graphic Work, by Franz Meyer, Harry Abrams, New York.

The Fantastic Engravings of Wendel Dietterlin, Dover reprint, paperback. Inventive, baroque architectural studies.

Durer, Complete Engravings, Etchings, and Woodcuts, by Karl-Adolf Knappe, Harry Abrams, New York.

The Graphic Art of M. C. Escher, Meredith Press 1961. A craftsman of the first rank creates some ingenious illusions with incredible precision.

Der Liebesspiegel (Gavarni), by E. Wieser, Aehren Verlag Affaltern 1953.

Goya Caprichos, by M. Micko, Spring Books, London.

Complete Etchings of Goya, Crown, New York 1943.

Wood Engravings of Winslow Homer, by B. Gelman, Crown, New York 1969.

Kirchner, His Graphic Art, by Annemarie Dube-Heynig, New York Graphic Society 1961. Many well-printed, large color plates.

Prints and Drawings of Kathe Kollwitz, by Carl Zigrosser, Dover, paperback, 1969.

Marino Marini, Graphic Work and Paintings, Harry Abrams, New York.

Joan Miro, His Graphic Work, by Sam Hunter, Harry Abrams, New York.

Rolf Nesch, Universe Books, New York 1969. A presentation of the work of a fresh creative spirit.

The Graphic Art of Rolf Nesch, Detroit Institute Arts 1969 paperback. Excellent catalog covers a retrospective of the innovator of collage prints.

Pablo Picasso: Fifty-five years of his graphic work, Harry Abrams, New York 1965.

Picasso: Sixty Years of Graphic Works, Introductions by D-H Kahnweiler and B. Geiser, Los Angeles County Mus. of Art paper. Catalog of a large exhibition, well illustrated.

Jose Guadalupe Posada, Hans Secker, Verlag der Kunst Dresden 1961.

Odilon Redon, by Andre Mellerio, Da Capo Press New York 1968. Reprint of a standard work.

The Graphic Works of Odilon Redon, Dover, paperback New York 1969.

Rembrandt, by K. G. Boon, Harry Abrams. Good reproductions.

The Complete Engravings of Martin Schongauer, by Alan Shestack, Dover paperback 1969.

E. Vuillard, L'Oeuvre Gravé, by Claude Roger Marx, Andre Sauret, Monte Carlo 1952.

Ward, Lynd, God's Man, A Novel in Woodcuts, Johnathan Cape and Harrison Smith, New York 1929.

Scholarly Treatises

Delteil, Loys, *Le Peintre-Graveur Illustre',* Collector's Editions, New York Reprint of 32 columes, Major work of 19th-century and early 20th-century French artists.

Dortu, M. G., *Toulouse-Lautrec et son oeuvre,* Collector's Editions, New York 1970 6 volume reprint.

Harris, Jean, *Edouard Manet, Graphic Works: A Definite Catalogue Raisonne,* Collector's Editions, New York 1970 reprint.

Hind, Arthur M., *A Catalog of Rembrandt's Etchings,* Da Capo reprint in two volumes. 1967.

Hind, Arthur M., *A History of Engraving and Etching from the 15th century* to 1914, Dover reprint, paperback. Many astute observations and evaluations.

Hind, Arthur M., *An Introduction to the History of Woodcut,* Dover reprint, in two volumes, paperback.

Hollstein, F. W. H., *Dutch & Flemish Etchings, Engravings & Woodcuts, 1450–1700,* Menno Hertzberger, Amsterdam, various dates in 19 volumes. A detailed survey of an enormous body of work.

Hallstein, F. W. H., *German Engravings, Etchings & Woodcuts 1400–1700,* Menno Hertzberger, Amsterdam, various dates in 7 volumes. A thorough and effective study of the scene. A monumental work.

Laran, *Jean, L'Estampe,* Presses Universitaires de France, 1959 in 2 volumes. Beautifully printed, with large heliogravure and color reproductions.

Lehrs, Max, *History and Critical Catalog of German, Netherlandish and French Copper Engravings in the 15th Century,* Collector's Edition, New York 1970. Reprint of 9 volumes.

Lehrs, Max, *Late Gothic Engravings of Germany and the Netherlands,* Dover paperback 1969. Marvelous source material for this era.

Lieure, Jules, *Jacques Callot: La Vie Artisique et Catalogue Raissone,* Collectors Editions, New York 1970. Reprint of 9 volumes.

Massar, Phyllis Dearborn, *Stefano della Bella: Catalogue Raisonne,* Collectors Edition reprint, New York 1970—two volumes.

Minott, Charles I., *The Engravings of Martin Schongauer: Studies and Illustrated Catalogue,* Collectors Edition Reprint, New York 1970.

Mourlot, Fernand, *Picasso Lithographe 1919–1956,* Monte Carlo: Andre Sauret 1949–1964 4 vols. Beautifully printed but rare and expensive because original lithos are included.

Panofsky, Erwin, *Albecht Durer,* Princeton, 1943 2 vols. The definitive study of Durer and his work.

INDEX

Zinc Etching Plate
John Ross
"Znamenja"